My War Memories

General Ludendorff

MY WAR MEMORIES

1914–1918

VOLUME 2

The Naval & Military Press Ltd

Published by

The Naval & Military Press Ltd

Unit 10, Ridgewood Industrial Park,

Uckfield, East Sussex,

TN22 5QE England

Tel: +44 (0) 1825 749494

Fax: +44 (0) 1825 765701

www.naval-military-press.com

Printed and bound by Antony Rowe Ltd, Eastbourne

TO THE HEROES
WHO FELL BELIEVING
IN
GERMANY'S GREATNESS
THIS BOOK IS DEDICATED

CONTENTS OF VOL. II.

MAPS TO VOL. II.

SKETCH MAPS IN THE TEXT (VOL. II.)

MY WAR MEMORIES,
1914-1918.

THE ENTENTE ATTACK, JANUARY— JUNE, 1917

I

AS far as human judgment could foresee everything pointed to the Western Front as the scene of our chief defensive fighting in 1917, however severe the struggle might be in the East. Direct co-operation with the Austro-Hungarian G.H.Q. was not so necessary as it had been during the campaign against Rumania, after the command on the Eastern Front had been reorganized in a less complicated form. The supreme importance of the Western theatre of war now demanded the presence there of the Commander-in-Chief. I suggested Spa or Kreuznach as the new headquarters. Spa was rejected; Kreuznach was particularly favourable, as many of the cables to the Front passed near the town, and it had suitable hotel and other accommodation. Orders were accordingly given for General Headquarters to be established at Kreuznach, Münster am Stein and Bingen, and the second fortnight of February was contemplated as the time when the transfer should take place. Meanwhile, the possibility of having to return to Pless had to be kept in view.

The Austro-Hungarian Headquarters was transferred to Baden, near Vienna.

The submarine-cruiser campaign opened on February 1st, 1917, and as soon as it became evident that the troops that had been concentrated on the frontiers of Holland and Denmark, to meet a possible attack from these quarters, would not be required, these forces and their staffs, which had been held in reserve for the purpose, were liberated for use on the Western Front.

In the West a continuation of the British attack on the Somme, perhaps extending to the north, had to be reckoned with. It was possible that this would be accompanied by a French offensive between Roye and Noyon, but the probabilities were that France would choose our Soissons-Rheims-Argonne front for attack, as she had done in the autumn of 1915. The Entente would thus have gained a strategic advantage by pressing in both flanks of the salient we had pushed into French territory It was impossible to foresee which part of the front the French would select. They might try a diversion at Roye, and reports also pointed to the possibility of an offensive on the Lorraine front and in the Sundgau, where we had made very little progress towards the consolidation of our lines. We had always been conscious of a certain weakness in this sector, as local engagements were to be expected here, and it was only with difficulty that we could bring up reinforcements. Verdun was also occasionally mentioned, as the French were always in a position to open an attack at this point. Lastly, an extension of the British offensive towards the north was indicated. Consequently we had to be prepared to offer a stubborn resistance at any point along our whole front. It was impossible to tell what was going to happen.

There was no doubt about the continuation of the struggle on the Izonzo front. Trieste was Italy's goal. Attacks were more than likely in Macedonia and on the Vardar, and certain in Turkey, Palestine and Bagdad.

In the East I anticipated an attack on the Austro-Hungarian troops in the southern section of the front. A sudden Russian advance in the direction of Mitau at the end of January alarmed both ourselves and the Commander-in-Chief on the Eastern

Front. It was, however, stemmed by reserves, which were rapidly brought up.

It was not yet possible to foresee when the great offensive would take place. On the Eastern Front it was scarcely to be expected before April. The big Russian advance in the spring of 1916 began in March, and was considerably hampered by the bad weather and the condition of the ground. It was unlikely that the Russians would repeat this attempt so early in the year. It was also possible that the Entente would accordingly postpone their offensive in the West. The situation on the Somme, however, was so tense that we had to be prepared for an earlier attack.

The general situation made it necessary for us to postpone the struggle in the West as long as possible, in order to allow the submarine campaign time to produce decisive results. Tactical reasons and a shortage of ammunition provided additional reasons for delay. At the same time it was necessary to shorten our front in order to secure a more favourable grouping of our forces and create larger reserves. In France and Belgium we had 154 divisions facing 190 divisions, some of which were considerably stronger than ours. In view of our extensive front, this was an exceedingly unfavourable balance of forces. Moreover, we had on certain sectors of our line to endeavour to avoid heavy enemy attacks as long as possible, by preventing our adversaries from concentrating strong forces in front of them. At the same time we secured positions in which weaker divisions, wearied by fighting, could be employed.

These considerations, taken in close connection with the opening of the submarine campaign, led to the decision to straighten our front by withdrawing to the Siegfried line, which was to be in a state of defence by the beginning of March, and methodically to carry out the work of demolition over an area of 15 kilometres in breadth in front of our new position.

Under the rubric " Alberich " the Army Group of the Crown Prince Rupprecht had worked out a programme for the work of clearance and demolition, which was to be spread over five

weeks. If an attack on the part of the enemy made it necessary we could at any moment interrupt this programme and
begin our retreat. Our first object was to avoid a battle,
our second to effect the salvage of all our raw material of war

Fig. 15. The "Alberich Movement" between Arras and Soissons,
March, 1917.

and technical and other equipment that was not actually built
into the position, and finally the destruction of all high roads,
villages, towns and wells, so as to prevent the enemy establishing
himself in force in the near future in front of our new position.
Poisoning of the wells was forbidden.

The Entente Offensive in the First Half of 1917

The decision to retreat was not reached without a painful struggle. It implied a confession of weakness bound to raise the *moral* of the enemy and lower our own. But as it was necessary for military reasons, we had no choice; it had to be carried out. General von Kuhl and I were in constant communication on the subject. The Field-Marshal and the Kaiser gave their consent. On February 4th the order was given to carry out " Alberich " according to plan. The first Alberich day was February 9th. The retreat was to begin on March 16th, but under enemy pressure might start at any earlier date. This would, however, have involved great loss of material, not to mention the partial abandonment of the work of demolition. At the same time Lieut.-Colonel Nicolai received instructions to mislead the enemy by furnishing them with special news. He and Colonel von Haeften had so to influence the home and neutral Press that no inkling of the intentions above described should be given. I myself personally informed the Chancellor of our scheme.

The Alberich programme was carried out according to plan. It was successful in every detail. Many treasures of art were removed from the zone we were evacuating, and in accordance with the terms of the Hague Convention stored in places of safety in the occupied territory. The fact that much property belonging to the inhabitants was destroyed was to be deplored, but it could not be helped. The bulk of the population was transferred eastward, only a small proportion being collected in certain places, such as Noyon, Ham and Nesle, and provided with rations for several days and left behind. On the one hand it was desirable not to make a present to the enemy of too much fresh strength in the form of recruits and labourers, and on the other we wanted to foist on him as many mouths to feed as possible.

On the Somme front fighting with the British had never quite come to a standstill. At the beginning of March signs were not wanting that the battle north of the Somme might break out afresh. South of Roye, too, French preparations for attack became ever more conspicuous. Whether the attitude of both armies was the outcome of the measures we had taken it is impossible to say. It was a severe strain on the nerves of the local commanders to keep, in spite of everything, to the date originally fixed upon for the retreat to begin. In the event this did not prove entirely practicable, as in the north from about the 11th, and in the south from about the 13th, minor modifications of the line were effected in order to evade the attack, which seemed every day more and more imminent.

The great retreat began on March 16th, according to plan, and was carried through without a break in a few great stages. The object of G.H.Q. was in general to avoid battle, and to allow the troops time to prepare the Siegfried line before the enemy reached it in superior force. Some of the divisions in reserve at the time were ordered to the new position, in other places divisions had to remain at their places in the front line.

Only south of St. Quentin was the enemy to be attacked after crossing the Somme and the Crozat canal ; this was done, but the attack was not carried out with sufficient energy. Its success was not conspicuous. The Crown Prince Rupprecht's Army Group and we at G.H.Q. had weighed the possibility of a general counter-attack along the whole of the Siegfried line, for we should have liked to wipe out our confession of weakness by a great tactical success. The condition and numbers of our troops, however, were such that it was impossible for us to throw in sufficient forces to guarantee a real victory on a battle-field rendered impassable, and G.H.Q. had, therefore, for better or worse, to give up the idea of a great counter-attack.

The Entente armies followed closely on the heels of our retiring forces and tried to make out that our retreat was a great success for themselves. But the Press had been so cleverly and effectively manipulated that they did not succeed. As a matter of fact they had not gained any military triumph. Thanks also to the false intelligence we had circulated, they had not even interfered with our work of demolition and clearance. The whole movement was a brilliant achievement on the part of both commanders and troops, and is evidence of the careful foresight and work of the German General Staff.

The Entente Offensive in the First Half of 1917

We were now more compactly and firmly established than we had been along our previous extended line. The tactical measures of the enemy had been frustrated. He was no longer able to attack in the same directions as before. The country we had traversed was devastated, and before military operations could be made possible upon it a certain amount of restoration was essential. For an attack to be launched over it an infinite amount of road and bridge building would have to be done The enemy, therefore, established himself in relatively low strength in front of our new line. We, for our part, could now thin out our forces by taking away whole divisions.

We had completely achieved the objects we had had in view in carrying out the Alberich programme, and occupying the Siegfried line. It stood us in good stead for some considerable time. The retreat had been well worth while. Indeed, all our commanders wished that the German Army had possessed many another Siegfried line, with its concrete dug-outs, for the conduct of the war during 1918 would then have been easier. The labour required for their construction, however, was not available. Moreover, the best lines ultimately gave way before the tanks, which were able to overcome the greatest obstacles.

We had to put up with the fact that the Entente turned our exceedingly thorough demolition of the territory and dispersal of the population to account, in order once more to call us Huns, and to play the organ of their propaganda with all the stops pulled out. One cannot blame them. Nevertheless, we had acted in accordance with the laws of warfare, and had not even gone as far as the belligerents in the American Civil War.

During our retreat in Poland in 1914 we had spared the country as far as possible, for there, on account of the vast distances, I had set all my hopes on the destruction of the railways. But in the present case the area evacuated was so small that the country had to be more severely handled. In Poland we were able to leave the inhabitants of enemy territory alone ; here both humanity and prudence demanded that we should remove them. Ought we to have left them to perish in the devastated districts ? In all the measures we took, the exigencies

409

of war alone proved the decisive factor. Otherwise the dictates of humanity were obeyed as far as possible. We were too great to wish to increase the suffering of others by unjustifiable harshness and spite. This was the case not only here, but everywhere. We only acted with severity where military security demanded it—in matters of contre-espionage for instance.

II

In considering the strategic value of our retreat, I counted on the British offensive developing to the north at the end of March. It was impossible to foretell with certainty where it would take place. An attack near Arras seemed likely.

In the middle of February, 1917, in order to improve its position, the Third Army had undertaken a local operation on the Champagne battle-fields of September, 1915. This operation was successful. Amongst the captured material there was found an order of the 2nd French Infantry Division, dated January 29th, clearly pointing to a great French offensive on the Aisne for April. This gave us an extremely important clue. Little attention was now paid to rumours of attacks in Lorraine and the Sundgau.

Thanks to their ample labour supply, the Entente had been in a position to furnish, not only the Verdun sector, but also a large portion of their front with all the means of communication and munitions necessary for an attack. It was, therefore, possible for them in the shortest space of time, and at various parts of the front, to develop an offensive without betraying their plans by their preparations. The photographs of the enemy's field defences and works, and the continual checking and verification by new photographs secured by our aviators, could therefore only give general indications of his intended movements.

The French front between Vailly on the Aisne and the Argonne was particularly well constructed, so that special preparations for attack were not necessary. We saw the works that were actually built south of the Chemin des Dames when we advanced in 1918. Their construction seems to have dated from 1915–16. It is possible that the French had intended to make an offensive here in 1916, but were prevented by the German onslaught on Verdun.

Conditions on the Western Front had become more secure, but the depression due to the battles on the Somme and at Verdun still weighed down the minds of our people, and increased the nerve-racking tension inseparable from the defensive. The organization of the commands had been improved. Crown Prince Rupprecht's command included the 4th, 6th, 1st and 2nd Armies, between the channel and La Fère. Next to this was the German Crown Prince's command, with the 7th, 3rd and 5th Armies, which extended almost as far as the Orne, east of Verdun. Then came the group of Field-Marshal Duke Albrecht of Würtemberg—who had handed over the 4th Army to General Sixt von Arnim—Army detachments C., A., B., whose Chief of Staff was General Kraft von Dellmensingen. Thanks to the establishment of this Army Group, conditions on the Alsace-Lorraine front were very considerably improved.

The shortening of the line between Arras and Laon made it possible to release the Headquarters Staff of the 1st Army. It was transferred to the group of armies under the German Crown Prince, on either side of Rheims, between the 7th and 3rd Armies. Such a transfer and readjustment of an army command is a troublesome undertaking, on account of the changes it entails in the lines of communications. It cannot be done in a day if serious friction is to be avoided.

I hoped that this Staff would be fixed up, with head-quarters in Rethel, before the French attack on the group of armies under the German Crown Prince was opened. The troops had had two extra months for rest and training, as a result of the successful carrying out of the Alberich programme. They had certainly gained considerably in strength, but in the group of armies under the Crown Prince Rupprecht there were still some divisions that required rest.

Training was suspended. Some of the new formations were

already being employed in quiet sectors of the line, others were only just fit for use as reinforcements. Divisions from Rumania had arrived in Belgium. G.H.Q. had also exchanged divisions unfit for the Western Front for good fighting forces from the East, although this necessarily involved a weakening of our defences there. The consolidation of the front was pushed on. The labour which had been liberated by the occupation of the Siegfried line was employed behind those sectors where attack was anticipated, and the completion of the support and rearward trenches had to be accelerated. The supply of ammunition had improved, the increase being due chiefly to the diminished consumption during several months. A reserve had been created, which gave a certain security as long as the battles east and west did not last too long. The Hindenburg programme gradually began to show results, and the further supply of ammunition was assured.

On the Italian Front all was quiet. In Macedonia local attacks by the Entente in February and March at Monastir and in the bend of the Cerna were repulsed with heavy loss. In Turkey's Asiatic theatre fighting had begun again with the fine weather. The British had finished their preparations and opened an offensive. In Palestine the British attacks on Gaza failed, thanks to the efforts of Colonel von Kresz. In Mesopotamia it soon became evident that the Turkish Army in Irak had lost all power of resistance. Kut el Amara fell on February 25th, and by March 11th Bagdad was occupied by the British, a severe blow for Turkey, which was thereby forced to evacuate the Persian frontier district. In consequence of these events Enver approached G.H.Q. with the request that a German Army Group Headquarters with a German auxiliary corps might be put at his disposal for the recapture of Bagdad. This undertaking involved months of preparation. The organization of the lines of communication had to be complete before the troops arrived. The completion of the Amanus tunnel for standard gauge traffic in January, 1917, and that of the narrow gauge line through the Taurus tunnel, to be opened in the autumn, improved communications in Asia Minor. Enver's projected enterprise seemed practicable. There was a likelihood of bringing strong Turkish forces into action again, supported by a few German battalions, which would compel the British to increase their effectives in Irak.

G.H.Q. agreed to Enver's request, though not exactly with enthusiasm, and at his desire General von Falkenhayn was given command of the group of armies. The Ministry of War began the formation of the weak Asiatic Corps.

In the East vast changes had taken place. In March the Tsar was overthrown by the Revolution, which was favoured by the Entente. A Government of pronounced Socialist leanings came into power. The Entente's reasons for backing the Revolution are not clear. They may have imagined they were confronted by a national movement which they could not ignore, and with which they consequently threw in their lot, or they may have thought that the Tsar had become inclined for peace, owing to fear of an internal collapse, and were therefore in favour of getting rid of him. Possibly there were other reasons. At all events, it is certain that the Entente expected the Revolution to bring them some advantage in the war. They wished at least to save anything that could be saved, and consequently did not hesitate to act. The Tsar, who had begun the war in order to please the Entente, had to be removed, This line of conduct revealed infinite will-power, which would stick at nothing in order to win the war. The same thing would have happened if Stürmer had really favoured peace in 1916.

The outbreak of the Revolution threw a strong side-light on conditions in Russia. The army and nation were rotten to the core, or it would never have taken place. In Russia, as with us, the army was part of the nation ; there, too, nation and army were one. How often had I not hoped for a revolution in Russia in order that our military burden might be alleviated ! But my desire had been merely a castle in the air. Now it had come true, and as a surprise. I felt as though a weight had been removed from my chest. At that time I never contemplated the possibility that it might undermine our own position later on.

It was impossible to tell to what extent the position in the East would be relieved, and for the moment attacks had to be expected. Nevertheless the Revolution was a serious blow for the Entente, as it inevitably entailed a diminution of Russia's fighting capacity and brought considerable relief to us in the extremely difficult position in which we were placed. For G.H.Q. this consisted first of all in the saving of troops and munitions in the East ; and the exchange of worn-out divisions from the West for fresh troops from the East was undertaken on a large scale.

Orders were given for propaganda to be set on foot at once to encourage a strong movement for peace in the Russian Army.

The outbreak of the Russian Revolution was a factor in the war upon which no general could dare to count with certainty. Now at last it was no longer a hope, but a reality with which I could deal as a soldier. Our general position had considerably improved, and I could look forward with confidence to the battles in the West. The results of the submarine campaign were distinctly favourable, and far exceeded the expectations of the Navy. The loss of tonnage and material sunk was bound to tell. The *Economist* of September 7th, 1918, calls the spring of 1917 the most critical and perilous period through which England had passed since the outbreak of war. The Entente found itself forced to employ for naval warfare men and material hitherto destined for the conflict on land, and this continued in an ever-increasing degree.

The United States declared war on us on April 5th. The collapse of Russia, the success of our submarine campaign and the desire to use their forces to combat the U boats, must have been factors in their decision. On February 3rd America had broken off diplomatic relations with us, and I doubt whether it would have been possible to come to terms with her in the meantime without disturbing the basis upon which the submarine campaign was being conducted. The attempt on the part of our Foreign Office to establish military relations with Mexico strengthened public opinion against us in the United States. In spite of my warnings the Foreign Office had used an antiquated and easily decipherable secret code.

Soon after America's declaration of war the whole world was

ranged against us, only a few States, including the Argentine and Chile, preserving their neutrality in face of enemy pressure. The American declaration of war included all the States of the Quadruple Alliance, with the exception of Bulgaria, where the American representative continued to hold his post at Sofia. The German Government failed to secure his recall through the Bulgarian Government, although I requested them several times to do so. This failure brought heavy retribution upon us later on.

It was not a matter of surprise to me that the United States joined the ranks of our enemies. I had reckoned upon her doing so, provided the balance of war continued in our favour, even if the unrestricted submarine campaign had never been opened. As far back as the spring of 1915 an American correspondent on the Eastern Front had expressed views to this effect, and they certainly did not reflect his own personal opinion alone. America had never known Germany in time of peace, and she now viewed us and all the events taking place in Europe through the glasses of Entente propaganda, strengthened by her ties of blood with England. The German American population had little influence. To appeal to their loyalty to the country of their birth, as against the country of their adoption, as we did for a time, was clumsy and bound to produce an unfavourable effect. I have not been able to get a clear account of the attitude of the Irish section of the population. The oppression of this unfortunate country left the United States cold.

Wilson's reply to the Kaiser's letter of the autumn of 1914, in which the latter appealed to America's sense of justice with regard to the Belgian atrocities, gave food for thought. America was led by economic interests ever more and more to the side of the Entente, for England had surrendered to her the position she had hitherto enjoyed as the first capitalist Power in the world. The Entente was deeply in America's debt, and their defeat would have involved her in heavy loss.

The attitude of the United States in regard to the question of the supply of munitions left no doubt about their one-sided conception of neutrality. England's monstrous violations of international law at sea were only possible so long as America connived at them. In a conversation at the Foreign Office several years before the war I was assured that America would never agree to such tactics. We reckoned with certainty on unlimited imports through Holland.

As a matter of fact the American Government did actually raise objections to the arbitrary methods of English naval warfare. The American note of protest of March 30th, 1915, was couched in serious language. It asserted in unequivocal terms that the so-called British blockade was " an almost unqualified denial of the sovereign rights of the nations now at peace," and continued with the warning that to tolerate England's procedure in this respect would be to assume " an attitude of unneutrality to the present enemies of Great Britain which would be obviously inconsistent with the solemn obligations of this [the U.S.A.] Government in the present circumstances." This declaration was perfectly plain. A second American Note of November 5th, 1915, emphasized the fact that the so-called blockade of March 11th of the same year must be considered ineffective, and therefore illegal. Both protests were bluntly rejected by England. The United States Government accepted the rebuff. According to her own verdict her attitude to Germany for nearly two years was unneutral.

The opinion of the German Ambassador, Count Bernstorff, on these proceedings is contained in a memorandum to the Government and people of the United States, published in the *Times* of April 13th, 1915. It runs as follows : " If the American people desire to observe true neutrality, they will find the means to stop the exclusive export of arms to one side, or, at least, use this export trade as a means to uphold legitimate trade with Germany, especially trade in foodstuffs."

From one-sided favouritism to open partisanship was but a small step. I will mention only two instances : Mr. Choate, the late American Ambassador in London, wrote on April 7th, 1917, to Earl Grey : " As you know, I have thought from the beginning that while for the time being we might better serve the cause of the Allies by remaining neutral and supplying all that we could in the way of arms and munitions, and, I am happy to say, some men, as our neutral right was ; that nevertheless, when by entering into the war with all our might and with the aid of all our boundless resources, we could help to bring it to an end in the right way by the complete suppression of Prussian militarism and the triumph of civilization, it would be our duty to do so. That time has now come." And on June 3rd the American Admiral Sims spoke as follows in London : " In 1910, when our Fleet visited England, I made a small but very undiplomatic speech. . . . In that speech I expressed an opinion which is now being translated into action. . . . This is what I said : ' In my opinion, if the time ever comes when the integrity of the British Empire is seriously threatened by a European coalition, you may count on every ship, every dollar, every man and every drop of blood of your kinsmen across the sea.' "

Very characteristic of the views of American official circles is the following conversation, which took place between a certain reliable personage and an American Consul-General, and it is in complete harmony with the opinions given above. Asked whether the *Lusitania* affair had really led to American intervention, the Consul-General replied : " No, that was only the match that set fire to the straw, and it has been fully exploited as propaganda. But for this we should have had to find other convincing reasons for coming into this business ! If we had not joined the Allies we should have been nowhere after the war. Now we expect to be number one—and we shall be number one ! " To the question as to what part America would play as number one, he replied : " Germany was undoubtedly the most industrious country in Europe before the war. We in America and England saw to what an exalted height Germany was climbing, and realized that in a few decades she would reach the pinnacle of power and be in a position to dictate, not only to Europe, but to the whole world. She had become a menace and we in America recognized the fact. For this reason we tackled the problem and thought we understood it. We are convinced that our people will take the lead after the war. It is we who are going to dictate, not only to Germany, but to the whole of Europe. The nations will expect great things from us, above all, peace. And they will get it, but on our conditions, and at our price ! "

" Will America impose her will on her Allies ? "

" Yes, indeed she will ! But they will get better conditions than other countries (the Central Powers), just as we (America) shall get better conditions from them (the Allies). It is all a matter of business. That is what war has always been ! "

The American consul's prediction regarding his country's position after the war was ill-founded, though only because the Revolution rendered Germany defenceless and gave world domination to Great Britain. For America could no longer count upon any opposition to England in Europe. However that may be, the war was certainly no matter of business for Germany. It was forced upon us. Our economic future and independence were bound up in it ; to us it was a question of life or death.

I will not discuss how far the above opinions coincided with those of President Wilson and the majority of the American people. All that need be said is that they became supreme. Under the pretext of the submarine campaign America entered the war against us at a period critical for the Entente. Whether, without the excuse afforded by the U boats, she would have done so in time to prevent our winning the war in 1918 is open to doubt. But it is impossible to say how events on land would have turned out if the submarine campaign had never been opened.

As a matter of fact, on January 9th, 1917, no one could have foretold the collapse of Russia, and nobody calculated upon it. With the help of our submarines we reckoned on a decision in our favour, at the latest before America, with her new armies, could intervene in the war. Without the U boats we calculated that the Quadruple Alliance must be defeated in 1917. As it was, the history of this year took a completely different turn : the Western Front held firm, but the submarine campaign brought no decision and Russia collapsed.

On the Eastern Front we were in a condition of neither peace nor war. A solution then became possible of which no one could have dreamt before the autumn of 1917 : namely, to aim at a decision of the war on land in the year 1918 by means of an offensive, which must succeed if the submarines had by that time been able at least to reduce enemy tonnage to such an extent as to render the quick transport of the new American armies impossible, or even to sink only a certain proportion of the transports. The Navy counted upon being able to do this.

III

G.H.Q. began to reckon on the great Entente offensive in France, Macedonia and on the Isonzo for the middle of April. From Kreuznach, whither we had moved at the end of February, I had often visited the Western Front, and had discussed the situation with the Headquarters Staffs of the Groups and Armies as well as with the Staffs of the corps in the most dangerous positions. We had exchanged views on tactics. The Army Groups of the Crown Prince Rupprecht and the German Crown Prince were strengthened with divisions, artillery and ammunition, and were provided with everything necessary for successful defence. Where help was desired I gave it to the best of my ability.

The 6th Army wanted to make a rectification of its line by means of a local advance at Souchez between Lens and Arras, and prepared to carry it out at the beginning of April. On the 6th of April I had no doubt that a great British offensive was imminent at Arras. The operation at Souchez was abandoned. I begged the Group Headquarters to bring up their reserves nearer to the line in the area of the 6th Army. The last attacks at Verdun in October and December had confirmed the old adage that the right place for reserves is close to the firing-line. The " Defensive Battle " manual laid down that, in many places on the front under attack, counter-attack divisions should be held in readiness in the second line to meet and throw back the enemy if he broke through the first line.

The divisions which constituted the second and third waves were indeed moved up by the 6th Army, but on the 8th were not close enough up. On the 9th, after a short but extraordinarily intense artillery preparation, our army encountered a powerful attack, led by tanks, on both sides of the Scarpe. Some

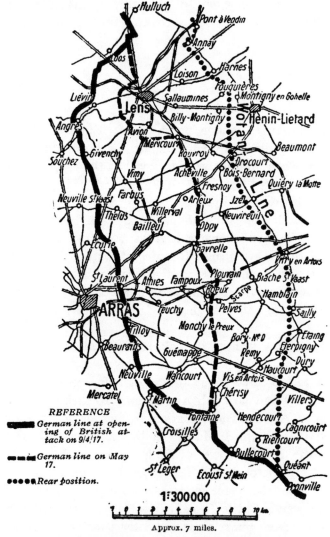

REFERENCE

▬▬▬ German line at opening of British attack on 9/4/17.

▬ ▬ ▬ German line on May 17.

●●●●● Rear position.

1:300000

Approx. 7 miles.

Fig. 16. The Battle of Arras. Spring, 1917.

of our advanced divisions gave way. The neighbouring divisions which stood firm suffered heavy losses. The enemy succeeded before noon in reaching our battery positions and seizing heights which dominated the country far to the east. The counter-attacking divisions were not there to throw the enemy back, only portions of the troops could be brought up by motor transport. The situation was extremely critical, and might have had far-reaching and serious consequences if the enemy had pushed further forward. But the British contented themselves with their great success and did not continue the attack, at least not on April 9th.

On that day I celebrated my birthday at Kreuznach. I had looked forward to the expected offensive with confidence, and was now deeply depressed. Was this to be the result of all our care and trouble during the past half-year? Had our principles of defensive tactics proved false, and if so what was to be done? I was not at that time able to get a clear view of all the details of the battle. I sent for officers who had taken part in the conflict in the front line, and by means of conversations with them and telephonic communications gained the impression that the principles laid down by G.H.Q. were sound. But the whole art of leadership lies in applying them correctly. Moreover, a division had failed here which had previously enjoyed a high reputation. The battle of Arras on April 9th was a bad beginning for the decisive struggle of this year.

April 10th and the following days were critical. The consequences of a break through of 12 to 15 kilometres wide and 6 or more kilometres deep are not easy to meet. In view of the heavy losses in men, guns and ammunition resulting from such a break through, colossal efforts are needed to make good the damage. It was the business of G.H.Q. to provide reserves on a large scale. But it was absolutely impossible, with the troops at our disposal and in view of the military situation, to have a second division immediately behind every division that might possibly fall out. A day like April 9th threw all calculations to the winds. Many days had to pass before a new line could really be formed and consolidated. The end of the crisis, even if the troops were available, depended very largely, as it generally does in such cases, on whether the enemy, after his first victory would attack again, and by further success aggravate the difficulty of forming a new line. Our position having been weakened, such victories were to be won only too easily.

The British attacked again at the same spot from the 10th onwards in great strength, but not really on a grand scale. They extended their offensive on both sides, especially to the south, as far as Bullecourt. On the 11th they took Monchy, and during the following night we evacuated Vimy ridge. April 23rd and 28th and May 3rd were again days of severe fighting, and in the intervals sharp local engagements took place. The battles continued ; we launched minor counter-attacks, which were successful, but also suffered slight losses of ground here and there.

The Army Commander of the 6th Army, General von Falkenhausen, whose Chief of Staff was Colonel von Loszberg, was very energetic in organizing the defence of the new position, and was supported in his efforts by the Staffs of the Groups and G.H.Q. A further withdrawal to the Wotan position, which was still under construction, was not found to be necessary, though contemplated for a time by the 6th Army.

The battle of Arras was at its height in the second half of April, and was swallowing up a liberal supply of reserves and material, when, on April 16th, the French also opened their formidable offensives on the Aisne and in Champagne. No doubt exceedingly important strategic objects lay behind the British attack, but I have never been able to discover what they were. I took for granted, in spite of the restricted area of their onslaught, that a great break through was planned, and not merely a battle of attrition and diversion. But possibly the British Army had not quite recovered from the battle of the Somme and had undertaken a diversion here whilst the French Army was to gain a decision.

The ultimate strategic object of General Nivelle was to break through the German line between Vailly and Rheims in the first few days. Following on this a push east of Rheims as far as Suippe, was to widen the breach and shatter our front for 70 kilometres ! The decisive blow was to be struck by the French Army against the group of armies under the German Crown Prince. The pressure from Arras eastwards on Douai and the

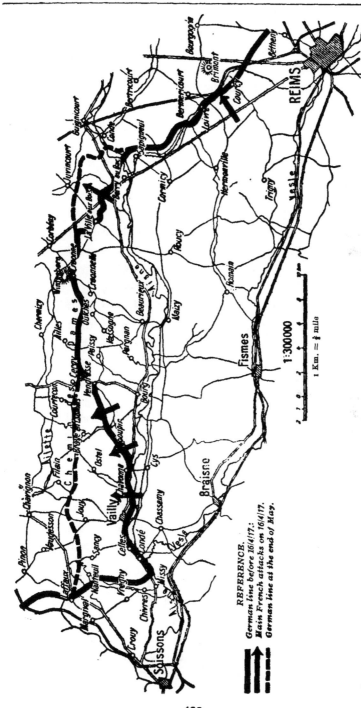

The Double Battle of the Aisne and Champagne. Spring, 1917.

REFERENCE.

German line before 16/4/17.
Main French attacks on 16/4/17.
German line at the end of May.

break through on both sides of Rheims via Rethel in the direction of Mezières was to envelop the Siegfried position, the construction of which had been surveyed by hosts of aeroplanes. The Entente intended to make our whole front reel as far as the sea.

The preparations for defence were carried out with extraordinary care by the German Crown Prince's Army Group and the 7th and 3rd Armies. The Crown Prince and his Chief of Staff, Colonel Count Schulenburg, were indefatigable. The command of the 7th Army was in the hands of General von Boehn, one of the best generals in the German Army, a Prussian officer of the old school, a good trainer of troops and a man of untiring energy. His Chief of Staff, Colonel Reinhardt, was a clever man, whose careful work made him a useful complement to his commanding officer. General von Einem, who was in command of the 3rd Army, is well known as Minister of War, an able and far-sighted officer who knew the army well and understood the psychology of the troops. His Chief of Staff, Colonel, later General, von Oldershausen, was a man of irrepressible vitality and loved his work; he too was the right complement to his superior. The Headquarters Staff of the 3rd Army was afterwards eliminated for the battle. In the first fortnight of April the Headquarters Staff of the 1st Army took over the command under General Fritz von Below. He had as his assistant Lieut.-Colonel von Klüber, who had gained valuable experience in the battle of the Somme, and, like his general, was a particularly sound judge of tactics. He was afterwards murdered at Halle by Sparticists in the discharge of his duties !

At first the troops would not believe in the possibility of an offensive, as they had seen no preparations for it. But gradually they nerved themselves to face the severe fighting that lay before them.

After several days' artillery preparation the French attacked early on April 16th between Vailly and Brimont, to the northwest of Rheims. They broke through at various points on the Chemin des Dames and forced us to withdraw with heavy losses from the Vailly salient to the heights of the Chemin des Dames. Further to the east the French clung firmly to the ridge that to the north falls sharply into the Ailette valley. Between the Winterberg and the Aisne the French pressed forward with tanks to the outskirts of Juvincourt, but were here held up by a counter-attack division. Due east of the Aisne our troops held their ground. Towards Brimont another break through was made, but was neutralized by a push on the part of our counter-attack forces. On April 17th and 18th the enemy renewed the assault, but was unable to gain any advantage.

Meanwhile offensives in Champagne had also been opened, directed against the heights of Moronvilliers. One division gave way, and we lost the heights which formed a key position.

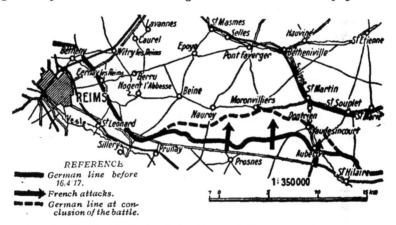

REFERENCE

▬▬▬ German line before 16,4 17.
▬▬▶ French attacks.
▬ ▬ ▬ German line at con-clusion of the battle.

1 : 350000

Fig. 18. The Double Battle of the Aisne and Champagne. Spring, 1917.

When the French attempted to descend the northern slope they were exposed to our artillery fire, which mowed them down and brought them to a standstill. Our counter-attack divisions, as I subsequently ascertained in personal conversation with the regimental commanders, were thrown in too hastily, so that on the 19th we failed to recapture the heights. The loss of them was a severe blow, as they afforded a view, to the north, right over the whole country ; but we had to make the best of it. The crisis of the April battle had been survived. In these battles the French infantry had attacked in close formation, and its losses had been appalling. Both on the Aisne and in Champagne General Nivelle again attempted to score a victory. By this time

425

our line was once more re-established and consolidated, so that on both fields of this great double battle the new offensive came to grief with heavy loss.

The 7th May saw fierce fighting all along the front, after which the attack on the Aisne died down, and after the 9th it waned in Champagne also, though it blazed up again at this point on the 20th. The French offensive had collapsed with terrible loss of life, and although France was obliged to celebrate it as a victory it caused great depression. The Minister of War admitted in July that the attack had failed with losses that must not be incurred again. These losses were so great that the *moral* of the army began to suffer and mutinies broke out, though we heard but little about them, and that only by degrees. Only later on did we learn the whole truth.

Changes were also made in the French High Command. General Nivelle was replaced by General Pétain. Both had made their reputation at Verdun, General Pétain by his defence in the spring and summer of 1916, General Nivelle by his offensive of October to December. The tactics which had succeeded then were expected to lead the French Army to final victory in the spring of 1917.

Thanks to the measures we had taken for defence and the resistance of the German Crown Prince's Army Group, this promised victory was turned into a defeat. By superhuman efforts we gained a great success and showed ourselves superior to the enemy in training. Our losses in men and material were extraordinarily high. It was impossible to foresee what turn the conflict might take and what claims we might have to meet.

In spite of the seriousness of our position on the Western Front, the absence of any Russian attacks in the spring of 1917 prevented a general crisis in our situation such as we had experienced in September, 1916. I had never been one to indulge in fruitless speculation, but I could not help considering what our position must inevitably have been had the Russians attacked in April and May and met with even minor successes. We should then, as in the autumn of 1916, have had a desperate struggle. Our supply of munitions would have been diminished to an alarming extent. If the Russian successes of July had occurred in April and May I do not see, as I look back, how G.H.Q. could have mastered the situation. During these two months of 1917, in spite of our Aisne–Champagne victory, it was the Russian Revolution alone that saved us from serious trouble.

The Russian offensive took place later on, in July, two months after the Anglo-French attack. This was not a joint blow such as we had had to meet in the autumn of 1916. It was a question of two disconnected attacks, and operating, as we did, from interior lines, we were able to repel and overcome our separate opponents one by one.

On the Italian Front, too, there was violent fighting in May. The tenth battle of the Isonzo once more closed without victory for the Italian Army. In Macedonia an enemy offensive on a large scale collapsed before the Bulgarian lines. The submarine campaign again achieved good results in April and May and relieved our Western Front.

IV

After their great failure in April and May and the collapse of Russia in the interval, England and France saw themselves faced with a new situation. They decided on a second great offensive, with the object of winning the war before the end of 1917. At the same time they wished to secure guarantees that final victory might be assured, at any rate by 1918. The chief weight of the blow was directed against Ypres, with a view to capturing the German submarine bases in Flanders. The transport of the new American troops to France in 1918 had to be safeguarded by a war against our U boats.

For the moment the French Army remained inactive, in order to recuperate after its recent defeat. Later on it confined itself only to local engagements, although these were of considerable intensity. The main forces of the British and Belgian Armies, supported by French troops, were held in readiness for the attack in Flanders. Fresh offensives were also to be opened on the Isonzo, in Macedonia and Palestine.

In the summer of 1917 I was naturally unable to form such a clear idea of the intentions and measures the enemy were then maturing as I did in the previous July and August.

A weakening in the French attacks was perceptible in the second half of May, and the French Army continued to be comparatively inactive. Meanwhile I had to reckon on a resumption of their offensive, which was possible at any moment, either here or at some other point. The British Army continued fighting on the old battle-field east of Arras in the second half of May, not, indeed, with the vigour displayed in the Somme battles, but still pursuing its tactics of attrition.

At the beginning of June increased activity on the part of the enemy was noticeable in the neighbourhood of our salient at Wytschaete, south of Ypres. The straightening of this salient really ushered in the great Flanders battle in June. As long as it remained in German hands every British attack at Ypres and to the north of that town was outflanked from the south. The tactical position of the German troops in the Wytschaete salient was by no means favourable. There were some thoughts of evacuating it and withdrawing to the chord position. The Army, however, was of opinion that it could be held. Repulsed attacks are always to the advantage of the defending side, owing to the immensely heavy losses they entail for the enemy. The Group Headquarters and G.H.Q. therefore agreed that the salient should be held. We should have succeeded in retaining the position but for the exceptionally powerful mines used by the British, which paved the way for their attack, consisting, as usual, of fierce artillery fire supporting a closely massed infantry advance. The result of these successful mining operations was that the enemy broke through on June 7th.

The heights of Wytschaete and Messines had been the site of active mine warfare in the early days of the war. For a long time past, however, both sides had ceased to use such tactics ; all had been quiet, and no sound of underground work on the part of the enemy could be heard at our listening posts. The mines must, therefore, have been in position long before. The moral effect of the explosions was simply staggering; at several points our troops fell back before the onslaught of the enemy infantry. Powerful artillery fire raining down on the Wytschaete salient hindered effective intervention by our reserves and the recovery of the position. The line following the chord of the arc was then taken up with our consent. I refused to

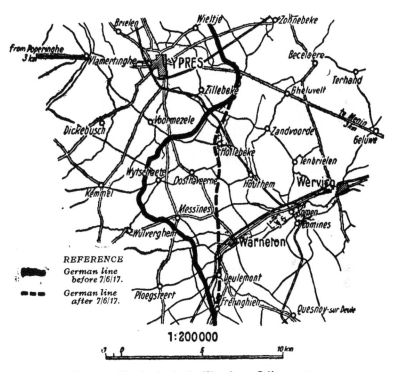

Fig. 19. The Battles in the Wytschaete Salient, 1917.

countenance any suggestion of further withdrawals. The 7th of June cost us dear, and owing to the success of the enemy attack the drain on our reserves was very heavy. Here, too, it was many days before the front was again secure. The British Army did not press its advantage; apparently it only intended to improve its position for the launching of the great Flanders offensive.

It thereupon resumed operations on the old Arras battle-field, and also between La Bassée and Lens. The object of the enemy was to wear us down and distract our attention from Ypres.

The command of the 6th Army had been changed. General von Falkenhausen had taken the place of the late General von Bissing as Governor-General of Belgium. He was a particularly striking personality who, on taking up his new position, retained our complete confidence. The 6th Army had been given to General Otto von Below who relinquished the command of the Army Group in Macedonia to General von Scholz, who had latterly commanded an army on the Eastern Front.

The end of the Aisne-Champagne battle had left the 7th and 1st Armies on a very unfavourable line, particularly at many points along the Chemin des Dames. To give up the ridge would have meant a French success and would have had a depressing effect on the troops who had held it so bravely. The group of armies under the German Crown Prince and the 7th Army wished to secure improved positions by a series of minor engagements, so as to establish a line suitable for a permanent position. This plan coincided with the views of G.H.Q. As the result of various actions, prepared with the greatest care by the Staffs which took part in them, and skilfully carried out by the forces engaged, a more favourable line was gradually secured here and fresh life was put into the troops.

General von Gallwitz, too, the Commander of the 5th Army, wished for the same reason to undertake a local improvement of position on the west bank of the Meuse, which the Army Group there considered particularly important. The German Crown Prince's Group supported the proposal and G.H.Q. gave its consent. The attacks on the 18th and 19th of June succeeded. But here again we realized, as we had done before, that to attack is easier than to hold what has been won.

In all these engagements, undertaken by the 7th and 5th Armies in order to improve their position, the possibility of enemy counter-attacks was reckoned with and their repulse provided for, in the estimates for men and ammunition furnished to G.H.Q. We wished to avoid anything in the way of a wild gamble. Although everything was done to meet these enemy counter-attacks they succeeded far too often. The 7th Army had been equal to them. Before Verdun the French deprived us of the greater part of our gains. I was glad when the battles there came to an end, and sorry that I had ever allowed the attacks to be made. I was as little in favour, as when Chief of Staff on the Eastern Front, of continuous battering tactics in which the gain does not counterbalance the loss.

On the front of the 4th Army the British had been established ever since 1914 in a narrow bridgehead close to the coast on the right bank of the Yser. This point had always been the Naval Corps' weak spot. The 4th Army, which was supported by this Corps, received permission to take this bridgehead. The attack took place on July 10th, and was successful. The Yser effectively prevented all enemy counter-attacks.

In spite of the severe fighting for the Wytschaete salient in the first half of June and other engagements on the British front, the activity in the West from the middle of May till June was such that some of the troops at least were able to recuperate, and we were in a position to form reserves. The Western Army was well prepared when events in the East came to a head.

V

Events turned out as we had expected ; the Russian Revolution had weakened the enemy's fighting strength. The wish for peace seemed to be gaining ground in Russia, but the attitude of the new Russian Government and of the Russian people and Army towards this question was not uniform. The Minister for Foreign Affairs, Miliukoff, pressed for the continuation of the war and the recasting of the map of Europe at the expense of the Quadruple Alliance. Other ministers talked about a peace without annexations or indemnities and the right of nations to self-determination. But they were all unanimous in demanding adherence to the alliance with the Entente Powers, and we had to reckon with their deliberate efforts to quell any desire for peace in Russia. There was not the faintest ground for expecting any relaxation of their desire to annihilate us.

The attitude of the Russian troops was in some places friendly, and we gladly met them half-way. On other parts of the front active fighting continued, but we kept as quiet as we could. In April and May, and right on into June, the general military position was not such as to encourage us to activity on the Eastern Front. The Government were also afraid that an attack on our part might check the disintegration of Russia. At the beginning of April events there were developing very rapidly. Linsingen's Army Group carried out a local attack on a bridgehead on the Stochod, north-east of Kovel, which had survived the fighting of 1916. This was in itself an unimportant operation, but the number of prisoners we took was so large that even I was astonished. The Imperial Chancellor approached me with the request to make as little as possible of this success, and I did as he asked, though extremely unwillingly. The troops who had carried out the attack did not deserve to be passed over in silence. In the Press our reserve about the Stochod battle gave rise to a certain amount of criticism. I understood that, but considered it my duty to accede to the Chancellor's request, in order not to disturb in any way the prospects of peace which at this moment really were looming into view G.H.Q. forbade any further demonstrations of force.

When Kerensky came on the scenes in May the great danger of the Russian Army being reorganized increased. England, France and the United States spared no effort to achieve this object. In view of this, frequent discussions took place at G.H.Q. as to whether a rapid attack on the Eastern Front with troops that the Commander-in-Chief there had on the spot, strengthened by a few divisions from the West, would not be better policy than continuing to play the part of inactive spectators; for now was the moment to level a blow at the Russian Army, while its fighting powers were reduced. I did not agree with that policy, although the position in the West had improved. I was unwilling to do anything which, even in appearance, might injure a real prospect of peace. From a

The Entente Offensive in the First Half of 1917

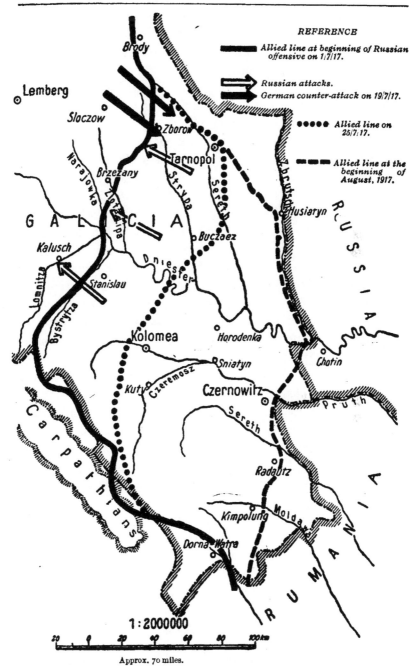

REFERENCE

━━━━ Allied line at beginning of Russian offensive on 1/7/17.

⇒ Russian attacks. German counter-attack on 19/7/17.

●●●●● Allied line on 25/7/17.

▬ ▬ ▬ Allied line at the beginning of August, 1917.

Brody

Lemberg

Sloczow

Zborow

Tarnopol

Brzezany

Narajowka

Zlota Lipa

Stryba

Sereth

Zbrutsch

Husiaryn

RUSSIA

GALICIA

Kalusch

Lomnitze

Bystrytza

Stanislau

Dniester

Buczoez

Kolomea

Horodenka

Sniatyn

Chotin

Kuty

Czeremosz

Czernowitz

Pruth

Sereth

Radautz

Kimpolung

Molda

Dorna Watra

Carpathians

RUMANIA

1 : 2000000

20 | 20   40   60   80   100 km

Approx. 70 miles.

Fig. 20.   The Battles in East Galicia in the Summer of 1917.

433

military point of view, too, this line of conduct was justified, because every revolution undermines and disintegrates the fighting strength of an army. Anyhow, I was still wondering whether this would happen, when on July 1st the first Russian attack took place in Galicia. The time of tedious waiting in the East was over and G.H.Q. no longer had their hands tied, but were given full freedom of action.

The Russian offensive was planned on a large scale. The attack was to be made from the Riga bridgehead, at Dvinsk, Lake Narotch, at and south of Smorgon, and in the whole of Galicia, from the Tarnapol–Zborow–Lemberg railway as far as the Carpathians. The centre of gravity of the whole operation lay here in the south. The Commander-in-Chief in the East was not unaware by the end of June of the projected offensive. Numerous deserters had kept him well informed and he took all the necessary defensive measures. To carry out the counter-attack he had planned he needed reinforcements from the West. It is true that for the moment things were quieter there, but it had to be assumed that fighting would continue. Nevertheless, whatever might happen there, G.H.Q. were bound to exploit the opportunity offered in the East. In order, if it were by any means possible, to deal with Russia once and for all, and so gain a free hand on one side, six divisions were set free for the East. More was not possible at the moment, and it was only very unwillingly that the army commanders on the Western Front gave up the divisions for the other front. They were unable to grasp the magnitude of the undertaking.

Next to a crossing of the Dvina above Riga, the most favourable point of attack on the Eastern Front, was the Zborow—valley of the Sereth line in East Galicia. From here an attempt might be made to envelop the southern portion of the Russian Army, and it was the intention of the Commander-in-Chief to put this plan into action at once. G.H.Q. was able to give its consent. How the attack would turn out, and whether it was to be regarded as a major operation, as I secretly hoped, or merely as a tactical counter-attack, and how the Russian and also the Austrian armies would fight, remained questions the solution of which I awaited with the keenest anxiety.

The Russian attack in East Galicia was made in dense masses with a vast expenditure of ammunition. It succeeded against Austrian troops, but not against German and Turkish. On July 1st strong Russian forces broke through the Austro-Hungarian line between Zborow and Brzezany. Austrian troops deserted to the enemy in large numbers. On July 2nd the C.-in-C. in the East had to throw in substantial reserves to ease the pressure. Further Russian attacks collapsed. The offensive against the southern army began on July 4th. The fierce struggle lasted for several days, and ended with a complete success for the defence of General Count von Bothmer's army, which consisted almost exclusively of German troops.

South of the Dniester the Russian attack against the Austrian 3rd Army on July 6th and 7th was completely successful. The Austrian troops gave way ; a German division which had but recently arrived tried to stem the retreat, but was carried along by it. The Russians pressed forward to the Lomnitza and occupied Kalusch. The position was critical for the Commander-in-Chief. He had collected his reserves for the intended counter-attack between Zborow and the Sereth, in the direction of Tarnopol, and the Western divisions were being moved to this area. Just as in the previous year the Archduke Charles's front had to be strengthened before we could concentrate against Rumania, so now the C.-in-C. in the East had to stiffen the Austrian troops, and especially the 3rd Army, before he could carry out his preparations for the counter-attack. He is the more to be congratulated inasmuch as, in spite of the retreat south of the Dniester and the violent attacks which now began in the north, he made his thrust north of Zborow and carried through the operation without a hitch.

At Kalusch luck favoured us. The Russian Army had already paid too dearly for its early keenness in attack and had made no further progress on the Lomnitza. The first German troops to arrive were consequently able, thanks in part to the energetic intervention of Major Freiherr von dem Busche, of my staff, to hold the position. On July 15th they succeeded in gaining ground, and the crisis was overcome.

The most violent of the attacks on the C.-in-C. in the East's old front took place on July 21st and the following days at Krevo, south of Smorgon; here the Russians broke through a division of the Landwehr occupying a very long front, though it defended itself with extraordinary courage.

For a few days things looked extremely serious, until our reserves and artillery fire restored the situation. The Russians evacuated our trenches. They were no longer what they had been.

Meanwhile our counter-attack group had finished their concentration between Zborow and the Sereth. Unfortunately the attack had to be postponed two or three days, until July 19th, on account of extremely bad weather. This was the day on which the peace resolution was debated in the German Reichstag. The attack was a brilliant success; ground was gained over an area twenty kilometres in breadth and fifteen kilometres in depth. The whole army was in high spirits. In the Reichstag this victory for German arms was described as a stimulant.

The next day the thrust was continued in the direction of Tarnopol, which fell on July 25th, and the Russians began to with draw from before our positions south of the Zborow-Tarnopol railway. The tactical counter-attack developed into an operation on a grand scale. The disorganization of the Russian front extended further and further to the south. The southern army, the Austrian 3rd and 7th Armies, which had a specially strong stiffening of German troops, moved up. The whole of the Eastern Front as far as the Bukovina was now in motion. The Russian Army retired in disorder; the Revolution had broken its backbone.

On August 2nd and 3rd we succeeded by steady fighting in reaching the Zbrucz, and took Czernowitz and Kimpolung. This was the utmost to which we could effectively develop the counter-attack of the 19th of July. It is true that for a time I hoped that the Austrian 3rd and 7th Armies would press forward into Moldavia, but the Austrian powers of attack were not equal to the task, and the Germans alone were not strong enough. Communications turned out to be so difficult that the proper supply of the armies could not be managed until the railways had been repaired. Large bodies of men were set to work at this, but the destruction was so thorough that weeks elapsed before we could think of extending operations to the south of the Dniester.

The German troops, as in the previous autumn, had done splendidly in this open fighting ; they felt relieved from the terrible grip of trench warfare. But the Austrian Army, in spite of all the care lavished on it, showed a diminution of fighting power which was in the highest degree alarming.

On the Zbrucz the struggle swayed backwards and forwards for a few days longer ; south of Czernowitz the group of armies under the Archduke Joseph, who had taken over the chief command in Hungary from the Emperor Charles, pressed a little bit further eastward ; but although battles had begun on the Rumanian front, the major operation was over.

Here, in the mountains between Focsani and the frontier, a Russo–Rumanian offensive had opened on July 24th to relieve pressure elsewhere. It chanced to strike a weak spot in our line and won a local success.

Our advance north of the Carpathians, down from the Dniester and through the Bukovina towards Moldavia, suggested the idea of resuming operations against the Rumanian troops and an attack on the lower Sereth, whilst the Austrian armies continued their march past and south of Czernowitz. Various considerations led us to send the Alpine Corps to Rumania in July and still further weaken the Western Front. This attack was still under contemplation when the Russo-Rumanian thrust mentioned above took pace. It was arranged that Mackensen's Army Group was to make an advance northwards on the west bank of the Sereth, and the southern group of armies, under the Archduke Joseph, from the Oitoz Pass towards Ocna. The battles began in the first half of August and lasted into the second half. They scored local successes in both places, and forced the enemy to surrender the ground won on July 31st.

Thanks to the influence of the French the Rumanian Army had become so much stronger that strategic successes seemed out of the question for us as long as the offensive in Bukovina remained at a standstill. For the present it was impossible to continue it. The attacks of the Army Groups under Mackensen and the Archduke Joseph were held up. The Rumanians, in their turn, now made unsuccessful attacks. Gradually the fighting died down here also.

The great Entente offensive to which we were to succumb in the early summer of 1917 had petered out; owing to the Russian Revolution there had been no concerted action. When the Anglo-French-Italian advance was made Russia fell out, and when Russia took the offensive the Western Front had weakened. We had held out, though we had suffered heavily, and on the Eastern Front we had won a notable success. The military collapse of Russia was patent to the whole world.

Six months of the submarine campaign had gone by. It had accomplished much; judging by mere numbers more, but in its final result less, than had been anticipated. I still hoped that the expectations of the Navy would be realized in the near future. But I began to wonder whether as many U boats as possible were really being built. It was imperative that every effort should be made to increase the effect of the submarine campaign. It is true that, in view of the anxious military and economic situation, G.H.Q. was not in a position to transfer skilled workmen to any great extent from the army to the navy, or to curtail the Hindenburg programme for the sake of the latter.

VI

Hard work and an unflinching determination, helped by the Russian Revolution, had enabled us to relieve the military situation. But meanwhile, as had already been the case in Austria-Hungary, the disintegration of the moral resolution of the

The Entente Offensive in the First Half of 1917

German people, under pressure of this upheaval and of economic privations, combined with the growing influence of enemy propaganda, was to bring about events which steadily lowered the fighting strength of both the allied States and jeopardized our military gains. From this time onwards the hope of the Entente for the internal collapse of their enemies was continually fed. Peace was to be made immeasurably more difficult, and the end of the war postponed.

Chancellor von Bethmann and Count Czernin were both completely obsessed by the influence of the Russian Revolution. They both feared a similar catastrophe in their own countries, and thought of nothing but possibilities of peace, which had unfortunately receded into the dim distance, whereas until peace had been attained they should have taken energetic measures to prosecute the war. They ought to have raised the *moral* of the nation by creative activity, just as G.H.Q. had succeeded in improving the army's fighting strength in a desperate struggle against a powerful adversary. As it was, their policy led to perpetual concessions at home, and they gave up the task of leading the nation. The whole tendency of their ideas made them overlook the unspeakable harm they were doing to the strength of their respective countries, which ought to have shown a united front to the enemy, and they did not realize how they were prejudicing the conduct of the war. Neither of these men, whom destiny had placed at the head of their people at this terrible crisis, possessed the strong character that events demanded. No doubt they had to face serious internal difficulties. Count Czernin, with his conglomerate Empire, had an infinitely complex task. The problems presented to Herr von Bethmann were probably easier ; he had only to act in accordance with the conclusions that could be drawn with overwhelming force from the nature of the war and from our position in face of a foe determined to destroy us. Instead of harping ever more and more on the idea of a peace of reconciliation, which was always out of the question, he ought to have knitted the nation together and pointed out to it the great tasks before it and the objects to be attained, and then have given us in the army a free hand. The German people ought to have been shown again and again what they were fighting for, and what the enemy in his heart of hearts really wanted. The majority would then have followed him as they had done in 1914. There are always some who can never be taught. Was there really any room for doubt regarding the ideas and objects of our enemies, as interpreted in the light of their whole history and their whole mentality, not to mention their answer to our peace offer of December 12th and to Wilson's Note of December 18th? Could anyone fail to realize that the weakening of the war spirit at home must cripple the conduct of the war?

How seriously the position was regarded by G.H.Q. the decision for the submarine campaign and the retreat to the Siegfried line had shown drastically and clearly enough, even to the lay mind. It must have been obvious to the Government that earnest and thoroughly conscientious effort alone could pull us through.

At the beginning of April, 1917, the Kaiser received the Emperor Charles at Homburg. The latter was accompanied by Count Czernin and General von Arz. The Chancellor, the Field-Marshal and I were also summoned.

Herr von Bethmann and Count Czernin had already met. On March 27th these gentlemen had come to an agreement, recorded in the " Vienna Document " of that date. It comprised a minimum peace programme, based on the *status quo ante,* and a programme for bringing the war to a favourable conclusion on the lines I had advocated. No mention was made of any renunciation whatever.

This important document was first known to the Secretaries of State and G.H.Q. on February 5th, 1918.

While kings and councillors were discussing affairs at Homburg, General von Arz, the Field-Marshal and I held a consultation on the situation. We had occupied the Siegfried line and were expecting the great April offensives. I considered the British attack imminent. The result of the submarine campaign in March had been good and the Ministry of the Interior began to build high hopes upon it. The importance of America was given due weight. Our verdict on the situation was grave but confident ; we hoped to repulse the Entente attacks in the near future, but for the rest had to await the results of the submarine campaign and the development of events in Russia.

General von Arz had similar hopes for the Austro–Hungarian Front, but added that in consequence of lack of raw materials and of the heavy demands on man power, the Austro–Hungarian Army could only fight on until the winter. There was no difference of opinion as to the necessity for prosecuting the war for the present with the utmost energy. It was impossible to foresee how events might have developed by the winter.

About midday there was a consultation between the German Imperial Chancellor, Count Czernin, the Field-Marshal, General von Arz and myself. The Chancellor asked me before the discussion began whether I thought the time had come to make a move for peace. I could only answer that the Entente were about to make an immense effort and that I did not think the moment favourable from the military point of view. The question was not further discussed, even in connection with the Russian Revolution. Count Czernin proposed that in order to obtain an early peace we should give Alsace–Lorraine to France. Austria–Hungary was to hand over Galicia to Poland and support a union of Poland and Germany. At this moment our meeting with the two statesmen, which had lasted about ten minutes, was interrupted. The Chancellor and Count Czernin were summoned to the two Emperors. This ended the official part of the Imperial meeting as far as I was concerned. In the afternoon I was received by the Emperor Charles.

After lunch Count Czernin explained his views to me in a private conversation. He based his wish for peace upon the internal condition of the Dual Monarchy. I had no reason to conceal my personal opinion. After all, I was the son of my Fatherland and had a perfect right to say what I thought. I told Count Czernin that he ought to lead the peoples of the Dual Monarchy more firmly and raise their *moral.* He replied that this was impossible. I then turned to his proposals. His

Polish project seemed to me very dubious. What would Poland's attitude towards it be? What effect would it have on our eastern provinces? I was all the more astonished at this whole scheme, as Austro–Hungarian policy in Warsaw showed no signs of honest concern about German interests. The Polish project was quite indefinite; the surrender of Alsace–Lorraine to France, however, presented a perfectly clear issue, of which, in my opinion, there could be no question as long as we were not beaten. Every nation stands or falls by its honour. All German parties—even the Independent Socialists—were united in regarding Alsace–Lorraine as German, and in considering it a point of honour for us to fight to the utmost in defence of this possession. Any Government, or even the General Staff, which failed to recognize this would have been rightly swept away by indignant public opinion. Our situation was certainly serious, but we were still capable of putting up a stiff fight; we only needed the will to do so. The surrender of Alsace–Lorraine would have been an open confession of weakness and certainly condemned as such even by peace-lovers. At that time there was no need for such a sacrifice. It might confidently be expected that the Entente would see nothing in all these proposals but a trap or a confession of military defeat that would make them raise their demands considerably.

Count Czernin could give no definite answer to my inquiry as to whether the Entente would really be satisfied with the surrender of Alsace-Lorraine.

He expressed views of the gravest kind on Germany's internal conditions. He must have been in possession of excellent information. This closed our interview.

Count Czernin did not again mention the separation of Galicia from the Austrian Empire, though he continued for some time to urge that Rumania should be included in Austria-Hungary's sphere of influence, and the East, including Poland, in that of Germany. These were broad and clear generalizations with which G.H.Q. could only agree. They were recorded in the Kreuznach Agreement of May 17th and 18th.

Soon afterwards, however, Count Czernin supported the Austro–

Polish solution with great energy and skill, and thus revealed the real character of his country. For Austria to renounce Poland would have produced disastrous effects in the Monarchy. The prestige of the young Emperor was also at stake. It was obviously Count Czernin's intention to oust us from Poland as well as from Rumania. The Austro-Polish solution entailed grave dangers for Prussia and Germany. The Field-Marshal and I feared that it meant the break-up of the Alliance, and was a direct threat to our eastern provinces. The Poles would always pursue their claims to German territory, and the Prussian Poles would play into their hands. The Vienna Government would find itself forced to become the agent of their wishes. As long as these views were advanced by an isolated Poland Germany could deal with them, but if a Slav Austria stood behind them the whole matter assumed a different aspect. Germany's vital interests would be seriously threatened, conflict would arise between the two Empires, and would find Germany in an extraordinarily difficult position, both from the military and political point of view. The province of Silesia would have been encircled and our communications with East Prussia, Lithuania and Courland threatened. The annexation of these two districts was at that time by no means a fantastic dream. Neither did I see how, from the economic point of view, Germany could reconcile herself to the Austro–Polish solution, which in Poland itself was bound to entail the gravest difficulties and to cut us off from the Russian market. We knew from experience what an obstacle Austria–Hungary presented as a route for our trade to the Balkans. The question was often to be discussed by us in the future, and the verdict passed upon it by the German Government to undergo strange transformations.

Austria-Hungary was constantly discussing the early conclusion of peace. Thus, about the middle of April, the Emperor Charles, in a letter addressed to His Majesty, dealt with the possibility of having to make great sacrifices in order to obtain it. The dangers of an international revolution were described in great detail, and the urgent need for such a peace deduced from it. These and similar letters were handed by His Majesty to the Imperial Chancellor to answer. The Field-Marshal and I had to comment upon them from the military point of view, and the Chief of the Naval Staff from the naval. Of course we said, as in duty bound, what we thought was right ; how our comments were made use of was the business of the Imperial Chancellor. In this instance his ideas coincided with ours and with those of the Chief of the Naval Staff.

Early in May the Chancellor replied to the effect that, considering the great hopes the Entente had at the moment, both of the success of their offensive and of the re-establishment of Russia, our efforts would be doomed to absolute failure if we made our readiness for peace too obvious. It would merely make the Central Powers appear hopelessly exhausted and thereby make the enemy intensify his efforts. At the moment peace was only obtainable by submitting to the will of our enemies, but that kind of peace the people would neither understand nor permit.

Conditions in Russia had so far developed favourably for us. In that country the demand for peace was becoming more and more insistent. Our difficult task was to follow the process of development and disintegration in Russia with the closest attention, hasten it if we could, and deal with any approaches from that quarter in such a way that actual peace negotiations might follow. Possibly such negotiations might then become the prelude of a general peace.

This constituted the official reply to the Emperor Charles' letter.

On many other occasions Count Czernin pressed for peace. He continued to advocate the surrender of German territory to France, but he was never able to say whether the Entente was inclined for peace, or whether any tangible method of attaining it had presented itself. Count Czernin would surely have told us if he had discovered it.

In his speech of the 11th December, 1918, he discussed the questions of war and peace at great length ; presumably merely in order to show that he had seen disaster coming. That is an unproductive occupation.

Pessimists are always clever people. When the evil day arrives

they are gaped at for their wisdom. The mob offers them in-
cense—and to itself at the same time. The mob has always
anticipated disaster. If it does not come, the pessimists
and the mob are more satisfied than ever. So they both enjoy
themselves, anyhow. Men of action are not so fortunate ; they
are only right when they are successful. Then the mob cheers
them. But if they are not successful, or worse, meet with disaster,
the same mob stones them. Pessimists and the mob do not ask
what they themselves, or the men of action, have done to avert
disaster. The mob lacks judgment and cannot be expected to
ask.

But I am surprised to find Count Czernin behaving in the same
way. Has he really fairly told himself and the world what
he actually did, in the situation in which he found himself, to
avoid losing the war and so save his own and his Allies' countries
from disaster and shame ?

Unfortunately Count Czernin omitted to inform us earlier of
those facts which did not come to my knowledge until I read his
speech. He said : " On several occasions our representatives
got into touch with those of the Entente, but unfortunately these
feelers never got to the stage of concrete proposals. We frequently had the impression that we should be able to make a
separate peace without Germany, but we were never informed of
the definite conditions on which Germany, on her side, might
have peace.

" Above all, we were never told that Germany would be allowed
to retain the possessions she held before the war. . . . As the
Entente never declared their willingness to negotiate with a
Germany that had no desire for conquest, but kept reiterating
their desire to destroy Germany, we were forced into a defensive
war on Germany's behalf and our rôle in Berlin was made amazingly difficult."

These words, if spoken earlier, would have silenced all our talk
about a peace of reconciliation and have revived the warlike
spirit and so brought blessing to our people.

Count Czernin, however, held his peace, and so took on himself
an enormous responsibility. Or perhaps he informed the Im-

perial Chancellor and the latter neglected to enlighten the people. The German people has the right to know the truth.

It was not only in Berlin, as Count Czernin thinks, but in Vienna also, that a statesman was lacking who was equal to the demands of this war, and could collaborate with the military leaders in securing victory.

The leading statesmen had no faith in victory, failed to find the road to peace, and yet remained in office.

VII

I deeply regretted the events which took place in Germany in the spring and summer of 1917, as I did all other manifestations of weakness. They were bound to react unfavourably on our conduct of the war, and therefore on the subsequent peace. Looking back I can see that our decline obviously began with the outbreak of the Revolution in Russia. The Government was oppressed on the one hand by the fear that it might spread to Germany and on the other by the knowledge of their inability to revive the resolution and warlike ardour of the people, waning as they were through the combination of innumerable circumstances. No doubt our precarious military position and, later, the want of success achieved in the submarine war, of which some people had unfortunately been too confident, made it more difficult to rouse our energy. It was obvious that it suffered from these causes.

But after all, owing to the collapse of Russia, our position in the summer of 1917 was better than that of the Entente. We were justified in being hopeful. But there were other reasons for our spiritual decline. The Government lacked the resolution to deal energetically with abuses. And behind it there was the Reichstag, with no united will, in part sincerely anxious about our future, in part merely striving for power from selfish reasons.

On the 7th April there was published a decree by His Majesty on the franchise. I only heard of it after the publication. Neither the Emperor nor the Imperial Chancellor, von Bethmann, ever spoke to me about internal affairs. Nor was it my business to originate discussions on these subjects, as internal politics had nothing to do with me.

The connection between the franchise decree and the Russian Revolution was too obvious. That was what made it so ill-advised. If a change in the franchise was necessary—as it doubtless was—it should have been made before the war, at the latest in August, 1914, with a *grand geste*, as the free gift of a strong Government. Worst of all, the Government now made the Crown the centre of political discussion, instead of keeping it clear of party strife. Besides, apart from a small section, this step pleased only the enemy, who probably grasped the reason for it with gusto. At every step the Government should have considered its probable effect on the enemy, as well as at home.

During the war home politics should have been dominated and directed by consideration of the effect on the enemy. The greater the prominence given to questions of internal politics, the lower the warlike ardour of the nation will sink. Any statesman should know that. The decrees of 7th April and 11th July disclosed our weakness to the enemy and revealed our fear of revolution. The enemy must have said to himself that there is no smoke without fire and a conflagration is therefore possible. Revolution will come. He must therefore have concluded that he had only to hold out and fan the flame to attain his object— revolution in Germany and her ultimate destruction.

The effect of the April decree at home was very much what it was abroad. The revolutionary elements perceived the Government's anxiety and became more exacting. Their reply was the strikes of the second half of April. They were an echo of the Russian Revolution and proved how dreadful was the lack of sympathy with the fighting men at the front. They also showed to what extent the mass of the workers had escaped from the control of their leaders. The decree produced no soothing effect, as the Government had hoped. It was too late for that and the Government itself was too weak and too incapable of producing anything new from its own resources.

The people were not much affected by the Prussian franchise ; only a few politicians and newspapers took a lively interest in it. Unfortunately it proved an instrument to widen the split at home and intensify the secret agitation. No one in the Army took any interest in the question. The Navy, which was nearer home and not engaged in active operations, is said to have been less apathetic. The thought of elections in time of war only filled me with anxiety. They were bound to reduce our strength still further. I also considered an election to be an injustice towards the soldier at the front who could, of course, according to the ideas prevalent at that time, take no part in it. I was drawn into the party conflict by partisans and opponents of the right to vote, although I never expressed my opinion on the matter in public. I often spoke of this to the Ministers.

Personally, I hoped a solution of the franchise difficulty might be found in a professional qualification such as Bismarck had had in mind. This, perhaps, might have imparted new vigour to our stagnant and sterile public life. At that time we had not yet reached that stage. Now we have a new, vague catchword : " Anchoring the workmen's councils in the constitution," which again points to some sort of representation by professions, at any rate in the First Chamber. It is inconceivable that only one class should have constitutional rights and the rest be sent empty away.

Further events announced the waning of our ardour—which had been alluded to with such kindling words in the Reichstag on the 27th February—before the Russian Revolution. In utter disregard of the destructive intentions of the enemy, the idea of peace by reconciliation made ever greater progress among the German people. It was swallowed most eagerly by those who feared the effects of victory on their political aspirations. During May and June a number of delegates, with facilities from the Government, undertook journeys to Stockholm, Austria-Hungary and Switzerland. We walked into the traps of the Entente. I was against these journeys and so was the Commander-in-Chief in the Marches. The Emperor decided in favour of them, and the deputies of the General Staff in Berlin had to prepare the passports. Count Czernin also sent the Socialist leaders of Austria-Hungary to Stockholm.

From there, supported by the Russian Revolution, the labour. ing classes of the hostile states were to be called upon to proclaim and carry out the " Reconciliation of Mankind." These endeavours revealed woeful ignorance of human nature, and certainly took no account of the spirit of the enemy nations, nor of our own ; they did, however, in some cases pursue decidedly revolutionary objects. No impression was produced on the enemy, but with us and in Austria the fighting spirit was weakened more and more. Confidence in our own strength was lost. Government allowed the conduct of affairs to slip more and more from its grasp ; and the worst of it was, it abandoned them, not to the people as a whole, but to certain groups which, throughout their history, had always displayed critical and never constructive faculties.

These assemblies and all the talk of peace by understanding suited the Entente very well. They disclosed our state of mind. But, with a clear idea of national feeling, they allowed no Socialist leaders to go to the meetings and declined to be bound in any way. They pursued quite different aims.

In the summer of 1917 the French Premier, Ribot, expressed his country's intention of destroying Germany so clearly that no misunderstanding was possible without deliberate self-deception. No one with the slightest sense of reality could doubt that for the Entente all the beautiful catchwords were mere window-dressing, intended to deceive the multitude, and to give might the appearance of right. The Government, the Reichstag and most of the people took it all for gospel. In the Reichstag, for the first time in the war, Socialist representatives openly threatened revolution. The " helots' peace " (of which the Imperial Chancellor spoke to G.H.Q. about this time), which would come if we gave in before the enemy felt any inclination to peace, was on its way.

General Headquarters observed the great spiritual decline with increasing anxiety, and in view of the uncompromising attitude of the enemy Governments felt bound to draw attention to the harm that was being done to the people and the army, especially in Berlin. More than once the Field-Marshal reported to His Majesty how greatly G.H.Q. missed the support of the Imperial Chancellor. We had urged the latter more and more frequently to strengthen the war-spirit of the nation.

On the 19th June, 1917, Field-Marshal von Hindenburg wrote to him as follows, to warn him against the view that the war would be over that autumn at the latest :

" These dangers " (of submarine warfare) " are undoubtedly recognized by clear-thinking people among our enemies. If in spite of this they advocate continuation of the war, it is because they expect the collapse of Germany and her allies to take place before their own. It may be that they hope to bring about this collapse by a victory on land, but they rely far more on economic and political causes, such as food difficulties, shortage of raw materials, disunion, discontent, and the supremacy of the German Radical Social Democracy. They base this expectation on the waning of our power of resistance at home, the growth of international sentiments, the state of our food supply, and the longing for peace to which we unfortunately give expression so often.

" A revival of our internal strength would be the most potent means of persuading our enemies of the futility of prolonging the war until their own means of existence are in danger of destruction. On the other hand, every complaint of disappointed hopes, every sign of exhaustion and longing for peace on our part, or that of our allies, any talk of the alleged impossibility of standing another winter campaign, can only have the effect of prolonging the war."

The wording of the Chancellor's reply, dated the 25th June, revealed extraordinary depression. His way of thinking differed from ours. He could find no way out of the situation, and still less could he summon up the energy to act. He was afraid of that " helots' peace," but talked about a peace by understanding, although he considered England's readiness for peace to be the necessary condition precedent and despaired of getting Lloyd George to agree to it.

However, his view of internal conditions soon became more

hopeful, as we may see from a telegram to the Emperor of the 5th July.

In the meanwhile, on the 27th June, the Field-Marshal had himself written to the Emperor : " Our greatest anxiety at this moment, however, is the decline in the national spirit. It must be revived, or we shall lose the war. Even our allies need a powerful tonic, otherwise there is a danger of their deserting us. For this it is necessary to solve those economic problems which are the most difficult and are of the greatest importance for the future. . . . The question arises whether the Chancellor is capable of solving these problems—and they must be correctly solved, or we are lost ! "

An outward indication of the falling-off of our spiritual capacity for war was afforded at the session of the Main Committee of the Reichstag on the 6th of July. Deputy Erzberger made a speech which utterly surprised us, in which he maintained that the submarine war was perfectly hopeless and that it was quite impossible for us to win the war at all. On this the spirit of the Reichstag broke down completely. The Imperial Chancellor had apparently been under a delusion when he changed his mind so suddenly on the 5th July. Now it was perfectly clear how far we had sunk. If things continued in this way in Germany, if nothing was done to encourage and strengthen the people, military defeat was indeed inevitable.

The War Minister agreed with us as to the bad effect of the events in Berlin on our military position and considered it necessary for the Field-Marshal to make a report to the Emperor on the subject. So the Field-Marshal and I proceeded to Berlin on the evening of the 6th. The Emperor, however, regarded those events as an entirely domestic affair which had nothing to do with the military authorities, and further considered that the latter should, constitutionally, be represented by the War Minister. So our presence in Berlin on the 7th produced no result in any direction and we returned to Kreuznach that evening.

The situation in Berlin became more acute. On the 8th of July the Chancellor, although at that time he accurately gauged the enemy's destructive intentions, agreed to the peace resolution which was to be put forward by the Majority parties and, at the same time, definitely promised them to apply the Reichstag franchise law to the elections for the Prussian Diet. Both these measures must have strengthened the enemy's will to an incalculable extent. On the afternoon of the 10th the Imperial Chancellor felt obliged to hand in his resignation, which was, however, refused on the 11th.

At Kreuznach we thought for a time that Prince von Bülow would succeed him. Further confusion was caused when, suddenly, the Austro–Hungarian Government openly sided with the Imperial Chancellor von Bethmann and against Prince von Bülow.

The Emperor had decided that Chancellor von Bethmann was to stay and the Crown Prince, who had arrived in Berlin, had given way. After all that had happened I could no longer believe that the Chancellor was the right man to perform the task demanded of him by this war and lead the country out of the depths of its depression to victory. It had become evident to me that, in order to conquer in the field, the General Staff needed the co-operation of the statesmen at home, and the better acquainted I became with the general situation after assuming duty the more convinced I was. This co-operation we had not obtained ; national thought and feeling at home had fallen off. The political leaders lacked creative force ; they had no ideal which would take hold of the people and thus develop their powers.

In 1914 we were aglow with patriotism, self-sacrifice and confidence in our own strength. We now needed fresh energy and impulse to make the German people forget the years of suffering and distress, of bitterness and disappointment, replenish it with holy ardour, strength and confidence, and enable it to imbue its fighting forces with fresh enthusiasm. The Imperial Chancellor underestimated the value of these moral forces. But the German people had to go on starving.

The Chancellor had permitted the enemy's refusal of our peace offer to pass by without letting the people know that, owing to the enemy's will, no just peace was possible, but that, on the contrary, as he believed and put it himself, a " helots' peace " was to be our lot. He had failed to imbue them with fresh warlike resolution and call upon them to fight for life and honour against a strong-willed enemy, striving for our destruction.

No, he himself despaired of victory and allowed the talk of an unattainable peace by understanding to shake our nerve, while it put all the trumps in the enemy's hand.

England's defiance of the laws of nations in employing the blockade against our very flesh and blood was not met by fiery protest ; the heart of the people was not filled with strong, manly hatred ; its holy ire was not directed against the inhuman enemy. Far from it. Discontent with the conditions at home, which were directly caused by the blockade, was permitted to spend its force internally, increase the effect of the blockade and disintegrate our national life.

The inhuman ill-treatment of our prisoners, the very flesh of our flesh, was not allowed to arouse any feelings which could be vented outside—though not, of course, against the prisoners in our hands. Instead, every expression of anger was suppressed, and the seeds of bitterness were sown.

When Wilson, on the entry of the United States into the war, attempted to drive a wedge between the Emperor, the princes and the people, the Chancellor did not arise to protect his Imperial Master. The Reichstag protested, but the Imperial Chancellor held his peace. He never called upon the people to defend the monarchical idea which, then as now, had its roots firmly fixed in millions of German hearts—he never prevented the axe being laid to the tree of the Imperial Office and the glory of the Empire.

Moreover, the political leaders lacked the strength to govern with firmness. At that time the mass of the people were not yet greedy for cheap phrases. They wanted to be sure that no unfair privileges were allowed as to living and conduct, and that in these respects everything was justly and equitably regulated. They also wanted peace, but never a peace such as we are now getting and could only have got even then. The

Government had lost the determination to win and its faith in German strength, which had so brilliantly manifested itself in the past three years and had only commenced to totter for want of leading. So the army did not receive what it needed for victory. I no longer believed that a change would take place under that Chancellor. The hope of being able to collaborate in complete accord with the Imperial Chancellor, which I had cherished when I went to General Headquarters, had broken down. So I wrote out my resignation.

The constitutional problems did not affect my military action. Personally, I considered the barrier which the Imperial Chancellor erected between the Emperor and the people to be deplorable. The Emperor could not become sufficiently acquainted with men. Several times, though in vain, I had asked Chancellor von Bethmann to let him meet leading men ; it could only serve to smooth matters over in a satisfactory manner. For this reason I thought it advantageous to include Parliamentary Secretaries of State in the Cabinet. I hoped, too, that through them the country would be more likely to receive what it needed for the war.

The Field-Marshal joined me and submitted his resignation at the same time. Our applications were dispatched to Berlin on the evening of the 12th, after we had sent a preliminary notification to General von Lyncker in the afternoon. Simultaneously we received an urgent telegram from the War Minister who considered it necessary, in view of the military situation, for the Field-Marshal to make a further personal report in Berlin. The Emperor also wished to see us.

In the meantime the Crown Prince had had a conference on the morning of the 12th with the party leaders of the Reichstag, the majority of whom either declared themselves in favour of the immediate resignation of the Chancellor or else asserted that they attached no importance to his remaining in office. No one took his side.

On the Crown Prince's report the Emperor now decided to accept the resignation of Chancellor von Bethmann.

When we arrived in Berlin on the 13th the Emperor had

already given his decision. I hoped that the man who was to assume office would be capable of concentrating the whole energy of the German people for a united effort.

On our first visit to Berlin, on the 7th of July, the Field-Marshal and I had been prepared to meet members of the Reichstag at the General Staff offices and give them information about the military situation in an informal manner. I was anxious to reassure them. This conversation took place in the afternoon of the 13th. Before the conference began, the Secretary of State, Dr. Helfferich, and Under-Secretary of State Wahnschaffe talked with me in a very excited manner about the possibility of a peace resolution.

Our defensive attitude throughout the first half of 1917, the various failures near Arras, in the Wytschaete salient and in Galicia, where we had not yet attacked, the absence up to date of any decisive result from the submarine war and our serious situation as regards food and raw materials, had caused great anxiety. These were the matters we were to discuss. But everyone was thinking about the peace resolution which the Reichstag was to introduce with the co-operation of Count Czernin, possibly even at his instigation. This gave rise in Berlin to the completely erroneous idea that we had come to take part in the deliberations on the peace resolution. As a matter of fact, the deputies kept on coming back to it.

We summed up our view of the situation more or less to the effect that on land it was serious, but secure. We simply must hold out, since our enemies did not want peace. The ammunition supply had improved and there was sufficient raw material. We made no reference to the impending operations in Galicia, both for the sake of secrecy and because their development could not possibly be foreseen. We had faith in the success of the submarine war, although up to date it had not produced the decisive effect that we had hoped for. In discussing the possibility of transferring the American Army to France, we put forward the naval opinion that it could only be considered feasible to a limited extent. To the peace resolution we were unable to give any support ; we explained that it did not meet with our views, since it was bound to exercise an adverse influence on the spirit of the troops and on the determination of the people, while the enemy would construe it as a confession of weakness. Its full effect must therefore be injurious. We also pointed out the evil consequences that might result from it in Bulgaria, where the demands for peace went very far.

The text of my argument was this : We shall win if the Army is backed up by a united people. That is where the people's representatives must help.

The meeting was quite informal. Herr von Helfferich requested the deputies to take no steps with regard to the peace resolution for the present. He invited them to meet him at the Ministry of the Interior the next day and the day after for a conference at which the new Imperial Chancellor would be present. The gentlemen accepted. However, early the next morning the peace resolution appeared in the *Vorwärts*. At the suggestion of Under-Secretary of State Wahnschaffe I had tried to prevent it, and had asked Deputy Südekum to exert his influence on *Vorwärts* in the same sense. The publication could, however, no longer be delayed. With that the Majority parties in the Reichstag had absolutely committed themselves Further discussion could serve no useful purpose.

Dr. Michaelis became Imperial Chancellor. Herr von Valentini, Chief of the Emperor's Civil Cabinet, had given the Field-Marshal the names of several gentlemen, of whom His Majesty would select one. Prince Bülow, whom the Field-Marshal had on occasion suggested to the Emperor, was not among them. Count Hertling had refused and declared he could not co-operate with the General Staff, at which I was not particularly surprised.

From correspondence I had had with him through the Bavarian War Minister, von Hellingrath, I had unfortunately acquired the conviction that he and everyone else in Munich regarded the General Staff in the same light as did the Wilhelmstrasse. Count Hertling became Chancellor later and on his retirement he expressed to me his satisfaction at the hearty co-operation that had marked the relations between his office and General

Headquarters. The Field-Marshal told Herr von Valentini that he should welcome any gentleman His Majesty might nominate. I was surprised to find that the authorities concerned did not have a successor to the Imperial Chancellor always in readiness, and that in a matter of such decisive importance for its destiny, Germany had to live from hand to mouth.

The path of our internal development had not afforded scope for the growth of strong personalities. It was quite striking to see how the officer class, the members of which were always thought to be the most narrow-minded, had produced men of decision, whilst the civil official class, on the contrary, had unfortunately so conspicuously failed in this respect. Men who were prominent in public life kept out of the way and followed their own professions. There may have been men of strong character in the Reichstag who could have guided the destiny of the country. The party sytem prevented their coming to the front. We were poor in men. Our political system had not produced new creative brains and by its barrenness it pronounced its own sentence.

Our participation in further parliamentary discussions of the peace resolution at the Ministry of the Interior had been suggested by the new Imperial Chancellor. I requested him to dispense with our attendance. I was convinced that we had fulfilled our task the day before and that it would only drag us into political controversy. The Chancellor persisted. As far as possible, we wished to support him in taking over his burdensome heritage, and therefore decided to comply. At the same time, we were desirous of showing Dr. Michaelis what value we attached to confidential collaboration with the Imperial Government. Both the Field-Marshal and I frequently wrote in this sense to the new Chancellor.

At the meeting we thought it most remarkable that the Majority parties based their demand for the peace resolution on the spirit of the country at the moment. Only by this means could the masses be rendered capable of holding out, if the wished-for peace did not materialize. This was a melancholy picture, far worse than I had expected. At the same time, the hope of a collapse of the enemy was expressed. The Russian Socialists were said to be desirous of forcing the other States of the Entente to stop the war. Otherwise no new points were raised.

As senior representative of the General Staff, the Field-Marshal again spoke against the resolution. I merely pointed out to the gentlemen sitting next me that the resolution contained not a single allusion to the Army. They therefore included a sentence expressing the thanks of the people to the Army.

When we left I requested Deputy Erzberger to stop the peace resolution. Beyond that I felt that my presence had not been necessary at this discussion of the question, and that I should have done better not to go. I said so later to the Deputy Müller-Meiningen, among others.

From the tribune of the Reichstag the peace resolution went out into the world. As anticipated, it produced on our enemies no political effect whatever; they took it as a confession of weakness. Bulgaria and Turkey began to doubt our victory. Nor was the effect in the country what the movers had hoped.

Instead of drawing the proper conclusion from the refusal of the enemy and strengthening the fighting spirit of the people, the Government gave no thought to the enemy, but entangled itself further and further in the unfortunate idea of a peace by understanding that could be had at any time. This was to prove the curse of the peace resolution. The General Staff considered it a mistake from the military point of view. But the Field-Marshal and I authorized the Imperial Chancellor to announce our concurrence in his attitude towards it, because he wished to avoid a conflict with the majority of the Reichstag in the interests of the prosecution of the war. And so we also shouldered the responsibility for the resolution which we thought a lesser evil than internal confusion. To that pitch had things come in Germany. We hoped the new Imperial Chancellor might improve matters, even if only gradually, and therefore thought it necessary to meet his wishes.

In Berlin the deterioration of *moral* at home had literally thrust itself on my notice. I could not fold my hands and watch the spirit of our people fall still further and undermine our fighting capacity altogether. Consequently, I laid before the new Chancellor the request I had made to his predecessor in the previous December, that the direction of the Press and the education of public opinion should be put in the hands of an authority under his immediate control. He promised to discuss this application at the end of August.

VIII

The spirit of the people at home rendered action imperative. We had the best prospects of winning the war, but it was not over and what we had won had to be kept. We were still a long way from that. The popular state of mind jeopardized everything. Besides, efforts at direct propaganda in the Army were observable. The Quartermaster-General wrote on the 25th of July : " It is certain that the Independent Social Democrats are carrying on an agitation in the Army which is in the highest degree detrimental to discipline." That this was the case at that early date is corroborated by the leader of the Independent Social Democratic Party—Ledebour.

Speaking at a conference of the Soldiers' and Workmen's Councils in connection with the events that took place between the 5th and 9th of November, 1918, he said :

" These four days, up to the 9th of November, were utilized by Scheidemann and his associates to reap the fruit of nearly two years' work by the Independents."

Another leader, Richard Müller, asserted : " The preparations for revolution were made as long ago as June, 1916, though the object was at the time not so clearly apparent."

The Independent Socialists had definitely paved the way for revolution for a long time. The majority of the Reichstag, and a section of the Press and the public, unfortunately helped on this work, often unconsciously.

In July, 1917, I had definitely come to the conclusion that

459

under the circumstances General Headquarters could not remain inactive until the end of August. Whatever it could do to revive our spiritual capacity for war must be undertaken at once. I was aware that, so long as the Government did not itself take energetic steps in this direction, whatever we did would only be patch-work.

Nor, owing to the slowness and confusion of ideas prevailing in the Civil Government, had I any guarantee that the work would be done thoroughly, even if the new Chancellor were to take charge of the work of educating public opinion personally. It was not easy for him, either, to carry through innovations and establish some entirely new machinery, since most of the Government departments were dominated by the same spirit which had hitherto radiated from the Imperial Chancellor's office, or, at any rate, did not oppose it—the same thing, in its effects.

For a long time past I had been thinking over the problem of diffusing a knowledge of the national aims and needs in the Army. It now became a burning question.

In accordance with the proposal submitted to me by Lieut.-Colonel Nicolai, General Headquarters arranged for patriotic instruction in the Field Army. But this was only a poor substitute for the work of enlightening public opinion at home, work which was done so consistently and effectively in the Entente countries.

The importance of patriotic instruction, or, as we first called it, the " work of enlightenment among the troops," was summed up in the following sentences :

" The German Army, owing to the spirit which animates it, is superior to its enemies and a powerful support to its Allies.

" At the beginning of the war the foundations of this spirit were enthusiasm and the discipline which had been inculcated during prolonged peace training. The three years of war have changed and enlarged these foundations. A comprehensible longing for home, family and calling, may weaken its war resolution and take the edge off the will to hold out till the final victory is gained.

The Entente Offensive in the First Half of 1917

" The long duration of the war has also brought with it want and sacrifice in increasing measure, both at home and in the Army. The more these burdens oppress the spirit of the Army, the more must the foundations of fighting power be laid on conviction, sense of duty and definite resolve.

" To supply this need is the task of patriotic instruction in the Army."

On the 15th of September, 1917, I wrote :

" The enemy's determination to destroy us and the necessity for us to go on fighting are less obvious to the troops employed on the lines of communication, on garrison duty and at home, than to the fighting forces themselves. For this reason special attention must be given to the *moral* of the troops on the lines of communication, and patriotic instruction must be specially fostered among them.

" The proper course is to concentrate on the relationship between the home and the Army. From the spiritual point of view and for the fulfilment of the national tasks, the people and the Army are one. Consequently, great importance attaches to the cultivation of patriotic feeling among the people at home, a duty which is carried on in conjunction with the civil authorities. The prosecution of this task must be regarded as one of the most important duties of the military authorities at home."

I intentionally extended this patriotic instruction to the home territory, although in other respects I refrained from direct action there. But I could not sit still and let everything slide before my very eyes. I expected to produce a stimulating effect, but received not the very slightest assistance from the civil authorities, although the Imperial Chancellor, Dr. Michaelis, and Secretary of State von Kühlmann recognized that some sort of machinery had to be created in order to raise the national spirit. An impression prevailed that nothing should be undertaken which might inflame national passions, for we had reached a point at which the development of national feeling was regarded as a damnable crime.

The War Minister agreed to the work of patriotic instruction being extended to the domain of the G.O.C.'s of the Corps Dis tricts. In the summer of 1918, at his request, he was given wide powers over these officers.

As the first object of instruction I recommended discussion of the causes of the war, Germany's economic development and its importance, the consequences of a lost war, especially for the German workman, and the necessity for continuing the struggle until we had broken the will of our enemies and created a safe foundation for further economic development.

I further laid stress on our justifiable hope of final victory, and the need for leadership and authority on the one hand and discipline on the other.

" Thoughts of self must be suppressed in view of the great common aim. Strikes endanger the success of the war and are paid for by the blood of the troops. Dreams of peace prolong the war, and so does discontent. Unity at home makes us strong ; everything else is weakening."

I designated as our object in the war the " safeguarding of our future," and closed with the words : " Army and people must unite in backing up the leaders of the Empire with all their strength until peace is finally concluded."

These instructions were based on the military situation at the time. They were the natural counter-measure to the wretched ideas prevailing at home. I believed in our final victory and feared disaster. I did all I could to show the people how serious was the situation without still further depressing them. I set great value on the moral factor, like many others ; but among them were men who deliberately undermined the fighting capacity of the German people and with it discipline in the Army. Between these two extremes stood the great bulk of the nation who had no conception of the spirit of their own people nor of that of the enemy.

In my view the War Press Office ought insistently to direct the authorities responsible for the work of enlightenment to describe the dangers of a lost war.

Patriotic instruction was to be kept away from all party intrigue. In this I included attack on, or defence of, the peace resolution and discussion of our war aims   I tolerated no departure from this principle. But I had no objection to superior officers expressing their own opinion on war aims to their men in a calm and objective manner, provided the latter approached them on the subject in a spirit of confidence.

It was a bad sign that in October this subject of instruction was approached in the Reichstag solely from the point of view of narrow party politics, while its real significance was misunderstood. The regulations for the instruction were closely examined and nothing objectionable was found in them. I was curious to see whether any demand for Government action would be put forward, or whether it might feel itself called upon to take up the matter. But the Reichstag was content merely to criticize; useful work was no part of its programme. The Government was glad to have steered past an obvious reef. But the public remained ignorant of the dangers which menaced it.

There were still men in Germany who had correctly gauged the enemy's mind. They desired to strengthen the fighting spirit and founded the " Fatherland Party " (*Vaterlandspartei*). I had no connection with them. But their work was most welcome to me in the interests of the war ; that their objects went too far did not matter. The storms of war guarantee that no trees grow up to the sky.

I began to hope that the Fatherland Party would at last do some good but my hope was short-lived, for it was soon dragged into the orbit of domestic politics. We were going in for internal politics instead of war politics. Its name may have been unfortunate and various circumstances attending its foundation may have been detrimental to the cause, but its energy was broken by its opponents and by the Government. In this Count Hertling not only followed the lead of the Majority parties. To my horror I found it coincided with his own private opinions. Instead of providing allies for those who were carrying on the war the Government took away those we had without supplying their place itself. Such was the state of affairs ; the Lord in Heaven forsook His German people, because it had forsaken itself.

I attached importance to gaining a personal knowledge of

the working of patriotic instruction. Accordingly, I arranged for the Propaganda Officer at Saarbrücken to give a lecture at Kreuznach of the same nature as he was delivering in public. The lecturer, Lieutenant Schmetzer, described the effects of an unsuccessful war on our working classes most effectively. He showed that they would be deprived of work and food or become the slaves of international capital. I can only say that all of us who heard the lecture were deeply impressed. I considered it to be of general interest, especially to the Secretary of State for Foreign Affairs, and had it repeated in his presence. Unfortunately, the hopes I had based on it were not realized.

It was not to be expected that the regimental officers, particularly the young company commanders, who were fully occupied with their daily duties, would display a sufficient grasp of the possibilities and requirements of patriotic instruction. I therefore wished it to be directed by officers who were in touch with the state of feeling both in the Army and at home, and who were particularly qualified to enter into the way of thinking of the men at the Front. They in turn were to get into touch with suitable officers, non-commissioned officers and men, and obtain the assistance of men from home. We were confronted with an entirely novel task and had to overcome suspicion and numerous difficulties in the Army itself. Nor was it easy to find suitable propaganda officers. Much time was bound to elapse before everything was working smoothly.

Even after patriotic instruction was instituted I continued to receive reports from the Army Headquarters as to the spirit and feeling of the Army and made use of every opportunity of obtaining an insight into its state of mind. Incidentally I heard that the chaplains were fulfilling their responsible office with devotion and ability and gave valuable support to the troops in the trenches.

In the Corps Districts at home the work was naturally even more difficult than in the Army. There also men of all parties helped us. The Government, however, held absolutely aloof.

The soldier was particularly concerned about his future after the war. This was natural considering the economic conditions at home, the ever-increasing selfishness and the ruthless profiteering. While I was still Chief of Staff to the Commander-in-Chief in the East, at a time when conditions at home had not yet become acute, I had, by means of communications to the Army newspapers, endeavoured to inform the troops of what was being done for disabled men and for dependents. I took much interest in these questions and observed with regret that the people at home showed less and less gratitude towards the disabled, and that the feelings of the latter were very often insufficiently considered. The question was one that concerned the whole German people, and should not have been exploited for party purposes.

Care for the soldier and for the dependents of the fallen was to me of vital importance. It could best be assured by final victory which alone would place it upon a sound foundation. But I wanted to do something more personal than that. A und for the disabled was started in May, 1918, in which I collaborated and which was then called after me. The Ludendorff Fund was a brilliant success. It was originated by an enthusiastic German lady, Fräulein Emma Tscheuschner, who was most energetically assisted in her great work by Director Henrich, and it raised far more than 150 million marks, a quite unprecedented result. During the Revolution it was renamed the "National Fund." Did the national delegates and the first Government of the German Republic object to my name being connected with a charitable institution which, mainly on account of my name, had brought in such great sums, and by which many thousands of disabled men have benefited? I leave this action to the judgment of humanity and the disabled who enjoy well-earned benefits from the " Ludendorff Fund," should they ever hear my name.

What has happened to the Fund under its new name I do not know. It is not in accordance with my ideas that advances have been made from it to take the place of state aid. That was not the intention. I wanted to help and it is now like a knife in my heart to see disabled soldiers, who are unable to earn their living, going begging. That also, however, passes for gratitude and the national sense of duty.

It seemed to me a particularly important branch of the care of the disabled to discover how brave men who had lost limbs could be re-educated so as to recover their joy in life and work and thus be reinstated in their former surroundings and given back to the country. All endeavours towards this object, as well as the progress made in the manufacture of artificial limbs, I followed with active interest.

Care for the soldier included not only provision for the dependents and the disabled, but also arrangements for ensuring economic security after the war for the sound men who wished to work. That was a duty of the State and the people at home towards the class that had unselfishly done so much for them. Soldiers ought to have been given cheap houses and cheap land, with proprietary rights, in which speculation should have been forbidden. This, of course, could only be effected very gradually, and should not involve harshness to the original owner nor loss of his rights. I was much impressed by the opinions of the land-reformer, Herr Damaschke, on the need for reducing the cost of housing, especially for the working classes, and for excluding profiteering, as also by his historical treatment of the subject. The information he gave about the scarcity of houses after the war of 1870–71 seemed to me of the greatest importance. G.H.Q. approached the Imperial Chancellor, pointed out the influence of the housing question on the after-effects of the war as regards national recuperation and requested him to bring in a bill to safeguard the rights and properties of soldiers. We also asked that means might be provided for building small houses and for securing them against speculation. G.H.Q. induced the Director-General of Medical Services, Lieutenant-General von Schjerning, to take an interest in the whole settlement policy to which he and his assistants, especially Major Dr. Hochheimer, devoted themselves with great enthusiasm. Their ideas were embodied in a memoir which was also sent to the Imperial Chancellor.

After the war I wanted to bring up a contented generation,

capable of self-defence. In the Baltic littoral I wanted to create a large settlement area for soldiers, and for the large number of Germans who were expected to re-emigrate from Russia. The vast uninhabited and untilled areas in those parts provided room for German settlements without crowding out the inhabitants· Alsace-Lorraine also was to be used for settlements, and in this way this ancient German territory would at last regain its German character. A wide field of labour of the greatest national importance was before us. General Hahndorff took up these questions in a far-sighted manner. Co-operative Settlement-Companies, assisted by the most experienced men in Germany, were started and set to work at once. At that time people got wildly excited about the settlement-companies. The soundness of the fundamental idea was proved later. One of the first measures of the Republican Government was to draft a settlement-law, of which the guiding principles were taken from the edicts for Courland drafted by Professor Ludwig Bernhard on behalf of G.H.Q. Its practical application is now impossible owing to the extraordinary rise in prices and to the difficulty of obtaining building materials. In the matter of helping the war victims, also, the Revolutionists have watered down the original schemes ; they have taken instead of giving. Money has been wasted, but the deserving soldier got none of it.

We also provided for the students and advanced schoolboys who were on active service, and whose future became more and more precarious as time went on. I hoped that the assistance afforded to them would prove of special benefit to the country. The Prussian Minister of Education, Dr. Schmidt, felt strongly on this subject and took the lead in the work.

IX

Besides the actual conduct of the war and the big questions connected with it I had a great many other duties to attend to at Kreuznach ; they were apparently unimportant, but yet formed part of the whole process. Life had settled down to the same sort of routine as at other headquarters. The Field-Marshal and I, with other officers, lived in a villa which had once formed the home of the Emperor William I., that great monarch and judge of men, under whose sceptre Germany's dream of union had been realized. Our office was in the Oranien-hof. The distance to it was short, and my regular walks to and fro afforded an opportunity to many kindly disposed people who wished to please me by their greetings and, at times, by gifts of flowers. Otherwise I led a secluded existence because—I know men.

Every day I went for exercise to the " Rose-garden " above the town, or perhaps merely into the grounds near the Oranienhof, rarely anywhere else. In the spring of 1918 this beautiful Rosengarten and the garden in front of the Oranienhof were destroyed in a few hours by tearing floods. As the Revolution passed over Germany in the autumn, so the flood passed over Kreuznach in the spring. What had taken the townspeople many years and an infinite amount of trouble was demolished in a few hours. It happened terribly quickly. The clearing up of the gardens and houses and the removal of the dirt and mud began at once, but it took a long, long time, and traces of the flood remained everywhere. Was that an omen ?

We had many visitors who came and went, and in spite of my enormous burden of work I had to find time to spare for all of them. I had also to confer with the representatives of the Prussian and Bavarian War Ministers on the maintenance and increase of the fighting capacity of the Army. *Moral* at home and the question of reinforcements were matters which never disappeared from the agenda. Questions relating to the future of the Army were also dealt with. Ideas on disarmament were as prevalent as those on peace by understanding, and as little in accord with the existing state of affairs. To disarm before changing the whole existing order of the world seemed to me, as a practical man, just as impossible as it did to the democratic Governments of England, France and the United States. Food and other problems of the home country often came before me. In a word, all the fundamental elements of warfare were continuously dealt with, revised and, as far as I was able, organized to meet our requirements. Applications for what we could not supply from our own resources were submitted to the Imperial Government ; with what sad results I have shown in reference to our most pressing need, that of arousing the warlike ardour of the German people.

As regards war politics, I had mainly to deal with the Dobrudja, the area administered by the Commander-in-Chief in the East, and Alsace-Lorraine.

In the Dobrudja the struggle between the Bulgarians and the German Line-of-Communication Administration continued, with all its many side-issues. In June the Tsar of Bulgaria came to Kreuznach with Radoslavoff, who now tried to get the line-of-communication area placed under Bulgarian administration, which amounted to his obtaining the Dobrudja for Bulgaria. This led once more to a great deal of argument. I raised the question of Germany's exploiting the rich coal-fields of Serbia for the common benefit of the Quadruple Alliance during the war ; some notes were made, but nothing more was done. It was a waste of time while my thoughts were so fully engaged with events at the Front. Owing to the enormous restraint I had often to impose upon myself this extra work was an intolerable thing to expect of any man. So stern a course of self-education would do many people good. In the present case G.H.Q. succeeded in defeating the Bulgarian project, or at any rate shelving the question indefinitely. Even now the Government failed to induce M. Radoslavoff to secure the recall of the U.S.A. Chargé d'Affaires from Sofia. I assume that it really made another serious attempt.

I had left the territory of the Commander-in-Chief in the East at the end of August, 1916. The administrative system I had introduced was only adapted to military needs ; it continued to work well in 1917. Its operations had now to be developed more on the political side.

It was to be expected that the proclamation of the Kingdom of Poland on the 5th November would have a depressing effect on the Lithuanians and would produce a Pan-Polish agitation in the territory under the Commander-in-Chief in the East. The guiding principles laid down for an impartial treatment of questions of nationality were by themselves no longer sufficient.

At my request Secretary of State von Jagow published an official announcement in the papers of the occupied territory, with the object of calming the Lithuanians. This announcement appeared simultaneously with the proclamation of the Kingdom of Poland. The Lithuanian movement, which had hitherto emanated exclusively from Switzerland, now began to be manifested in the country itself, and the Pan-Polish movement, of which the object was the union of Lithuania with Poland, grew at the same time. We had no reason to permit these agitations. Poland had clearly shown, in the matter of raising the Army, that she was merely a political war-profiteer. We could no longer consider anything but our own future, and the dangers which might threaten us from Poland. In accordance with our previous policy the Commander-in-Chief in the East was therefore instructed that any strengthening of the Poles, which could only come about at the cost of other nations, was undesirable.

The Lithuanians entered the lists against the Poles by expressing their feelings and wishes more forcibly. In March, 1917, they submitted a representation on the subject to the Commander-in-Chief in the East. The latter now sent in a memoir on the methods to be followed by German policy in the territory under his administration. We passed the memoir on to the Imperial Chancellor, with the request that he might give a definite decision as to the policy to be adopted in regard to the nationalities in the area administered by the Commander-in-Chief in the East. G.H.Q. considered it out of the question to pursue a purely Polish policy. The establishment of a Poland that would surround East and West Prussia was incompatible with the security of Germany. German rule in the territory under the Commander-in-Chief in the East must be based on the Lithuanians and the White Ruthenes. At the same time we suggested a conference on these questions, the early solution of which I very greatly desired. In this, as in all other matters, I maintained that the Imperial Chancellor must lay down the guiding principles of policy, with the sole limitation that they must be compatible with military security. The execution of the political instructions was in this case the duty of G.H.Q. and of the Commander-in-Chief in the East.

On the 5th April we had the first conference with representatives of the Imperial Chancellor, under the presidency of the Quartermaster-General, General Hahndorff, at Bingen.

The Field-Marshal and I considered that the territory administered by the Commander-in-Chief in the East should ultimately be divided into a Duchy of Courland and a Grand Duchy of Lithuania, and with the further object of adjusting their respective interests, both should be in the closest relationship to Germany, and united under the personal sovereignty of His Majesty, either in his capacity as King of Prussia or Emperor of Germany. In this way Germany would gain a military defence against further surprise attacks by Russia, and also land for the settlement of our troops after the war.

The boundaries of Courland were already fixed.

The settlement of the Lithuanian question was difficult. Generally speaking, the mass of the Lithuanian people, though interspersed with big Polish landowners, lives north of the line Dvinsk–Vilna–Olita–Suvalki. South of it they radiate into the country of the White Ruthenes, which, however, is permeated by Poles and very Polish in spirit. Vilna, Grodno and other towns were Polish. The solid mass of Polish population only began at Byalistok. Jews were to be found all through Lithuania. Germans lived mainly on the East Prussian border. In the territory under the Commander-in-Chief in the East, south of Courland, the Lithuanians were in a small majority, and so formed a counterpoise to the Poles. They were menaced by them in precisely the same way as we were on our eastern borders, and so were our natural allies, whom we must seek to strengthen and attach to ourselves by every possible means. On the 5th April my argument did not go as far as this. My immediate object was to obtain the Imperial Chancellor's consent to a pronounced pro-Lithuanian policy. Nothing definite resulted from this conference.

. On the 23rd April a second conference took place at Kreuznach. After the outbreak of the Revolution Russia had made extensive promises to the Lithuanians. Now even the Imperial Chancellor admitted the necessity of formulating a clear line of policy with regard to them. On the 30th April a general agreement was reached to the effect that in the whole of the territory under the Commander-in-Chief in the East our action was to be based on the following principles: Everything German was to receive favourable treatment, but even the merest appearance of forcible germanization, of which I had never approved, was to be avoided. The word " germanize " has always been abhorrent to me. The Lithuanians were to be won over by all possible means, and the White Ruthenes in the northern district to be brought more in touch with them. In consideration for the Poles the latter object was not to be pursued in the south.

Polish propaganda was to be prevented, but without coming into conflict with the policy of the Governor-General of Warsaw by combating it in public.

The enunciation of these principles did not finally commit the Imperial Government, but it did enable us to follow a settled policy with regard to the Lithuanians. On the 30th May the Commander-in-Chief in the East, in agreement with the Government, published a decree permitting the formation of a Lithuanian Confidential Council, in which the Lithuanians were to form the majority, the other nationalities being represented by single members. The Confidential Council was intended to be the official channel by which the wishes of the Lithuanians were to be communicated to the administration.

The general conditions made it more and more imperative clearly to define our intentions in the eastern territories. The catchwords " peace without annexations " and " self-determination of small nations," which had been invented by hostile propaganda, were likely to lead to a solution of the Lithuanian problem which would be detrimental to German interests. It opened the way for the Poles to become supreme in districts where they had not hitherto been so.

On the 21st July, when the Imperial Chancellor, Dr. Michaelis, had just attained his exalted position, G.H.Q. approached the

The Entente Offensive in the First Half of 1917

Foreign Office with the proposal to pursue a policy of local nationalism in Courland and Lithuania, that in Lithuania being definitely Lithuanian in character. We made a final attempt to carry out our ideas with regard to these two countries. In both of them " Local Councils " were to be instituted.

On the 25th July Secretary of State Zimmermann agreed to our policy being initiated at once. Our success in Galicia had cleared up the situation still further. The Secretary of State merely dissuaded us, " in view of the impossibility of foreseeing the future," from " binding ourselves publicly, or even only mentally, to the definite project of a personal union." Later on, however, he declared that he " by no means intended definitely to decline that form of organization." When the Government would publicly announce this policy was its own affair ; I was content with having obtained its consent to a definite policy. I expressed my satisfaction at our having reached an agreement as to the immediate policy to be followed in the territory under the Commander-in-Chief in the East. The latter received instructions early in August with a view to the formation of " Local Councils."

I hoped that, with the necessary firmness and perseverance, we should attain our object, and that by this arrangement the Lithuanians would obtain their rights better than by joining either Russia or Poland. Competent judges among them had perceived that they could only maintain their nationality with the aid of Germany. Among these were the clergy whose superior intelligence, and the fact that we had promoted the return of the Bishop of Kovno, made them well-disposed towards us. The Lithuanian democracy believed in the power of the catchword " self-determination," although, owing to the mixed pop ulation of the country, it could not possibly be applied with justice. Being tied up in political theories, they did not see the Polish danger which actually menaces their land.

The third problem which occupied me in the summer of 1917 was that of Alsace-Lorraine. G.H.Q. could of course approach it only from that point of view which it was our duty to represent, the military one. The impressions I had gained as a brigade commander at Strassburg, and the many sad experiences of this war relating to Alsace-Lorraine, had fully convinced me that its position as Imperial territory (*Reichsland*) was an anomaly which did not accord with the interests of the inhabitants. There was far too much meddling in its affairs by the Reichstag. The policy followed was weak and ill-defined, and could not satisfy anybody. I strove for a union of the country with Prussia, which by no means involved " Prussianizing " its inhabitants. Prussia had absorbed the Rhine Province, of which the population had retained its typical character and developed vigorously ; why should not the same path lead to the happiness of the people of Alsace-Lorraine who are by race and economic conditions closely allied to Germany. Other solutions also seemed possible. Whatever happened, it was necessary to make certain of ensuring a single control of the troops on the frontier, the frontier defence system, and the railways. On carefully examining the question it was found to be very difficult to achieve this end by any other than the " Prussian " solution.

From the military point of view I expressed the opinion that the granting of autonomy was the least satisfactory solution. But whichever one was to be adopted, the fundamental principle was really to oppose the unjustifiable French influence and to replace it by the German ; in my view this involved the employment of German clergy and civil officials. The clergy was still recruited from French institutions, as also were some bodies of Sisters and female teachers. This was really scandalous. Was not Germany just as well able to provide clergy and teachers ? The civil officials ought also to have been imbued with German feeling. There was no need to select the notorious " East Elbians," who had done so much for Germany's greatness, but whose natural hardness might possibly render them unsuitable for Alsace-Lorraine. The Rhine Province and South Germany could meet the demand.

Finally, French property in Alsace-Lorraine ought to be transferred to German possession, a transaction which the Entente had declared to be in accordance with the usage of war. In this way we should also acquire land for settling German soldiers.

The attack on private property was one of the abominations of this war. In 1870–71 Germans had been deported from France, an action which was at the time considered a special offence against international law, but France had left their private property untouched. Very soon after this war began England had proceeded to liquidate German businesses and by so doing had made plain why she had joined in the war. She wanted to remove the inconvenient German competition throughout the world and her example was followed by the other Powers of the Entente. The Black Lists served the same purpose ; they were also intended partly to increase the severity of the blockade. They caused the greatest suffering among the neutral countries, who—said nothing. The war of nations produced ever greater abominations.

It seemed to me necessary that the highest military and civil authorities should be in agreement as to the future of Alsace-Lorraine. Field-Marshal Duke Albrecht of Würtemberg, who represented the military authority in Alsace-Lorraine since the spring of 1917, required clear instructions. I therefore suggested to the Government that a conference should be held. It took place. Nothing definite was achieved.

THE BATTLE OF FLANDERS AND THE COL-
LAPSE OF RUSSIA IN THE SUMMER AND
AUTUMN OF 1917

I

FOLLOWING on the prelude in the Wytschaete salient on the 7th June, the battle of Flanders began on the 31st July, after an artillery preparation lasting several days. This formed the second great strategic action of the Entente in 1917; it was their bid for final victory and for our submarine base in Flanders. The fighting spread over large portions of the Western Front, the Italian and Macedonian Fronts, and finally as far as Palestine

The fighting on the Western Front became more severe and costly than any the German Army had yet experienced. In spite of this, the Western Armies could not be reinforced from the East, for there, at last, heavy work was to be done. Russia and Rumania were to be defeated, in order to enable us to force a decision in the West in 1918 by means of an attack on France combined with the submarine war, in case the latter should not achieve the desired result by itself. The situation required that I myself should undertake a great responsibility, so great that it shook even me. However, I had to do it, for in 1918 the dangers might otherwise become too much for us. It was, of course, obvious that G.H.Q. did not withhold from the armies of the West a single man who was not urgently needed elsewhere. During the further course of events the German Crown Prince often told me not to let the tension in the West become too great.

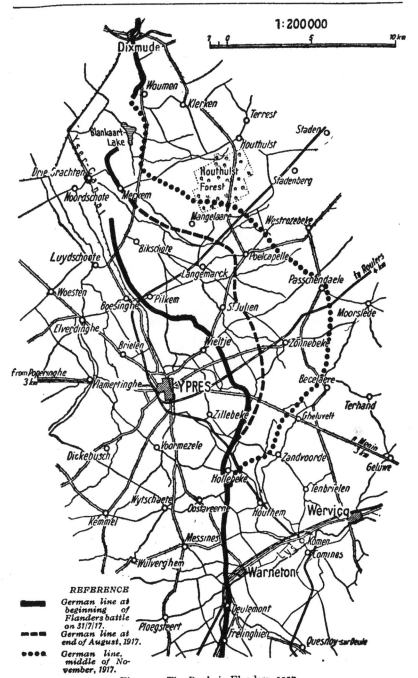

Fig. 21. The Battle in Flanders, 1917.

I knew well that G.H.Q., in imposing this enormous strain on the Western Front, had in view the possible situation in 1918. I saw what the danger would be if the submarine war did not work after all. But I am not one of those who give way in the face of dangers ; I was put in my position in order to overcome them and to employ every means to prevent a great misfortune overtaking our country.

In the East we had to keep on hammering at Russia in order to bring about the fall of the Colossus. While the operations in Eastern Galicia were yet in progress I had telephoned to Colonel Hoffmann to ask what he thought of a crossing of the Dvina above Riga. For that, of course, troops were required which were at the time still engaged in Galicia. The Colonel was all for it at once, and the Commander-in-Chief in the East issued the first preparatory orders without delay. In the first days of August it became evident that our advance would have to be stopped in Eastern Galicia and the Bukovina, and that the offensive could not be resumed there until the railways had been repaired ; he was therefore instructed to carry out the crossing of the Dvina. At the time I believed it might take place about the 20th August and hoped that some troops would soon become available from there. By the middle or end of September, after the repair of the railways south of the Dniester, I thought we might be able to commence operations from the Bukovina across the Sereth into Moldavia. For that purpose the troops would have to be railed back again from Riga to the south.

From July 31st till well into September was a period of tremendous anxiety. On the 31st July the English, assisted by a few French divisions on their left, had attacked on a front of about thirty-one kilometres. They had employed such quantities of artillery and ammunition as had been rare, even in the West. At many points along the whole front the enemy had penetrated with tanks. Cavalry divisions were in readiness to push through. With the assistance of the counter-attack divisions, the 4th Army, whose Chief of Staff was now Colonel von Loszberg, succeeded in checking the hostile success and ocalizing its effect. But, besides a loss of from two to four kilometres of ground along the whole front, it caused us very considerable losses in prisoners and stores, and a heavy expenditure of reserves.

In August fighting broke out on many parts of the Western Front. In Flanders the Entente attacked again on the 10th, although they must have suffered severely on the 31st July. The 10th August was a success for us, but on the 16th we sustained another great blow. The English pressed on beyond Poelcapelle and, even with an extreme exertion of strength on our part, could only be pushed back a short distance ! During the following days fighting continued with diminished intensity. The 22nd was another day of heavy fighting. The 25th August concluded the second phase of the Flanders Battle. It had cost us heavily.

Further to the south several English divisions broke into our position north of Lens on the 15th August and captured an important height.

On the old battle-field of Arras, on both banks of the Scarpe, a hostile attack failed on the 9th.

Towards the end of August the Siegfried Line north of St. Quentin was unsuccessfully attacked by the French. It was not a serious affair.

Subsidiary French attacks were made on the ridge of the Chemin des Dames.

The main French effort took place at Verdun on the 20th and 21st August. The 5th Army was not surprised. As had been provided for weeks before, certain areas, such as the Talou ridge, were abandoned in time. The assault, which was not accompanied by tanks, again penetrated far into our positions. On the left bank, close to the Meuse, one division had failed, nor had we been fortunate on the right bank ; and yet both here and in Flanders everything possible had probably been done to avoid failure. The 21st and 26th also brought success to the enemy and loss to us. The French Army was once more capable of the offensive. It had quickly overcome its depression. Just about this time the statesmen in Paris put forward peace conditions which did not accord with the military situation.

The costly August battles in Flanders and at Verdun imposed a heavy strain on the western troops. In spite of all the concrete protection they seemed more or less powerless under the enormous weight of the enemy's artillery. At some points they no longer displayed that firmness which I, in common with the local commanders, had hoped for.

The enemy managed to adapt himself to our method of employing counter-attack divisions. There were no more attacks

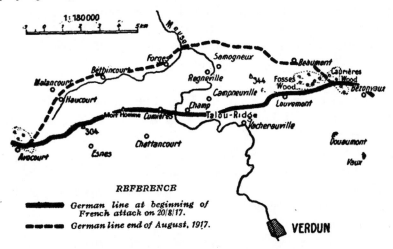

Fig. 22. The Battles at Verdun. August, 1917.

with unlimited objectives, such as General Nivelle had made in the Aisne-Champagne Battle. He was ready for our counter-attacks and prepared for them by exercising restraint in the exploitation of success. In other directions, of course, this suited us very well.

I myself was being put to a terrible strain. The state of affairs in the West appeared to prevent the execution of our plans elsewhere. Our wastage had been so high as to cause grave misgivings, and had exceeded all expectation. The attack on the Dvina had to be postponed repeatedly. Indeed, it became a question whether we could continue to bear the responsibility of retaining those divisions in the East.

The Crown Prince was not alone in his anxiety; several Chiefs of Staff of very cool judgment shook their heads. But, in estimating the strength of our enemies, I always said to myself that in this war the only alternatives were victory or defeat, that their determination to destroy us made any intermediate solution impossible. In spite of all, I was convinced that the West Front would stand even more battering, though fate might have even greater trials in store for it. This was another case where human wisdom failed.

General Headquarters allowed the Dvina attack, from which it expected great results, owing to the

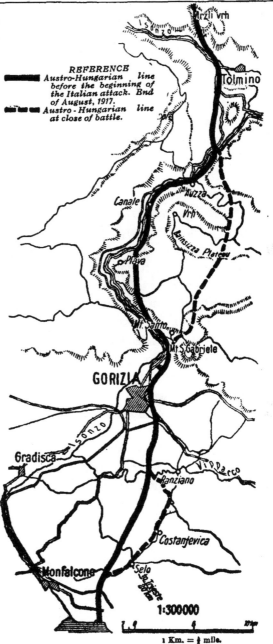

REFERENCE
▬▬ Austro-Hungarian line before the beginning of the Italian attack. End of August, 1917.
▬ ▬ ▬ Austro-Hungarian line at close of battle.

1:300000

1 Km. = ⅝ mile.

Fig. 23. The 11th Battle of the Isonzo in August and September, 1917.

proximity of Petrograd, to proceed, although it did not intend to push it very far. From the purely strategical point of view it was merely intended as a means to a wholesale improvement of our position which would enable us to economize troops.

The offensive in Moldavia was still kept in view as a second decisive stroke. But this operation, which was delayed by difficulties in railway construction, came to nothing.

At the end of August the Eleventh Battle of the Isonzo had begun on a front of seventy kilometres and proved successful for the Italians. Early in September the fighting was continued with determination. The Italians were again successful. The Austro–Hungarian Armies had indeed held their ground, but their losses on the Carso Plateau had been so heavy, and they were so shaken, that the responsible military and political authorities of the Dual Monarchy were convinced that they would not be able to stand a continuation of the battle and a twelfth attack on the Isonzo. The Austrian Army on the Italian Front needed stiffening by German troops. We could not carry our attack into Moldavia and to throw in German divisions in Italy for a pure defensive was not a measure which accorded with our critical situation. G.H.Q. had to take steps to carry out some offensive, if possible even a large-scale operation, so as to bring about an improvement in the general situation somehow.

To abandon the operation in Moldavia was a disappointment. It seemed to me more important than one in Italy. It might, considering the situation in Russia, prove a decisive step towards ending the war on the Eastern Front. It could not then be seen that this object could be attained without considerable military effort, owing to the disintegration of the Russian State and Army. The attack on Italy might no doubt have a great effect and immediately relieve the Western Front ; but whether it would, in conjunction with the shortage of coal, produce a crisis in Italy could not be foretold. The general opinion was that it would not.

In spite of the difference in the value of the possible results, in the middle of September it became necessary to decide for the attack on Italy in order to prevent the collapse of Austria-Hungary. We had now only to examine how Russia, after the attack on Riga, could be damaged further in a way likely to accelerate her dissolution. Moltke's saying: "Strategy is a system of expedients," remains as true as ever.

At the end of August and early in September I had much to endure. I had a great amount of business with Berlin. On a journey to the West I met with a railway accident. Another

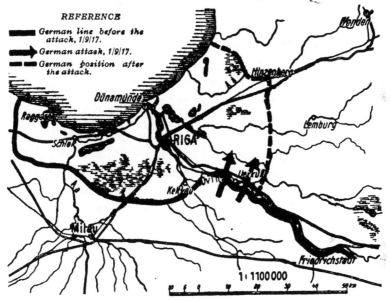

REFERENCE
German line before the attack, 1/9/17.
German attack, 1/9/17.
German position after the attack.

Fig. 24. Riga. 1917.

train ran into the coach in which I was dining with my officers and overturned it. But that only caused a momentary fright. A severe blow was the death of my eldest son, or, rather, the eldest son of my wife by her first marriage. I have no children of my own. I was deeply attached to my son, as to all my step-children, and had seen him at Lille only a short time before, fresh and strong and full of enthusiasm for his profession and his country.

He was shot down over the Channel. Not till weeks afterwards did we find his body washed up on the Dutch coast.

This high tension was followed by a period of inactivity,

commencing in Flanders at the end of August, at Verdun and in Italy at the beginning and middle of September. How long it would last no one knew.

Between the 30th August and 8th September the Entente had also made heavy attacks on several parts of the Macedonian Front, but without success. Local engagements in the mountains west of Lake Ochrida had an important bearing on the main operations inasmuch as they forced the Bulgarians to extend their line.

In Rumania there was some fighting between the Sereth and the frontier mountains. Otherwise there was but little activity on the whole Eastern Front right up to Riga. A local attack by German troops near Czernowitz was merely intended to rectify our line, which was urgently necessary.

The Front between the Carpathians and Tarnopol was now thinned out in order to obtain reserves for the next operations.

On the 1st September we effected the passage of the Dvina at Uxküll, south-east of Riga, opposite a strong enemy position. Helped by various higher commands, General von Hutier, commanding the 8th Army, and his Chief of Staff, General von Sauberzweig, had made very thorough preparations. The crossing was successful. The Russians had evacuated the bridge-head on the left bank in time and with few exceptions offered but slight resistance here also. I breathed again when the blow had at last fallen. We soon halted the 8th Army, and behind the furthest point of its advance it at once set about fortifying a position on the shortest line between the Dvina and the Gulf of Riga. Two divisions left immediately for the Western Front in order to relieve others for Italy. The Eastern Front had to send considerable forces there. In spite of our intention to strike at Italy and the extremely critical situation in the West, where fighting might flame up again at any moment, the Commander-in-Chief in the East still retained a certain surplus in order to keep Russia busy. It was a poor substitute for the offensive in Moldavia, but still better than nothing. If, after the event, I am charged with dispersion of force, I must put up with it. Things do not always work according to plan —and I achieved my object.

II

Apart from the lack of vigour shown by the troops, the defect of the Austro-Hungarian offensive from the Tyrol in 1916 was that the forces with which it was undertaken were too weak for the point at which it was made, and that the Army on the Isonzo did not attack at the same time. From a military point of view it was tempting to dally once more with these ideas and possibilities; but in September, 1917, I had to base our plan of campaign on the fact that the Austro-Hungarian Armies were very exhausted at the moment and that Germany could not spare more than six or eight divisions. With such forces an attack from the Tyrol would have been absurd. They could only achieve results by striking at a point where the enemy was particularly weak and not expecting attack. If, furthermore, the selected point admitted of a strategic exploitation of the break-through, as had been the case in Eastern Galicia, every immediate requirement would be met. Further developments would have to be left to careful preparation and the decision of arms.

The front between Flitsch and Canale was suitable for attack, although the difficulties of the ground seemed almost insurmountable, and the communications on the Austrian side were as bad as could be imagined. But the Italians themselves were not expecting to be attacked there and holding the line with weak forces. If we succeeded in surprising them and bursting over the mountains north of Cividale towards Udine, the Italian line on the Isonzo would totter.

We could now begin to consider the operation itself. The warmest supporter of the plan was Lieutenant-Colonel Wetzell. It was first necessary to determine whether the attack on this front was possible at all and if so, how it could be made. With the consent of General von Arz, General Krafft von Dellmensingen who was then Chief of Staff to the Army Group of Duke Albrecht, and Major Freiherr von Willisen were ordered to reconnoitre the ground. Their report showed the attack to be feasible, and formed the basis of further decisions by G.H.Q. I now gave myself up completely to this new great task.

General von Krafft and Major von Willisen had also made some excellent suggestions for the equipment of the troops. On this subject G.H.Q. at once communicated with the Austrian General Headquarters who were asked particularly to provide pack transport and mountain artillery for the German formations. Both before and during the war the German Army was often in difficulties for want of mountain artillery and a certain amount was provided. But of course what we had was insufficient for this campaign. Austria-Hungary was perfectly well able to help, and there was no reason why we should always provide everything ourselves.

The selection of the troops was most important. The first to be chosen were units like the Alpine Corps which had gained experience in mountain warfare in the Carpathians and were suitably equipped. These were the 117th and 200th Infantry Divisions, at that time in the Bukovina, which were to be set free by the Austro–Hungarian troops in that area taking over their front.

Generally speaking, G.H.Q. wanted to employ divisions which had fought only on the Western Front, or suffered particularly severely in operations in other theatres. But, owing to the importance of the Western Front, and the small numbers that could be drawn from it, the wishes of many formations to fight in other localities and be employed in an offensive, could only be met to a small extent. The choice now fell upon the 5th, 12th and 26th (Würtemberg) Divisions and a few Jäger Battalions, which were later formed into the German Jäger Division. Six to seven divisions were made available against Italy; two were taken from the Western Front, where they were replaced by the two from Riga.

In addition, the East was to release two more divisions, which, if the situation at all permitted, were to be sent later to Italy, otherwise to the West.

The divisions detailed were also provided with German formations of artillery, engineers, trench mortars, aeroplanes, balloons and signals, motor and horse transport, and lines of communication establishments; everything, in a word, which an army needs. The troops were given such mountain equipment as was necessary by the Intendant-Generals and their respective War Ministries. Training in mountain warfare began at once. The artillery required special training in shooting in mountainous districts.

It was arranged with General von Arz that the Germans, with a contingent of Austro-Hungarian troops, were to form the 14th Army, under General Otto von Below who had hitherto commanded the 6th Army. General von Krafft became his Chief of Staff, and Major von Willisen joined the 14th Army Headquarters as Senior General Staff Officer.

In the 6th Army, General von Below was succeeded by General von Quast, a man of clear judgment and a resolute leader. In the Army Group of Duke Albrecht General von Krafft was replaced by Colonel Heye, who had for a long time served with distinction as Chief of Staff to General von Woyrsch.

The preparations for the operation had involved a great deal of business with the Austro-Hungarian G.H.Q. at Baden. General von Waldstätten was often at Kreuznach. From the outset it was agreed that the German Army should make the main attack, on which everything depended. It was therefore assembled at the decisive point on both sides of Tolmino. The German Jäger were moved into the Flitsch Valley.

The Emperor Charles wished the operation to be conducted by the Austro–Hungarian High Command. I secured, however, a sufficient voice for our own General Staff through our preparations, the interspersion of a German Army Staff, and a system of telephonic communication.

Unfortunately it was clear that the operation could not begin until after the middle of October.

The operations in the East continued in September. The bridge-head of Jacobstadt was captured on the 21st by a powerful and well-planned attack. It was to be followed by the capture of the islands of Osel, Moon and Dagö. This would

require one division and a brigade of cyclists, which were temporarily withdrawn from the coast of Flanders. The operation had been in preparation, in conjunction with the Navy, since
the middle of September. At the end of the month the fleet,
transports and landing force were ready at Libau. Owing to
unfavourable winds the execution of the landing was also delayed
until the middle of October.

The postponement of the operation against Italy and the
attack on the islands until the middle and end of October was
to prove another enormous burden for us.

After a period of profound quiet in the West, which led some
to hope that the Battle of Flanders was over, another terrific
assault was made on our lines on the 20th September. The
third bloody act of the battle had begun. The main force of
the attack was directed against the Passchendaele-Gheluvelt
line. Obviously the English were trying to gain the high ground
between Ypres and the Roulers-Menin line, which affords an
extensive view in both directions. These heights were also
exceptionally important for us, as they afforded us ground
observation posts and a certain amount of cover from hostile
view.

The enemy's onslaught on the 20th was successful, which
proved the superiority of the attack over the defence. Its
strength did not consist in the tanks ; we found them inconvenient, but put them out of action all the same. The power of
the attack lay in the artillery, and in the fact that ours did not do
enough damage to the hostile infantry as they were assembling,
and, above all, at the actual time of the assault.

Another English attack on the 21st was repulsed ; but the
26th proved a day of heavy fighting, accompanied by every
circumstance that could cause us loss. We might be able to stand
the loss of ground, but the reduction of our fighting strength was
again all the heavier. Once more we were involved in a terrific
struggle in the West, and had to prepare for a continuation of
the attacks on many parts of the front.

October came, and with it one of the hardest months of the war.
The world at large—which began in my immediate neighbour-

hood—saw only Tarnopol, Czernovitz, Riga, and later Osel, Udine, the Tagliamento and the Piave. It did not see my anxiety, nor my deep sympathy with the sufferings of our troops in the West. My mind was in the East and Italy, my heart on the Western Front. My will had to bring mind and heart together. I had not known what joy meant for many a long day.

The actions in the Third Battle of Flanders had presented the same set-piece characteristics as those in the Second and the fighting at Verdun. The depth of penetration was limited so as to secure immunity from our counter-attacks, and the latter were then broken up by the massed fire of artillery.

After each attack I discussed the tactical experiences with General von Kuhl and Colonel von Loszberg, sometimes at the Front, sometimes on the telephone. This time I again went to Flanders in order to talk over the same questions with officers who had taken part in the fighting. Our defensive tactics had to be developed further, somehow or other. We were all agreed on that. The only thing was, it was so infinitely difficult to hit on the right remedy. We could only proceed by careful experiment. The proposals of the officers on the spot tended rather in the direction of our former tactics ; they amounted to a slight, but only a slight, reinforcement of our front lines, and the abandonment of the counter-attack by the counter-attack divisions, local counter-attacks being substituted for this. These local counter-attacks were to be made by a division in the second line, to be brought close up and spread over a wide front, before the enemy's attack began. So, while the front line was to be held rather more densely once more, in order to gain in power, the whole battle-field was to be given more depth than ever. G.H.Q. would thus, generally speaking, have to provide a second division for every fighting division in the front line, an unheard-of expenditure of force. That the employment of a second division in rear of practically every one in the front line would increase the power of the defence was a simple sum in arithmetic. But the second sum was equally simple ; that our lines on other fronts would have to be thinned out even more than they had been hitherto. I said I would see what I could do. I agreed to the tactical changes, although misgivings were expressed among my Staff at this departure from the " Defensive Battle." I thought I ought to give way to the experience of officers at the front.

Another tactical detail which was emphasized everywhere was the value of ground observation for artillery. Only by that means could the attacking hostile infantry be annihilated, particularly after penetrating our front, or fire be concentrated on decisive points of the battle-field.

As to the tanks, opinion was calm ; they were not thought particularly dangerous. I purposely made use of the expression " tank-fright," but the officers from the front would not admit there was any such thing.

I need not say that from the first the 4th Army was as well supplied as possible with artillery, ammunition, aircraft and other weapons ; and Colonel von Loszberg, who always wanted a lot, was in the end satisfied with his Army Group and with me.

The officers in the West followed the Eastern and Italian operations with ever increasing anxiety.

Early in October the artillery action revived, and on the 2nd and 3rd artillery engagements of great violence took place. The infantry battle commenced on the morning of the 4th. It was extraordinarily severe, and again we only came through it with enormous loss. It was evident that the idea of holding the front line more densely, adopted at my last visit to the front in September, was not the remedy. I now followed my own judgment without asking for further outside opinions, and recommended the 4th Army to form an advanced zone, that is to say, a narrow strip between the enemy's front line and the line which our troops were to hold by mobile defence. The enemy would have to cross this strip in making his attack, and our artillery would have time to get on to him before he could reach our main line of resistance. The great difficulty lay in withdrawing the garrison of the advanced zone in case of attack, and in bringing the artillery barrage back to our own line. The term " advanced zone " has been defined in various ways, and ideas often became confused. The principle of it was simple. The 4th Army complied with my suggestion somewhat reluctantly, and did not accept it with conviction for some time. I never ceased to lay stress on the principles of the employment of artillery in masses and the utmost possible concentration of artillery fire.

There were further severe engagements on the 9th and 12th October. The line held better than on the 4th, although in some places the enemy penetrated to a considerable distance. The wastage in the big actions of the Fourth Battle of Flanders was extraordinarily high. In the West we began to be short of troops. The two divisions that had been held in readiness in the East, and were already on the way to Italy, were diverted to Flanders. The attack on Osel, at any rate, had commenced, but the Italian operation could not be started before the 22nd, and the weather held it up until the 24th. These days were the culminating point of the crisis.

III

The fifth act of the great drama in Flanders opened on the 22nd October. Enormous masses of ammunition, such as the human mind had never imagined before the war, were hurled upon the bodies of men who passed a miserable existence scattered about in mud-filled shell-holes. The horror of the shell-hole area of Verdun was surpassed. It was no longer life at all. It was mere unspeakable suffering. And through this world of mud the attackers dragged themselves, slowly, but steadily, and in dense masses. Caught in the advanced zone by our hail of fire they often collapsed, and the lonely man in the shell-hole breathed again. Then the mass came on again. Rifle and machine-gun jammed with the mud. Man fought against man, and only too often the mass was successful.

What the German soldier experienced, achieved, and suffered in the Flanders Battle will be his everlasting monument of bronze, erected by himself in the enemy's land.

The enemy's losses were also heavy. When we occupied the battle-field in the spring of 1918 we encountered the horrible spectacle of many unburied corpses. They lay there in thousands

Two-thirds of them were enemies, one-third German soldiers who had found a hero's grave there.

And yet it must be admitted that certain units no longer triumphed over the demoralizing effects of the defensive battle as they had done formerly.

On the 26th and 30th October and 6th and 10th November the fighting was again of the severest description. The enemy charged like a wild bull against the iron wall which kept him from our submarine bases. He threw his weight against Houthulst Forest, Poelcapelle, Passchendaele, Becelaere, Gheluvelt and Zandvoorde. He dented it in many places, and it seemed as if he must knock it down. But it held, although a faint tremor ran through its foundations.

The impressions I continuously received were very terrible. In a tactical sense, everything possible had been done. The advanced zone was good. The effectiveness of our artillery had considerably improved. Behind almost every division in the front line there was another in support ; and we still had reserves in the third line. We knew that the enemy suffered heavily. But we also knew he was amazingly strong and, what was equally important, had an extraordinarily stubborn will. Lloyd George wanted victory. He held England in his hand. Only one thing we did not know ; how long the battle would continue. The enemy must tire some time.

The French had attacked simultaneously. For this they had selected the favourable salient south-west of Laon, known as the Laffaux corner. We discovered their intention early in October ; the Army took all measures for defence and was supplied with everything it deemed necessary. In spite of other advice it wished to hold the salient, feeling confident of success. It made all its arrangements with meticulous care. All the same, G.H.Q. ought to have ordered the evacuation of the salient.

The French attack on the 22nd October was successful. One division succumbed to the effects of an exceptionally heavy gas-bombardment and gave way before the hostile assault. The enemy advanced towards Chavignon and so caused a narrow but deep indentation in the salient. This forced us to order its evacuation, and the line was withdrawn behind the Oise–Aisne Canal. The losses were very serious ; once more several divisions were destroyed.

This withdrawal of our line inevitably entailed the evacuation of the Chemin des Dames ridge. It was ordered, and carried out on the night of the 1st–2nd November, after the stores and equipment had been removed. In itself it was of no consequence whether we stood north or south of the Ailette, but after having fought all through the summer for possession of the Chemin des

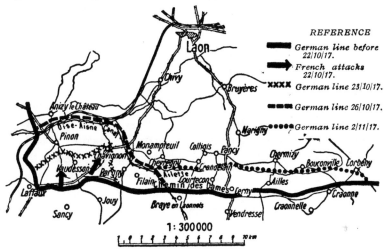

REFERENCE

━━ German line before 22/10/17.

➤ French attacks 22/10/17.

✕✕✕✕ German line 23/10/17.

▬▬▬ German line 26/10/17.

●●●● German line 2/11/17.

1 : 300000

Fig. 25. The Battle at the Laffaux Salient. October 22.

Dames it was very difficult to order it to be given up. To hold on, however, would only have involved continuous wastage.

In pushing on towards the Canal on the 23rd the enemy gained further successes, but later on all his attacks, which curled round towards the north and also extended further towards the east, were repulsed.

As at Verdun in August, the French, supported by remarkable masses of artillery, had fought very vigorously.

While the October battles continued in the West until the combatants were exhausted, in the East the expedition against the islands had terminated in our favour. The campaign against Italy had begun. There our troops raced from victory to victory.

In the West the crisis caused by the Battle of Flanders, the Battle of the Laffaux Salient and their after effects, passed away. We were expecting a continuation of the attacks in Flanders and on the French front, when on the 20th November we were surprised by a fresh blow at Cambrai.

The Siegfried position was but weakly held. The fighting further north, particularly the heavy concentration in Flanders, had induced the Army Group of Prince Rupprecht, with the consent of G.H.Q., to weaken the troops holding the Siegfried Line —tired, or Landwehr divisions—more and more. This brought about a serious element of danger, which we at once endeavoured to reduce. As things were, we had commenced the relief of tired Western divisions by strong Eastern ones in the East, and the 107th Division, which had entrained in the East about the middle of November, was intended for the neighbourhood of Cambrai. Its leading troops had just arrived when the blow fell.

Under cover of darkness and the great Havrincourt Wood, the English had, during several nights, concentrated a considerable number of tanks and cavalry divisions between the two roads converging on Cambrai from Bapaume and Péronne. On the morning of the 20th, after a short, heavy bombardment, they advanced to the attack. The tanks overcame obstacles and trenches, and so opened the way for the infantry and cavalry divisions. When, soon after 8 a.m., I spoke with the Chief of Staff of the 2nd Army he reported that the enemy had already broken into our line at several points. I at once ordered several divisions which were more or less rested, in rear of the group of the German Crown Prince, to be railed to the neighbourhood of Cambrai and south of it, and requested the group of Prince Rupprecht to move forces to the north of Cambrai. General von Kuhl had left by car for the 4th Army before hearing about the battle on the 2nd Army front. The divisions of this group were thereby delayed.

The order for a unit to entrain is by no means the same thing as its arrival. It has to march to the entraining stations, where trains have to be got ready for it. On the various lines the trains can only follow each other at certain definite intervals of time, and

the normal duration of the journey has to be added to all this.
So it generally took two or three days for a division, using some

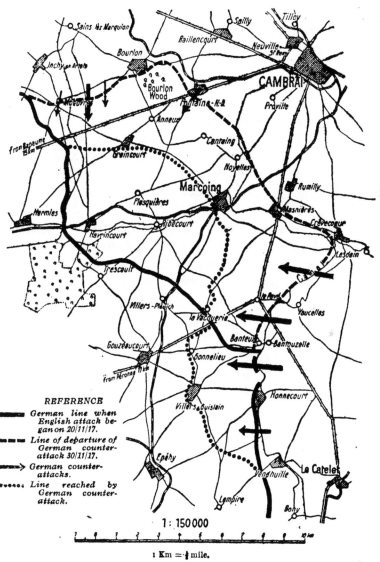

REFERENCE
▬▬ German line when
English attack be-
gan on 20/11/17.
▬ ▬ ▬ Line of departure of
German counter-
attack 30/11/17.
▬▬⇒ German counter-
attacks.
•••••◄ Line reached by
German counter-
attack.

1 : 150 000

1 Km = ⅝ mile.

Fig. 26. Cambrai. 1917.

thirty trains, to reach its destination. It could seldom be done
in less.

The first reinforcements could not reach Cambrai by train before the morning of the 21st ; not until the 23rd would sufficient troops be collected to oppose the attack. The lack of motor transport for moving troops was now much felt.

It was not until noon that I obtained a clear idea of the extent of the enemy's success. It made me very anxious. Everything possible, however, was already being done. So here again I had to leave things to take their course.

The English Army Commander did not exploit his great initial success, or we should not have been able to limit the extent of the gap. If he had done so, what would have been the judgment on the Italian campaign ? That was the sort of war we had to wage against the world. As a matter of fact, the blow was parried on the afternoon of the 22nd and on the 23rd, on the line Moeuvres —Bourlon—Fontaine—Noyelles—Masnières. Even the troops which had been run over by tanks on the first day fought well, and so did the newly arrived 107th Infantry Division. To its intervention the early check to the enemy's attack is mainly due. It was immediately decided, if possible, to take the English attack in flank. In theory, a decision of that kind is easy to make ; but in practice, its execution was enormously difficult in the West. The assembling of the troops, their disposal for attack and bringing up the huge quantities of ammunition required take time. In the meanwhile, the defence itself consumes troops.

At other points the English and French Armies undertook nothing of importance. In the re-entrant in our line the fighting died down without the employment of excessive numbers on our part. By the evening of the 29th the Commander of the 2nd Army, General von der Marwitz, had collected enough troops for a counter-attack. The main effort was to be made on the southern part of the battle-field, in the direction of Banteux and Gouzeaucourt, while a subsidiary attack was to be made west of Bourlon in a direction due south. This time the English were surprised. Our attack on the 30th was well supported by artillery and succeeded, though not quite as well as I had hoped. But it was at any rate at last an offensive victory on the Western

Front. The foresight of the Chief of Staff of the 2nd Army, Lieut.-Colonel Stapff, and the energy of the General had earned their just reward. The success was the more remarkable because it was in the main achieved by half-tired troops who had not been specially trained for attack.

There was only one serious feature. The success had not been as complete as it might have been, because a good division, instead of pressing on, stopped to go through an enemy supply-depot.

The English brought up reserves and counter-attacked. The battle went on until the 5th December, and during its course we regained a good deal of the ground we had lost and some new ground as well. We had won a complete victory over a considerable part of the British Army. It was a good ending to the extremely heavy fighting of 1917. Our action had given us valuable hints for an offensive battle in the West, if we wished to undertake one in 1918.

Neither the English nor the French attacked again in France. The second strategic scheme of 1917 had also resulted in failure for them. A quiet period, which our exhaustion rendered so imperatively necessary, supervened at last in the West.

IV

The offensive against Italy at Tolmino began on the 24th October.

The Flitsch Group, under the Austro-Hungarian General von Krausz, and the 14th German Army were to seize the mountain range which follows the right bank of the Isonzo from about Flitsch to Canale and reaches its highest point in Mount Matajur, 5,420 feet, south-west of Caporetto. While all the other divisions were to ascend the range, the 12th, under General Lequis, was to move from Tolmino on Caporetto and then advance round the Matajur by the valley road towards Cividale.

The Army Group of General Boroevic was to join in the advance

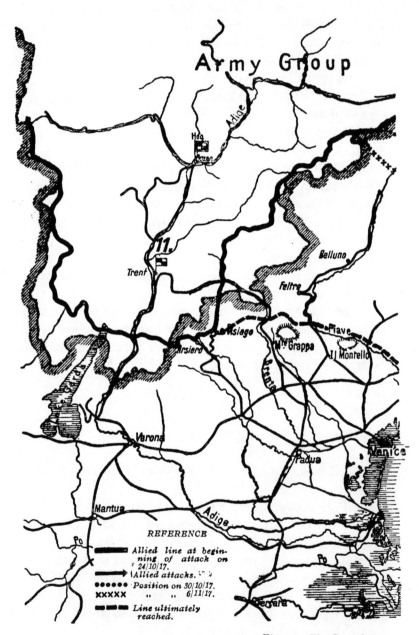

REFERENCE

▬▬▬	Allied line at beginning of attack on 24/10/17.
➤	Allied attacks.
●●●●●	Position on 30/10/17.
×××××	" " 6/11/17.
▬ ▬ ▬	Line ultimately reached.

Fig. 27.   The Campaign

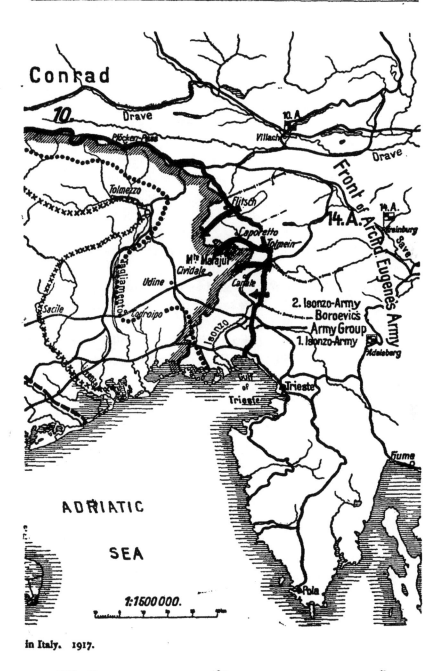

in Italy. 1917.

of the 14th Army, moving in a westerly direction from the Carso Mountains.

The deployment of the 14th Army had proved very difficult. Only two mountain roads were available and they were very narrow in places, so that movement in one direction only was possible. All the care and intelligence of the German staff officer was needed to ensure the movements taking place without friction and being completed to time. First of all the artillery and trench mortars, with large supplies of ammunition, were moved up in good time, under the feeble protection of a few Austro-Hungarian battalions. The infantry divisions were moved up last of all.

The deployment took days and was betrayed to the Italians. The desperate hostile attacks in the West in the second half of October had already some connection with our plans in Italy. Our weakness in the West was to be taken advantage of. Tactically, Cadorna seems to have taken no steps. Possibly he thought the attack was hopeless.

After a few hours' bombardment by artillery and trench mortars with high explosive and gas shells, the ascent of the mountains began on the morning of the 24th, while the 12th Division pushed ahead in the valley towards and beyond Caporetto with the greatest energy. On the 25th the decisive mountain range was already in our hands and the Matajur was taken from several sides.

On the 27th we had already gained more ground in the mountains towards the upper Tagliamento and occupied Cividale. The Italian North Front on the Carinthian frontier, and the Isonzo Front both began to give way. Unfortunately Boroevic's Group did not follow up with enough energy, so that more Italians escaped than should have been the case.

General von Below was instructed to keep his right wing in the mountains, but to advance with his left by Udine and press towards Codroipo and the south, so as to strike a decisive blow at the whole enemy force to the east of the Tagliamento. In this way another 60,000 Italians were captured east of that river, which was reached on the 1st December along its whole course below Tolmezzo.

Fighting in Flanders and Collapse of Russia

The 30th November was another good day. In France there was the victory of Cambrai and in Italy this fine success. As early as November I had requested General von Arz to reinforce General Conrad's Group in the Tyrol from that of General Boroevic and to make an energetic attack there, either down the Brenta or in the Asiago–Arsiero area. Now that the operation we had planned had succeeded, General von Boroevic was too strong, General von Conrad too weak. General von Arz consented. But the railways were too bad, and no movement worth mentioning could be effected.

The Tagliamento was crossed on the 6th December and the Piave, from the Montello downwards, was reached on the 11th. Other troops pressed on in the mountains towards Feltre. Before this advance the Italian Army on the upper Piave hurriedly fell back from the mountains through Belluno.

The right wing of the 14th Army was now deflected through Feltre towards the mountains between the Brenta and the Piave, in order to secure the exit into the plain. Elsewhere the Piave, being in flood, brought our advance to a halt. Beyond the Piave the Italians once more stood their ground in fair order. The first English and French reinforcements joined them.

Here, just as in August in the Bukovina and Eastern Galicia, the railways in rear of the armies had to be repaired before we could think of resuming operations in the plain. The weather in the mountains became unfavourable and the fighting there proved very exhausting. The troops continued to gain ground, but they did not succeed in capturing the critical Monte Grappa *massif*. The impulse of the offensive, begun on the Isonzo, had come to a natural end. Reinforcements would even now have carried it on some way, but General von Conrad had insufficient artillery, and his infantry were not strong enough to attack.

His advance began on the 4th December, much too late to affect the main operation, and very soon came to a standstill. The German General Staff would have been glad to send a division from the Western Front to the Trentino, but could not spare it in November. When this was eventually done it was too late. Here again the railways were too bad.

Early in December, after a discussion with General von Krafft, I came to the conclusion that nothing further was to be gained by continuing the operation beyond the Piave. We therefore suggested to General von Arz that he should order it to stop, and arrange for the German troops to be transported to the West.

The operation against Italy had achieved all that could possibly be expected of it. The Italian Army was thoroughly beaten and needed the support of its Allies. Both the Austro-Hungarian Army and the Western Front had been relieved. Austria-Hungary and her army had taken on a new lease of life. As Russia now concluded an armistice the Dual Monarchy appeared to be coming round to a more warlike frame of mind again. We were no longer told, as we used to be, that her army would have to drop out of the war at the beginning of winter. This campaign had once more revealed its poor fighting capacity. It badly needed the approaching period of rest for recuperation and training. Success had stimulated it.

German leadership and German troops had gained fresh laurels, and given further proofs of their superiority in the war of movement. On occasions our full force had not been developed owing to incidents arising from the lack of experience of young troops.

V

After the outburst of activity in September another period of quiet set in on the Macedonian Front, which was to last for some considerable time. General von Scholtz was untiring in his efforts to train the Bulgarian troops and keep them fit for battle. All German commands in Macedonia were working for the same end. The Bulgarian General Staff, however, as before, took no interest in these important questions.

In the meantime the Entente had not slackened in their endeavours to secure the services of the Royal Greek Army. King Constantine had been deposed, and his son Alexander had succeeded him. Venizelos ruled the country. The Greek Army had been mobilized, but the formation of troops fit for the battle-line proceeded only slowly.

In Palestine and Mesopotamia Turkish affairs became steadily worse.

Operations against Bagdad were to begin in the autumn of 1917 or the spring of 1918. A start had been made with the preparations, but in spite of the improvement in the traffic, which resulted from the opening of the tunnels, little progress was made. The service remained bad and irregular. The local commanders, however, believed that with the assistance given them by our General Staff, they would be able to overcome all these difficulties. In this they displayed too much confidence in the Turks.

The strategical basis of the enterprise against Bagdad was the security of the front in Palestine. I continually drew Enver's attention to this point and very often requested him to reinforce that front and pay particular attention to improving the service on the Syrian railways. G.H.Q. gave him all the help they could. What we gave him was not excessive, and this fell into the hands of incompetent Turks.

Colonel von Kresz was the leading spirit in all endeavours to improve the condition of the Turkish Armies in Palestine. As I afterwards discovered, he had a better idea of the troubles and anxieties of the local Headquarters than the gentlemen in Constantinople. The latter had far too optimistic an idea of the situation, and communicated it to their General Staff.

The authorities in Constantinople gradually came round to the idea of strengthening the Palestine Front, but now thought of achieving that object by an offensive. The operation against Bagdad was ingloriously consigned to the waste paper basket, and an attack in Palestine substituted for it. The Army Group Headquarters of von Falkenhayn was brought to this theatre.

In view of the poor communications and the condition of the Turkish troops Colonel von Kresz had doubted the possibility of their taking the offensive, and events proved that he was right. Instead of the Turks, the English attacked.

After the failure of their attack on Gaza in March, the Colonel

had attempted to operate against their communications in
the Sinai Peninsula by means of raids and aircraft. He did once
succeed in damaging their pipe-line, but he was unable to do
either it or the railway any serious harm.

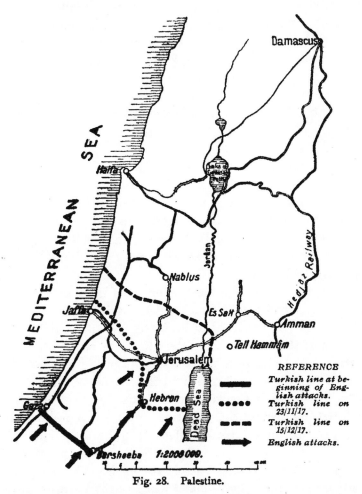

Fig. 28.   Palestine.

At the end of August large masses of English cavalry advanced
on Beersheba so as to work round the left flank of the Gaza
Front and reach the water-supply of Jerusalem. This enterprise failed, as did others on the 2nd and 18th October. Not
till the 2nd November did the English succeed in capturing Beer-

sheba. Simultaneously, with the assistance of the fleet, they attacked Gaza. The Turkish Army was forced to retire and was drawn up on the line Jaffa–Hebron–Dead Sea in order to protect Jerusalem. The English Army followed slowly. On the 17th it took Jaffa and deployed strong forces towards Jerusalem as well. On this line the Turks did not fight it out, but fell back to a position south of Nablus, between the sea and the Jordan. English troops occupied Jerusalem on the 9th December. The Turkish Army had suffered heavy losses. Its ability to offer further resistance could only be considered slight. However, the German Asiatic Corps arrived in Palestine by degrees and gave our ally some stiffening.

The defeat of the Turks greatly influenced the attitude of the Arabs who sided more and more with England.

After occupying Bagdad the English extended the area under their control further up the Euphrates and Tigris. In October they held the line Ramadieh–Samara, and in November they gained more ground towards Mosul.

On both fronts, in Palestine as in Mesopotamia, the strength of the Turks had considerably decreased. It was evident that the position there could only be maintained by means of further reinforcements.

The Russo-Turkish Front continued inactive. At my request, Enver was going to send reinforcements from there to Mesopotamia; but whether the troops ever started could not be ascertained.

VI

On the Rumanian Front the fighting continued without result into September, when it died down.

On the Eastern Front all was quiet. In the middle of October we withdrew our advanced troops east of Riga to their permanent positions. Along these extended fronts active communications between the two lines of trenches gradually set in. We continued our endeavours to increase the desire for peace in the Russian Army.

On the 11th October the fleet left Libau for the attack on the islands lying off the Gulf of Riga. The blow was aimed at Petrograd, and, since very many people have no idea of time and space, was bound to make a profound impression there. It was a peculiar satisfaction to me that in this way the fleet obtained an opportunity for active work.

During its long period of rest events had occurred which threw a most disquieting light not only on the agitation which the Independent Socialists had carried on in certain parts of the Navy, but also on the state of public opinion in Germany, and therefore on our fighting power. The aims of a small fraction of the people had been accomplished in the Navy. The outward conditions of its existence and its constant touch with the home country had favoured the spread of revolutionary ideas. Many, and often the best, of the regular officers and engineers of some length of service had been detached for duty with submarines, or in the High Seas Fleet, and this had not been good for discipline. A renewal of active operations could not fail to improve and fortify the spirit of the Navy.

The tasks of the Navy were to provide transports, cover the sea-passage and the landing, co-operate in the operations from seawards, and maintain the communications of the expeditionary force with Libau.

This force, consisting of the 42nd Infantry Division and the Cyclists' Brigade, was commanded by General von Kathen, whose Chief of Staff was Colonel von Tschischwitz. So the conduct of the operation had been entrusted to particularly capable hands.

The landing-place reconnoitred and selected was Tagga Bay, on the north-west corner of Ösel Island.

After neutralizing the batteries on the Sworbe Peninsula— the southern extremity of Ösel—the fleet steamed into the Gulf of Riga, and then advanced into Moon Sound, while torpedo craft steamed round the north side of the island. They were to bombard the long causeway which connects Ösel and Moon and cut off the enemy's retreat from Ösel. They were also to push into Moon Sound from the north. The Navy hoped to force an action on those portions of the enemy's naval forces which had their permanent stations there, or to cut them off altogether. The object of the troops landed on Ösel was to seize the causeway as soon as possible, capture the whole island and so take the defenders of the Sworbe Peninsula in rear.

Fig. 29. Dagö-Ösel. 1917.

This plan succeeded and only a small part of the garrison escaped by way of the causeway. On the 16th Ösel was in our possession, and Moon fell on the 18th. Soon afterwards we also secured Dagö. The Navy found an opportunity of engaging hostile craft.

507

This ended the fighting on the Eastern Front for the time being.

How far these last attacks accelerated matters in Russia I do not know. The fact is that simultaneously with the rise of the Bolshevists in the autumn the disintegration of the Russian Army proceeded very rapidly. The officers lost their privileged position and all authority was taken from them. They were not to be regarded as more important than the men in the ranks ; in a little while they were regarded as less and had no rights at all. These measures were approved by many people in Russia. There, as elsewhere, there were many short-sighted individuals who could not see that the strength of the Army, and all social order, rests upon authority, and that by shaking the authority of the officers they were undermining the social order of the whole world.

Hetman Skropadsky told me that he never noticed how his Corps, which he had commanded in the war, dissolved. It merely vanished all at once. This simple story made a tremendous impression on me.

In the army the Russian revolution did not stop at depriving the officer of his rights. It set up the Soldiers' Council in the place of Authority, and went even further. It disarmed all but the proletarian soldiers and created the Red Guard. In the purely political sphere it acted in the same way. The *bourgeois* counted for nothing at all ; the proletarian Workmen's Council was predominant.

The proletarian Society of Workers and Soldiers was now, by means of its Councils, to govern and reorganize the world. All that had existed hitherto was ruthlessly destroyed. Civilization was disintegrated. Private property was to be limited and all joy in work to be killed. Woman became public property. Bestial instincts soon became uppermost. The chaos developed more and more into the bloody dictatorship of a few men, who relied on troops faithful to themselves, and on whose passions, even when they were Chinese mercenaries, they placed no restraint. The country, dominated by this dictatorship, was ruined ; but that meant nothing to those in power.

A curious state of affairs was thus created. Those who never could cry out enough about violation of rights and against war, paid no regard to the rights of the majority, but violated them more than any Government had done, called the people to arms and made war, not against external enemies at first, it is true, but generally against every existing institution. Those who disagreed with them heard no word of reconciliation or understanding.

And soon all those who had previously done their utmost to destroy authority in the army and the nation recognized the danger into which they had plunged themselves and their whole country. Unfortunately it was found impossible in Russia to arm all the anti-Bolshevist parties and make them sink their sectarian differences and unite for the regeneration of the country.

The peasants and the middle-class found themselves exposed, unarmed, to violation by their oppressors and fell a prey to anarchist disruption. Who knows when, if ever, they will recover their vitality ? We can see no signs of it, and merely to hope for it seems almost dangerous self-deception. Possibly, like many people in Germany in the spring of 1919, they looked upon Bolshevism with fatalistic equanimity, as an inevitable doom which must of itself produce salvation. That is a cowardly thought, and in Russia it had terrible consequences. Salvation from Bolshevism is not to be found in looking on and doing nothing but in strong and wise action, accurate gauging of the enemy's strength and weakness, and also in far-sighted economic reforms which would have been imperative after the war in any event.

From October, 1917, onwards, Bolshevism in Russia obtained an ever firmer hold.

I could not doubt that the disintegration of the Russian Army and nation involved an extraordinary risk for Germany and Austria-Hungary. All the greater was my anxiety when I thought of the weakness of our Government and theirs.

By sending Lenin to Russia our Government had, moreover, assumed a great responsibility. From a military point of view his journey was justified, for Russia had to be laid low. But our Government should have seen to it that we also were not involved in her fall.

The events in Russia gave me no cause for complete satisfaction. They considerably eased the military situation, but elements of the greatest danger still remained.

As early as the summer I had drafted the armistice conditions. They were based on the desire to come to an understanding with Russia, for the needs of the war demanded peace in the East.

The fundamental idea of the armistice was to cease hostilities on the lines which each army held at the time. I demanded no cession of territory or surrender of arms. The conditions contained nothing that might make the armistice or the future peace more difficult. The draft was submitted to the Imperial Government and the Allied Headquarters and was agreed to. Minor changes involved no alteration in principle. It was agreed with the Imperial Government that if the armistice was negotiated between the contending armies, the conduct was to be in the hands of G.H.Q., assisted by a representative of the Imperial Chancellor. The latter agreed to include a representative of G.H.Q. in the commission to be appointed for the peace negotiations ; he was, of course, to be the subordinate, not the equal, of the Chancellor's plenipotentiary.

I had everything ready in case the Russians should make advances. By November the Russian Army was so far corroded by Bolshevism that G.H.Q. could seriously think of weakening the Eastern Front in order to strengthen the West. We had then about 80 divisions there, one-third of our whole force. I now proposed that the Austro-Hungarian troops should take over a larger part of the line. We discussed with their Headquarters, and with the Commander-in-Chief in the East, how we could set free the greatest number of German troops on the fronts in Transylvania, the Bukovina and Eastern Galicia. General von Arz also agreed to send Austro-Hungarian troops from Italy to the East. These measures would, of course, be carried out only in the somewhat remote future. But it was necessary to make preparation now, so that all movements might be completed by the coming spring, the decisive period for us. Otherwise the scheme would have been impracticable owing to the bad condition of the railways and the critical state of transport in the occupied territory and Germany. But affairs in Russia prevented our taking too drastic decisions as yet.

From the end of November onwards troop-trains were incessantly passing from East to West. It was no longer a case of replacing tired divisions in the West by fresh ones, but of really adding to the number of combatants in the West.

The training of the troops in the East for western conditions was pushed on, and the same was done in Rumania.

The idea of making an attack in France in 1918 attracted many of our generals as early as November, myself perhaps most of all. I therefore eagerly awaited the day when the Russian Government would ask for an armistice. At the front numerous local truces were made in November. Larger and larger formations made overtures to us and already individual Russian Armies made proposals for ceasing hostilities. Peace negotiations were attempted at Dvinsk, but came to nothing. In some places armistices were denounced. It was a confusing picture, half peace, half war.

On the 26th November the Russian Commander-in-Chief, People's Commissary Krylenko, inquired by wireless whether we were prepared to conclude an armistice. We agreed. On the 2nd December the Russian delegates crossed the German lines. Negotiations began without delay at Brest-Litovsk, where the Commander-in-Chief in the East still had his Headquarters. At the same time the four Allied Powers sent their representatives. By the 7th December a ten days' truce was agreed upon.

General Hoffmann conducted these negotiations very skilfully and kept the Bolshevist representatives to the point. The discussion was limited to the matter in hand. The Russians returned temporarily to Petrograd with the draft agreement in order to obtain fresh instructions. Negotiations were reopened on the 12th and the armistice was signed on the 15th. It was to begin at the termination of the truce at noon on the

17th, and continue until noon on 14th January, 1918. If not denounced at seven days' notice it would continue automatically.

The original draft had not been fundamentally modified; the Russian front had not changed, and no neutral zone was created. The respective wire entanglements were considered as the boundaries. Indeed, at the request of the Russians, communication between the two fronts had been arranged at certain points of passage. We clearly perceived their intention of carrying on propaganda. The Commander-in-Chief in the East was positive that he could frustrate this attempt by suitable measures. We therefore accepted this condition merely to make an end of the business. The agreement was officially binding on the whole Russian front; but the power of the Government of Councils did not extend so far.

It therefore became necessary to enter upon special negotiations on the same basis in Rumania and Asia Minor. These were also brought to a successful conclusion. The armistice of Focsani was concluded on the 9th December. It is useful to compare our conditions with those which the determination of the Entente to destroy us imposed upon the Powers of the Quadruple Alliance.

After three years of titanic contest, quiet reigned along the whole front. What German leadership and German troops accomplished in fighting throughout this long period against enormous superiority will always fill a glorious page in the history of our country and the German manhood which fought and bled here.

For the past six months I had devoted myself, and made others devote all their energies, to the attainment of the object we had now achieved. The Western Front had held, the Italian Army was defeated and the Austro-Hungarian Armies in Italy had been imbued with fresh vigour. Negotiations were to begin at Brest–Litovsk about Christmas. We had some prospect of gaining the final victory.

It was only in Asia Minor that all had not gone well, but compared with the great events in Europe that was of quite subsidiary importance.

The troops and leaders who had fought in the West could proudly say that their achievements had laid the foundation of this mighty result. By their steadfastness the campaign in the East and in Italy had been won. Here also the German had done a hero's work.

As in the year before, the co-operation between our General Staff and the Allies had produced great results.

The Entente was impressed by this change in the situation. They still had hopes of America. But in spite of that, feeling in France had remained shaken since the battle on the Aisne and in Champagne. In November Clemenceau became Prime Minister. He was the strongest man in France. He had been through 1870–71 and had since then been one of the most ardent protagonists of *Revanche*. Clemenceau knew what he wanted. His policy was a war policy ; he suppressed every sign of peace agitation and strengthened the spirit of his country. His proceedings against Caillaux showed clearly what we were to expect of him. He, too, thought only of victory and like Lloyd George had his country behind him. The enemy's conduct of the war gained immensely in vigour. In America also the fighting spirit became more and more pronounced. There, too, the Government took action against all thought of peace with the greatest ruthlessness. Under the powerful influence of Clemenceau and Lloyd George Italy survived the impression produced by her defeat, which had at first been very deep. In the hostile democratic States the Government assumed more and more the charac ter of a dictatorship.

VII

The Peace Resolution of the German Reichstag moved the Vatican to take special steps in the direction of peace. The Papal Peace Note of the 1st August appeared in the middle of that month, and was addre ssed to the heads of the various States at war.

The Note pronounc ed entirely in favour of a peace withou_t

annexations or indemnities and expected us to make considerable sacrifices, while the Entente got off very cheaply. German public opinion received it in the same way as the peace resolution in July. The Press of the Right declined it, that of the Majority Parties was in favour of it and invited the enemy to follow the sounder view and accept it also. The Press of the Entente unanimously refused it and adhered to that attitude, and the Government did the same.

The Imperial Chancellor, Dr. Michaelis, read his answer aloud to us at Kreuznach. I anticipated no results from this attempt at peace. Nor did the answer accord with my views. But I put my objections aside and only made unimportant counter-proposals. I could only wait and see what would come of these purely theoretical endeavours to make peace, notwithstanding my aversion to the perpetual peace-talk on account of its evil influence on the conduct of the war. Looking back I regret that I did not oppose all these ideas with more energy. To conclude peace, which I equally desired, was the business of diplomacy, but to be always talking to the public about it could do us no good so long as the enemy remained determined to destroy us. The foresight of the Entente in this respect was exemplary.

Our reply, like that of Austria-Hungary, accepted the Pope's advances although many points were diplomatically evaded. By a reference to the peace resolution of the Reichstag, which was included at the desire of the seven members who assisted in drawing it up, our position was clearly defined.

The reply of the Entente amounted to a refusal; otherwise it was not to the point. The Pope's step was entirely un-successful. It was always the same old story : the German people honestly desired peace, but the Entente refused it. In their quiet but penetrating propaganda they were continually making our public, and neutral countries, repeat the catchword : " Peace by understanding and reconciliation," but they always avoided committing themselves to it. Now, as ever, they pursued but one idea, to destroy Germany.

The Pope's step could not succeed. It is curious now to

observe the way in which the Pope was excluded from the negotiations at Versailles. The Entente are not grateful to him.

At his accession I had informed Dr. Michaelis that Herr Hugo
Stinnes was in communication with the Japanese Ambassador
in Stockholm and had told me he had some hope. He said he
was about to leave for Stockholm and was likely to see the Ambassador. The Imperial Chancellor thereupon received Herr
Stinnes. I took no further interest in the matter.

Suddenly, at the end of August, or early in September, we
heard there was an opportunity of opening discussion with the
Entente. The Imperial Chancellor and Herr von Kühlmann,
who had become Secretary of State for Foreign Affairs when
he was appointed, told us it was a secret. I had heard from
Colonel von Haeften that reports had come through neutral
countries, in connection with a speech by Mr. Asquith, the former
British Premier, and later statements by Lloyd George, that
England expected us to make a statement about Belgium. The
Chancellor now told me that England had suggested the possibility of some sort of discussion. I was naturally pleased; if
England had now become ready for peace its prospects were
brighter than before when we alone made the approaches. I
therefore considered the question of peace more favourably
than I had done hitherto.

The talk of peace led to various discussions with the Imperial
Chancellor on the question of Belgium.

We laid down as our goal the economic attachment of Belgium
to the German Empire, in view of the close relationship that had
existed before the war. The Imperial Government thought
that this gave them some basis on which to enter into communication with England. I expected that the Secretary of
State would make a public declaration in this sense in the form
of a speech in the Reichstag at the end of September. On the
20th September, Colonel von Haeften had a fairly long discussion
with him about it. But the Secretary of State did not agree,
and remarked: " Who told you that I am prepared to sell
the horse ' Belgium ? ' It is for me to decide that. At present
the horse is not for sale at all."

In his speech on the 9th October he did not mention Belgium, but amid the boisterous applause of the Reichstag alluded to Alsace-Lorraine in the following terms : " As long as a German fist can hold a rifle, the integrity of the German dominions, which we have received as a glorious heritage from our fathers, can never become the object of any negotiations or concessions."

That did not bring us a single step forward, as far as England was concerned.

We heard no more of the prospects of peace. On inquiry the General Staff received no definite answer from Secretary of State von Kühlmann. I was disappointed and regretted having momentarily believed in it. It was only for that reason that I had requested the Imperial Chancellor to refrain from a great speech which he wished to deliver at the end of September, as it seemed conceivable that it might lessen the possibility of peace. It would have been better for him to have spoken. It seems doubtful, however, whether he would have succeeded in uniting the whole Reichstag and people, in view of his relations with the various political parties. He opposed their desire for power, and his attitude towards the Reichstag itself was that of a stranger.

I also entertained some hopes of the efforts being made by the representative of the Foreign Office in Brussels, Herr von der Lancken, who sought to get into touch with French statesmen. He went to Switzerland, but the gentleman from France stayed away.

I also heard casually that Herr von Kühlmann was in communication regarding peace questions with the Spanish Ambassador in Brussels.

Such were the possibilities of peace of which I received information during 1917. Of President Wilson's so-called offer, which Herr Jaffé brought to the Foreign Office from Munich, I only heard from the papers after my resignation.

In connection with these mysterious peace rumours a Crown Council was held at Berlin on the 11th September. I considered it my duty, and it was within my province, once more to point out clearly what, according to the experience of this war, was necessary in order to secure Germany's future, and on this occasion, and later on in the autumn of 1917, I committed myself to the following opinions :

" According to the statements of the Departments concerned the food and coal situation at home is difficult. As regards coal this is unfortunately due in part to neglect in previous months. Our financial system is enormously strained. The Majority in the Reichstag has rendered the situation at home deplorable. The labour question, and therefore the recruiting question also, have become acute. But I consider that these internal difficulties must be overcome by firm statesmanship on the part of the present Government. It is possible."

In considering the requirements imposed upon us by the necessities of strategic and military economics, I based my considerations on our pre-war situation and developments during the war. A three-years' war was only possible because we had in Germany abundant coal, and so much iron and food that together with what we could obtain from occupied territory and neutral countries, we could, by practising the most rigid economy, manage to exist in spite of the hostile blockade.

Only by offensive action in this war which had been forced upon us, and by expanding to the East and West, had we been able to exist ; we should certainly have been lost had we remained within our own frontiers.

Defeat was inevitable if the enemy should succeed in occupying German territory for any length of time ; we might starve, and the back of our military economic system would be broken. The importance in war of coal, iron and food was known before this war ; but how absolutely decisive they would actually become was only demonstrated to all the world as hostilities proceeded. Before the war we had recognized the exposed position of the coalfields of Upper Silesia, and when we demanded the " Milliard Mark Bill " measures were taken to protect them. Our industrial areas in the West were considered to be secured by our strategical deployment.

No less unfavourable than our strategic situation in the centre of Europe was the position of our iron and coal fields, which were mostly near our frontiers. Every other country was better off in that way. The coal and iron of Upper Silesia were right on the Russian border. In the west, the iron of Lorraine and the coal of Saarbrücken were just as exposed. The industrial area of the Lower Rhine and of Westphalia was quite unprotected against Belgium. In comparison with these areas, the lignite deposits of central Germany were unimportant.

Destructive weapons had been perfected in the war. The range of guns had considerably increased, and the power of aircraft had been greatly extended. On the other hand their employment was limited by certain fundamental conditions. Every shot from a long-range gun did not stop all activity within reach. That we learned in the spring of 1918 when bombarding the French coal-mines, and on other occasions. Aircraft are dependent upon the weather; otherwise we would have bombed London more often. With these reservations I had to allow for all the new means of warfare in considering the characteristics of any future war. I took as a basis the same frontiers and the same political situation as in 1914.

It was to be expected that the enemy would, directly after the order to mobilize at the latest, attack our military factories with numerous aircraft well supplied with ammunition. A certain degree of security could be obtained by concentrating strong aircraft forces on the frontier, and good anti-aircraft protection; but these measures would not prevent attack or bomb-dropping. Nor could any protection be provided against long-range hostile guns. This sudden attack would be followed up by the main mass of the army. The course of the operations could not be foreseen in detail. But as far as the influence on our war industries was concerned it could be taken for granted that everywhere a marked reduction of output—decisive in its total effects—would follow, and that at the worst a great proportion of our labouring classes would be very hard hit. Without being unduly pessimistic I could foresee that we might in certain circumstances lose the war in the first few days. We should be killed like rats in a trap.

It was not possible to follow out all the conclusions which

this led to., *e.g.*, we could not aim at pushing our frontiers far into the interior of France. We must be content with meeting our most pressing needs. A protective belt of a few miles would have to suffice for safeguarding the Upper Silesian coalfield and the iron mines of Lorraine from the immediate effects of the operations. The fact that both coal and ore are found in these belts, both in Poland and near Briey, did not influence me. That these measures were insufficient by themselves but would have to be supplemented by elaborate military defences in time of peace was obvious. Whatever we might do, the security of our economic resources here would be inadequate, and it was therefore imperative to ensure the certain protection of the industrial area of Westphalia and the Lower Rhine. I had learned to know its importance as a peace and war industry when acting as Regimental Commander at Düsseldorf, and now again as First Quartermaster-General. The only possible conclusion was that Belgium must on no account be allowed to become a hostile area of deployment. Her neutrality I considered to be a mere phantom on which no practical man would rely. We must ensure that her economic interests became identical with those of Germany, with which she was already united by such strong commercial ties. She was to remain an independent State in which the Flemings also should enjoy their rights. The violation of this ancient Germanic race is another of the enormities of human history. For the first few years I considered it would be necessary to maintain a German army of occupation. The Meuse at Liége could only be given up, if at all, after Belgium had completed her economic union with Germany and, in accordance with her real interests, taken her place on our side.

The idea of German naval bases on the coast of Flanders did not appeal to me. It had not been thought out and was not the outcome of a definite military policy. I wrote as follows : " We would only become quite secure, *i.e.*, as regards the industrial area of the Lower Rhine, especially if the Channel Tunnel scheme is executed, by occupying the whole of Belgium and establishing our army on the coast of Flanders. This object is unattainable at present. The question is whether we should continue the war for the sake of achieving it. In my opinion we ought to do so if the English keep a strip of French territory, *e.g.*, Calais. If they do not, the acquisition of the coast of Flanders is not a sufficient reason for us to prolong the war through the winter."

The retention of Calais by England was at that time discussed in my presence more than once ; that is why I mentioned it.

I thought it important to bring Luxemburg into closer relationship to the Empire.

When we had arranged matters in the West more or less in the manner indicated we should have achieved what was necessary in that quarter for Germany's military and economic security.

In the East the whole German frontier was as unfavourable as possible, not only on account of the Upper Silesian coalfield. The campaign of 1914 had shown the difficulty of holding the country east of the Vistula. East Prussia, after its severe suffering, was certainly entitled to a protective belt.

The Polish re-entrant had proved exceedingly detrimental to our defence.

The full force of this disadvantage had again been felt in the autumn of 1914 when Grand Duke Nicholas struck his great blow at the Prussian frontier. To eliminate the danger altogether by territorial acquisitions appeared impossible. It was, however, strategically necessary to widen the narrow neck between Danzic and Thorn towards the south and to provide a protective belt for the Upper Silesian coalfield.

The desired union with Courland and Lithuania would not improve the frontier. But, once we had secured the protective belt east of the Vistula in the south and the widening of the neck on the south side of Thorn, a good deal could be made good by completing the railway system. Courland and Lithuania would improve our food supply, in case we should, in a future war, have to rely once more on our own resources.

This re-arrangement of the Eastern frontier would in this region also secure what seemed essential to the military and economic security of Germany ; provided always that the so-called " Austro-Polish solution " did not eventuate, and that

Poland established economic relations with Germany, and perhaps later with Russia.

My hopes went a step further. The inhabitants of Courland and Lithuania were to bring Germany additional man-power. That men meant power I felt more and more every day. It was in men that the superiority of the Entente consisted. The population of those countries could retain their nationality under the German Empire. An increase of the Polish population in the defensive belt, which would follow, was undesirable, but this grave objection would have to give way before military necessity. The German settlement, which we hoped would take place on a great scale, and the collection of Germans from abroad in those extensive Eastern territories, which the Imperial Chancellor had tried to establish as far back as 1915 in certain frontier areas, would in the future provide further increase.

For the benefit of Germany's economic position in relation to the rest of the world I contemplated commercial advantages in Rumania and the Balkans, and above all the return of our colonies, or their combination in one united Colonial Territory.

I was averse to the Central-European economic union; it did not appear capable of realization, as it postulated too great a position of superiority for Germany.

I never had serious hopes of indemnities.

These were the military necessities I aimed at; it was not, however, at all certain that we could secure them. If we could not, our demands would still not be unnecessary; but the failure to get them would be a disadvantage which would have to be accepted and remedied by greater safeguards in time of peace.

I never, on my own initiative, expressed in public my ideas regarding the conditions of peace. But, at the request of the Imperial Chancellor, Dr. Michaelis, I discussed them with several representatives of the most diverging political opinions.

My views on peace never formed the basis of any discussion with the enemy, as the Government never got so far as that. Later on, in the first negotiations at Brest, and at Bucharest, the Government went its own way, which did not coincide with mine.

The discussions on war aims between the Imperial Chancellor

and G.H.Q. were purely academic. Everyone knew that the terms of peace would be decided by the way the war ended, and by nothing else, and that we should have to make up our minds according to circumstances.

When concrete cases had to be dealt with, as in drafting the reply to Wilson on 29th January, 1917, our attitude towards Russia in the early summer or towards England in August and September of the same year, or in drawing up the terms of the armistice in the East, we acted according to the circumstances at the time. I did not think of taking my stand on purely theoretical ground.

As long as the enemy persisted in his determination to destroy us, this war could only end in victory or defeat. In any case, the Government was unable to indicate any other way of finishing it and obtaining peace.

To assert that we could have had peace earlier on some condition or other is a scandalous piece of frivolity and a wilful misleading of the German people. The Entente never made an offer; they never dreamt of giving us anything; they were not even satisfied with the conditions existing before the war; they only wanted to get something. Well then, did any single German put forward the idea that we should sacrifice Alsace-Lorraine, the Province of Posen, or our Colonies? Imperial Chancellor von Bethmann did in the autumn of 1916 allude casually to the cession or exchange of a few localities in Lorraine and the Sundgau.

Were we to hold a *plébiscite* in our own country, as a peace offering? That idea was surely not evolved in a German brain. If we wanted to render our defence even more difficult and weaken our political and economic position we ought to have taken it up. That is the kind of thing we are experiencing now.

The war was begun; our duty now was to seek a decision by force, or to accept a defeat which we had the strength to avert. If only Germany would realize this now, that it has been clearly shown that all the Entente's catchwords about self-determination of peoples, no annexations or indemnities, disarmament, freedom of the seas, are mere figments of the imagination and will ever remain so! Every human life is a battle on a small scale; within the various States parties struggle for supremacy, and so it is in the world of nations—so it will ever be. That is a natural law. Enlightenment and a higher morality can mitigate the struggle for power, as well as the means of waging it, but can never destroy the desire for power itself, for that goes against human nature and in the long run against Nature itself. Nature is war. If that which is strong and good does not win, then the ignoble powers gain the upper hand. If we want the good to survive we must be prepared to defend it, by fighting and even by violence. Even goodness can only live if it is strong.

VIII

The internal conditions in Germany continued to develop unsatisfactorily. In the Reichstag the struggle for power between the parties and the Government became more acute. The idea of "Parliamentarism," carried on by professional politicians and concealed under catchwords of every kind, grew daily more naked and unashamed. Dr. Michaelis opposed it with determination and thus very soon became the victim of his own actions. He wore out his strength in this struggle and had no time to work for the war.

In the answer of the United States to the Papal Note, Wilson had again attempted to interfere in Germany's internal affairs and to divide Government and people; this aroused protest in the Reichstag. But even thus we could not muster the strength to repudiate his action with the righteous indignation it deserved.

The occurrences in the Navy in the summer of 1917 showed clearly how far the spirit of revolution had spread. The idea was to enforce peace by a Naval strike. These conditions were not duly appreciated; the first warning was unheeded.

The attitude of the Government was not strong; it revealed the uncertainty of one who is conscious of his own weakness. Dr. Michaelis did certainly perceive the dangerous influence which the Independent Socialists exercised on the conduct of the war ; but he did not prevent their revolutionary activity. Their Press, the evil influence of which could be proved, was allowed to go on writing.

The Reichstag displayed no understanding of its duties in connection with the war. Well-known members protected those representatives whose close connection with affairs in the Navy was proved, who were fighting for revolution and destroying discipline. The German people was not sufficiently informed of the serious nature of these events.

In the Navy also they were dealt with in a way that was bound to do immense harm ; in the Army, too, they were discussed, and the settlement of the matter made a deep impression.

After a temporary rise, the warlike spirit of Germany had allen since July to a disquietingly low level. The spirit which was to disarm the German people in the summer of 1918, and in 1919, became apparent. Our offers to undertake the direction of the Press and of internal propaganda were not met in a manner at all compatible with the seriousness of the situation and this in spite of the revolutionary turmoil in Russia and the Naval mutiny.

After discussion with the War Ministry, G.H.Q. considered it imperative to create an organization for dealing with the instigators of revolution. Proposals to this effect went to Berlin, where they were discussed with the Imperial Authorities. Again nothing could be achieved. The representative of G.H.Q. now suggested that this Office should be established as part of the General Staff in Berlin. Everyone agreed to this. Its duty was limited to establishing facts ; but its field very soon became almost entirely political. It was significant that in spite of this, the Government refused to take over the new Department, though I considered, and had already recommended, that it should do so. G.H.Q. had thus no alternative but to assume another function that was no part of its duty.

The anomalies of our way of carrying on war-time government became more and more apparent and were bound to cause increasing irritation.

Our economic position had also become more acute and raw materials became scarcer.

We had managed to struggle through the food troubles, but it had been very difficult. In the winter of 1916-17 there had been no means of carting potatoes. We had to fall back on kohlrabi. At that time many people went hungry. In spring and summer supplies improved ; but they had only sufficed with the aid of Rumanian wheat and maize. By early threshing on a considerable scale we might yet tide over a period between the old harvest and the new. But that meant anticipating our credit.

Forage had become very scarce ; grazing started early and helped a good deal. The oat harvest had been bad and the hay crop scanty. Evidently the forage problem was going to become worse.

The coal supply seemed more certain than in the winter of 1916–17 ; that of house-coal was tolerable.

The stocks of oil were uncommonly low ; it was urgently necessary to increase the supply from Rumania. Lightless winter evenings were again in store for the country districts.

At the time of Dr. Michaelis' resignation the prospects for the future were exceedingly serious. I hoped that the collapse of Russia, about which there could no longer be any doubt, would at last remove the danger. That, in conjunction with our brilliant successes in Italy and our heroism on the Western Front, was surely enough to rouse us and to prevent disappointment at the absence of complete success in the Submarine war. The nations of the Entente could not point to similar results at that time. They had had nothing but failures, but they were as determined as their Governments and with strong national feeling backed up the great men who led them so vigorously. Opposition was ruthlessly suppressed. Germany, unfortunately for herself, had taken another road The Reichstag opposed firm government, and the opponents of war gained ground among the people. The political leadership of the Chancellors was a failure. Thus the balance of internal conditions in the various States that were at war altered to our disadvantage. The enemy's hope of our internal collapse balanced his military disappointments. We could not entertain such hopes in respect of our strongest enemies, and so, although the military situation was in our favour, there existed a profoundly different spirit between the two sets of opposing nations.

At the end of October Count Hertling succeeded Dr. Michaelis. He was the first Chancellor to be nominated by the Crown with the consent of the majority in the Reichstag. Thus far had the balance of power been altered in favour of Parliament ; and the same process was illustrated by several other ministerial appointments. From this time onward the Reichstag majority was, even more than formerly, jointly responsible for the country's misfortune.

G.H.Q. did not hear of the nomination until it had become an accomplished fact. In the meantime Count von Hertling had come to think better of us. He was unknown to me. We expected of him the fulfilment of the tasks which fell to the Government in the prosecution of the war ; these were, strong internal government, raising the warlike spirit of the people, the execution of the proposals as to recruiting which we had already made to Dr. Michaelis, and finally, the development of propaganda against the enemy.

Once more I entered into communication with the War Minister and the Head of the War Department, which had been for a considerable time in the hands of General von Scheüch, regarding the need of supplying the Army more liberally, but could not bring them to a decision. No doubt both these gentlemen were suffering fron the influence of the unsettled domestic conditions, but instead of overcoming them they allowed them to fetter their own judgment.

I constantly recurred to the subject which had prompted my proposals of the autumn of 1916, namely, the necessity for utilizing all the forces of the country to achieve victory. It had become perfectly evident that the Auxiliary Service Law did not fulfil its object ; on the contrary, it did harm. Besides that, it failed to place the working capacity of the individual at the disposal of the country and to return the temporarily exempted men to the Army in sufficient numbers. The question of drawing the employers and work-people closer together, which was so immensely important for the transition period and for the maintenance of order after the war, had made no progress.

At the request of General von Scheüch, the Field-Marshal and I received the representatives of the Free Unions, and later those of the Christian Unions and the Employees' Associations. We told these gentlemen how necessary it was to maintain and raise the spirit of the people at home, as otherwise that of the Army must inevitably suffer. It was not our business to deal with the Auxiliary Service Law itself. They promised to assist in improving *moral* and denounced the strikes ; to my satisfaction they realized their great responsibility. They made a number of suggestions regarding working conditions at home, which though they did not immediately concern me, interested me considerably, and were passed on to the Government departments concerned with the request that they might be adopted. I hope that in our discussion I clearly explained to them the connection between the Army and the people at home, and that they grasped the great importance I attached to the effect of the internal conditions of the country on the conduct of the war. They were our guests at luncheon and no doubt felt that we treated men of different opinions to our own with respect, and aimed at securing collaboration for the good of the country. The stupid gossip about our seeing none but the " captains of industry " died down somewhat after this visit. We had quite different ideas. We regarded ourselves as the leaders of the whole nation in arms and not of one section only of the nation, which was at that time still capable of defence. In this also we were, though not openly, in opposition to the Government, which depended consciously and definitely only upon that section of the people represented by the Left Majority of the Reichstag and had more or less democratic and radical ideas, while the other section was completely eliminated. The manner in which the law was weakened in favour of the Left, whereby strikes were facilitated and those who were willing to work rendered defenceless, and young men were allowed to combine and run wild instead of being kept under control, and the punitive measures promulgated simultaneously against the Right, show clearly the road the Government was travelling.

I discussed with the War Minister the regrettable phenomena at home, and among other things I pointed out that I did not consider the supervision of the Press to be adequate. The state of affairs in the home garrisons was discussed. The training and discipline of the men were not up to the required standard; saluting had become slack and was generally omitted. No doubt these garrisons had to contend with great difficulties. The shortage of suitable officers was increasing. The Army at the Front could not spare fit officers, but there were a number of unfit officers available who still retained their strength of will. But even these were trying to get to the Front, as they were often forced to do by the extremely low rates of pay prevailing at home. In this respect, too, nothing but drastic innovations could have brought any improvement. However, conditions in the training units led the War Ministry to fill up the Recruiting Depots of the Field Army as much as possible, with a view to getting the recruits away from home sooner and bringing them into touch with the Front, thus turning them into good soldiers. The 1919 Class was transferred to the Recruiting Depots during the winter of 1917-18.

I had again examined the question of securing the drafts required to continue the war. I considered it so important that I thought the public must at last take an active part in it. It could only be solved in a satisfactory manner if the people could be made to see the situation clearly and to decide its own fate. On the 10th September, 1917, G.H.Q. had made serious representations on the subject to the Imperial Chancellor. The Field-Marshal had written:

" The drafts for the Field Army are at present insufficient ; in particular, all arms are alarmingly short of trained reinforcements. . . .

" If we fail to provide the necessary drafts the success of the war will be jeopardized."

We considered that, besides raising the warlike spirit and

starting further propaganda, it was necessary in order to secure drafts to improve the Auxiliary Service Law, increase the individual output of labour, draw the largest possible number of fit men from the factories not later than the spring of 1918, and prolong the term of service. The document ended as follows : " But this it is my duty to emphasize : the situation must become critical if we do not act with energy, and at once. If we do the Army will yet bring the war to a satisfactory conclusion.

" An enormous responsibility rests, therefore, upon all departments concerned with the questions discussed above. In particular the Reichstag, the Trades Unions, etc., must not be left in doubt that they, too, will incur the most serious blame if they hesitate or refuse.

" It is unnecessary to point out that, after months of delay immediate action is necessary."

But this letter also produced no result. Whether the Reichstag was ever informed of it I do not know.

After I had come to know the Imperial Chancellor, Count von Hertling, I became convinced, and had to reckon with the fact, that he, too, was no War Chancellor. His platform was entirely that of the Majority, of which he was in a sense the product, and his programme was peace by understanding. He said so clearly and distinctly in his first great speeches, without finding any sort of echo in the countries of the Entente. He called himself the " Reconciliation Chancellor." I think the time was not yet ripe for reconciliation. We needed a Chancellor who would live only for the duties of his exalted position as war Minister, act with energy, and make the country see the dangers which threatened it. All this was contrary to the nature of Count von Hertling. He was skilful in manipulating the parties of the Reichstag, but gave in to them even in cases where the war demanded another course. Honest intentions had induced him to accept office ; but the times demanded a strong personality. The burden was too heavy for a man of his great age and frail physique. Was I once more to say so to His Majesty ? Who was to become Chancellor, since His Majesty had so often pronounced against Prince von Bülow and Grand Admiral von Tirpitz ? Who was the man who would throw himself into the breach and join in the fight, who would unite and lead the people by the compelling power of his aims? Many had already approached me with the suggestion that I should become Chancellor. This, though well-meant, was a mistaken idea. The work I had to compass was enormous. In order to carry on the world-war I had to control the machine. This alone required an unusual capacity for work. It was inconceivable that I should take over in addition the conduct of a Government which on account of its extremely clumsy working methods required even more than one man's whole time and strength. Lloyd George and Clemenceau might be dictators, but the details of the war did not concern them. Germany's dictator would have to be in Berlin, not at G.H.Q. He would have to be a man with an intimate knowledge of all home conditions. Such a man Berlin might have followed. I could not take over the task; of that I became convinced after a severe mental struggle. I was not deterred by fear of responsibility, but by the knowledge that the strength of one man would be insufficient both to lead the people at home and the Army at the Front in this world-wide war of nations and overcome all the opposition and friction which, as a representative of un-popular " Militarism," I should everywhere have encountered. Circumstances were very different from what they had been in previous wars. The analogies which were suggested to me at that time did not fit at all; times and circumstances could in no way be compared. Frederick the Great was a monarch and possessed his authority by the grace of God. Napoleon knew, at any rate, at the outset of his dazzling career, that he had all France behind him. One thing, however, was certain. Power must be in the hands of one man.

There was no alternative. I must, in addition to my tremendous task at the Front, continue the struggle with the Government in order to obtain what the Army needed for its last and final victory. I knew how arduous it would be, but hoped that the fall of Russia would make a satisfactory solution possible. This was where the situation differed from that at the time of the resignation of the first War Chancellor in July, 1917.

Fighting in Flanders and Collapse of Russia

IX

Besides the problems of peace, the most important political question was the Austro-Polish one. Count Czernin had succeeded first of all in winning over the Emperor, and then the Imperial Chancellor and Secretary of State Von Kühlmann, to his way of thinking. Directly after Count Hertling had taken over, a Crown Council was convened to deal with this matter, which the Field-Marshal and I were ordered to attend. The Imperial Chancellor and the Secretary of State were Bavarians, the Vice-Chancellor, Von Payer, a Würtemberger. They were strangers to the conditions of the Eastern provinces of Prussia and favoured the Austro-Polish solution ; the other Ministers and Secretaries of State agreed in the main with them. The Field-Marshal and I expressed serious dissent, based upon military objections. My arguments are corroborated by the conditions which now prevail and which illustrate in another form the danger I anticipated.

But the Field-Marshal and I were out-voted. The Emperor ordered us to report what military arrangements would make the Austro-Polish solution acceptable to us.

We therefore sought a way out of the difficulty ; it could only be found in a still wider protective belt along the whole Prussian frontier.

In the meantime, in the territory under the Commander-in-Chief in the East, matters had developed favourably in Courland as a result of the instructions issued in August ; in Lithuania, however, the situation had become unsatisfactory.

In September, in accordance with the instructions of the Commander-in-Chief, Major von Goszler had succeeded in forming a Diet at Mitau. He was able to revive to some extent the historic constitutional life of Courland. The nobles had the sense to follow his lead, and invited the Letts to take part in forming the Diet. They accepted. All those who think that the destruction of all existing institutions spells the salvation of a country considered that the Letts had been offered too little. It was indeed not much. But it did pave the way for steady future development ; at any rate, the Letts no longer stood aside. The Diet assembled with due ceremonial at Mitau and requested His Majesty in an address to protect Courland and accept the dignity of the Dukedom. The reply of the Imperial Government was favourable, although it refrained from finally committing itself.

In Lithuania the muddle-headed views of the local democratic party were expressed with increasing insistence. The Diet was formed at Vilna by transforming the old Confidential Council. But it proved incapable of performing its work and political life stagnated.

Before he resigned, Dr. Michaelis had visited Lithuania and Courland, and I expected that now affairs in the East could be brought to a conclusion. At his request I intended to go to Berlin early in November. His sudden resignation destroyed my hopes.

Early in November I was in Berlin. The intended conference on questions relating to the territory under the Commander-in-Chief in the East took place on the 4th, but under the presidency of the new Chancellor, Von Hertling. I intended to determine in his presence the fundamental principles of the relationship of Courland and Lithuania with Germany, and to assure myself that he agreed with the settlements arrived at with former Chancellors. At the same time I wished to strengthen the position of the Chief Administrators by ensuring that they alone should be the deciding authority in those countries, and not any Member of the Reichstag or the Imperial Chancellor or G.H.Q. As before, our policy in the territory of the Commander-in-Chief in the East aimed at joining Courland and Lithuania to Germany by means of personal union under the House of Hohenzollern. I now considered it desirable in the interests of our future that the two Diets should make a declaration on the subject. In Courland most of the work was already done ; nothing remained but formalities. In Vilna, on the other hand, extraordinary difficulties had still to be overcome. However, definite hopes were quite justified if the Administrator received clear instructions and the vacillation in our dealings with Lithuania was put an end to. Then it was intended in both countries to prepare the main outlines of the internal constitution, as well as for the military, economic and political union with Germany.

I met with no opposition at the Conference. The gentlemen sent by the Commander-in-Chief in the East, who did not know Berlin as I did, were glad to be able at last to go on with their work. I was sceptical; and it turned out I was right. The situation in Lithuania remained confused. The Lithuanian Democrats began an agitation against the Administrator, Lieutenant-Colonel Prince von Isenburg. The complaints were usually alleged to be founded on the war conditions, for which the administration could not in any way be blamed. But the conviction was already formed and, as is usual in political differences, no statements of fact could prevail against it. The democratic Lithuanians of Vilna were listened to by our Majority parties, and these again by the Foreign Office. The Lithuanians lost the habit of regarding the military administration as the embodiment of German authority, and very soon discovered that individual deputies were more powerful than the Government itself. These deputies again indulged their vanity by pursuing a Lithuanian policy of their own, although they did not know the country. The Government, anxiously engaged in preventing G.H.Q. from starting a policy on its own account, which it had no intention of doing, allowed the deputies to do as they liked. Under its influence the Foreign Office continued to deal with the Lithuanian question in Berlin exclusively in accordance with the alleged requirements of the internal political situation in Germany, and not in accordance with those of the country itself. So in this case also, party politics became the governing factor in matters of foreign policy. In this way it was impossible to secure healthy conditions in Lithuania; every action of the Administrator, whose authority was being undermined from Berlin, was foredoomed to failure. In view of this, the conference of the 4th November was my last attempt to bring order into the Lithuanian muddle. I afterwards restricted myself to preventing immediate damage.

Lieutenant-Colonel Prince von Isenburg found himself obliged to resign when he saw that the main principles of the policy which he knew to be right were being forsaken. I regretted his departure.

About the middle of December the Lithaunians were led by the Imperial Chancellor to expect that their country would be recognized as free and independent, with its capital at Vilna. It would have to promise to conclude certain conventions with Germany. That sort of Lithuania was in a fair way to fall into the hands of the Poles, unless the conventions contained conditions which secured German influence. But the attitude of the Lithuanians gave little promise of that. What prospect there was could only diminish, the more we gave way to their conflicting desires. Besides, some Lithuanians and one influential deputy from Würtemberg wanted a Prince of the Royal House of Würtemberg, while on the other hand the hopes of the Saxon House appear to have been raised also. Any prince at Vilna would have had the Polish nobility at his Court, the officers of the army would be Poles, and so would the majority of the civil officials. Only Prussia-Germany could keep Lithuania for the Lithuanians and provide officials and officers, which they themselves could not do in anything like sufficient numbers. States capable of an independent existence are not produced by political catchwords, nor are small nations kept alive thereby. I was, therefore, by no means pleased with this vague solution, which seemed so very dangerous for Germany's future. It was significant how quietly the Poles accepted it. They could afford to be satisfied.

G.H.Q. maintained the view formerly approved by the Imperial Chancellor, that Lithuania should be closely joined to Germany by personal union under the House of Hohenzollern.

The Eastern questions were again discussed at length in the conference which took place at Kreuznach on the 18th December under the presidency of His Majesty, in order to determine the peace conditions to be presented to Russia. On this occasion the Emperor expressed his agreement with the protective belt on the Prusso-Polish frontier which we had stated to be just, adequate, without protest from the Imperial Councillor or the Secretary of State for Foreign Affairs. The Imperial Chancellor agreed with the idea of establishing a personal union of Courland and Lithuania with Prussia or Germany, provided the Federal Princes agreed. His Majesty approved this opinion and insisted on the necessity of allowing the nations of other races which might be included to develop according to their own character. As regards our policy towards the people of Courland and Lithuania, this involved safeguarding the results we had secured hitherto, unless we wished to see fresh dangers arise on our Eastern frontier in the future.

Regarding Esthonia and Livonia, His Majesty decided to propose, without demanding, their evacuation by the Russians, so as to allow the Esthonians and Letts to exercise their right of self-determination.

This provided the Foreign Secretary with the necessary basis on which to conduct the coming negotiations.

In the interval, a change had been made in the administration of the territory under the Commander-in-Chief in the East At the head of it were placed a special Administrative General, General Count von Waldersee, and a high administrative official, Under-Secretary of State Freiherr von Falkenhausen. The intention was to make better provision for meeting the political needs of the country and to comply with the wishes of the Imperial Chancellor. General Count von Waldersee and Under-Secretary of State von Falkenhausen carried out their duties with prudence and skill. But, lacking clear orders from Berlin, they could undertake no constructive work.

Under the Chancellorship of Count von Hertling the question of Alsace-Lorraine assumed another aspect, inasmuch as he was a decided advocate of the idea of dividing that country, in which case Bavaria was to get Alsace and Prussia Lorraine. Imperial Chancellor von Bethmann had already had discussions with Bavaria about it. I could not see what good could come of the idea, and feared that this particular solution would cause irritation, particularly in Würtemberg. We could only ask the Chancellor to take the necessary steps to hold a conference

535

in which the fundamental principles of the question would be laid down. Since then the whole business has been dormant. I had, at least, hoped that he would take advantage of his influence in Rome as an established leader of the Centre Party and former Bavarian Prime Minister to settle the ecclesiastical affairs of the Reichsland in a national German sense, but he achieved nothing.

THE PREPARATIONS FOR THE ATTACK IN THE WEST IN 1918

I

OWING to the break-down of Russia the military situation was more favourable to us at New Year, 1918, than one could ever have expected. As in 1914 and 1915, we could think of deciding the war by an attack on land. Numerically we had never been so strong in comparison with our enemies.

The submarine war had not up to date produced those economic results which the Chief of the Naval Staff had expected, and which I, relying on the opinions of the experts, had hoped for. I had continued to take an interest in the problem of providing submarines, in spite of naval assurances that everything possible was being done. I actually received letters from Reichstag deputies, who informed me that more could be built. I was pleased to get these letters, for they amounted to a recognition of my will to carry on the war with all possible energy. On the other hand they surprised me. The building of submarines was constitutionally no business of mine. I had already been reproached by these gentlemen often enough for interfering in matters which did not concern me. It had, in fact, become quite the usual practice, when anything wanted doing at home, to appeal to me. In this instance, of course, I could unfortunately do nothing, except once more press the matter upon the Naval Authorities concerned. G.H.Q. had long before issued orders that every application for individual men by name was to be complied with immediately. Further than that we could not go in releasing workmen. On the list of requirements for the supply of raw materials the construction of submarines was the first item. Everything connected with it was of decisive importance to us. The question was : What will be the rate of supply of submarines in the spring of 1918 ? Will the submarines, even if they have been unable to damage England decisively, have so far reduced tonnage that the new American troops cannot come over in a short time, and will they be able to strike at American transports while engaged in destroying hostile tonnage generally ?

In July, 1917, the Deputy Erzberger had spoken to me about the importance of world-tonnage for the effect of the submarine war, and had also expressed his opinions in the Reichstag. No doubt the world-tonnage did greatly influence its effect, but it was not decisive by itself. If, for instance, England had to withdraw ships from the service between America and Australia in order to maintain the service with America, these ships could not be there as well ; the Australian grain, on which England depended, remained in Australia and the general supply available for the Entente fell short by that amount. In my opinion the expression " world-tonnage " does not fully answer the question why the submarine war did not conquer the Entente. England's economic situation was eased by increased agricultural production, and this delayed the effect of the submarine war. Whether the construction of new shipping in the Entente was greater than had originally been assumed, and thus rendered further help, I cannot decide. But it was of decisive importance that the Entente had had time in two years of war to adapt its economic life to the circumstances and to perfect its means of defence. " But," says the *Economist* of the 7th September, 1918, " the fleet (with American aid certainly) mastered the submarine danger and greatly reduced its efficiency." In war it is even harder to see into the future than in peace, especially when conditions are so complicated as in this case. These conditions were not perceived by the enemy either. This explains why our Navy did not obtain an absolutely clear view of all the determining factors.

Its responsible heads worked and calculated dutifully and conscientiously. Although by October, 1918, the submarines had not decided the war, their achievements nevertheless were of great influence. " It was the greatest danger that England ever faced," says the *Morning Post* of the 3rd October, 1918. It would also be a mistake to under-estimate its effect on the whole economic life of the Entente, and to disregard the extent to which it eased the strain on the Western Front. It will be the task of History to clear up these questions and to pursue this complicated problem further. The achievements of our submarine crews will remain heroic deeds for all time and the country and the Navy may be proud of them.

About New Year, 1918, the opinion of the Navy was as optimistic as ever. I had, however, become more sceptical, and felt obliged to count on the new American formations beginning to arrive in the spring of 1918. In what numbers they would appear could not be foreseen ; but it might be taken as certain that they would not balance the loss of Russia ; further, the relative strengths would be more in our favour in the spring than in the late summer and autumn, unless indeed we had by then gained a great victory.

In the late autumn, 1917, G.H.Q. was confronted by the decisive question : Should it utilize the favourable conditions of the spring to strike a great blow in the West, or should it deliberately restrict itself to the defensive and only make subsidiary attacks, say in Macedonia or Italy ?

The Quadruple Alliance was only held together by the hope of a victory by the Germans.

The Austro-Hungarian Army was worn out ; it had lost 1,800,000 prisoners ; it was short of recruits. Its fighting value was slight, though against Italy it had on the whole sufficed. If Russia actually dropped out we might hope that that Army would continue to be equal to its task. Whether it could spare forces for other objects was doubtful. In 1917 we had already received an intimation from the Imperial and Royal Government that the Army could only go on fighting for a limited period ; we might anticipate something similar in 1918.

We had to take into consideration that Austria-Hungary might actually arrive at the end of her military power. It was clear that her political power would not last one hour longer. Nothing but the Army held the Dual Monarchy together.

The Bulgarian Army had sufficient drafts; it was, however, found necessary to enrol numerous men of other races. In 1917 the troops had fought tolerably well; their spirit had improved. The communications had been put in order behind their whole front. The influence of the German Group Headquarters and of the other German commands had become more pronounced; it extended, however, no further than the limits of actual direct German command. The training of the Army as a whole was furthered by means of schools established by Group Headquarters. Thanks to its past work, the latter could anticipate the coming struggle with some confidence. I often conversed with General Gantsheff, and requested him to do his part in promoting the improvement of the Bulgarian Army. In view of the events of the previous year he considered its position secure; it was only the mobilization of the Greek Army that made him anxious. That he could, of course, never ask for enough German stores and German troops was inherent in his office. With every word he expressed the hope of a German victory in the West.

Bulgaria had occupied all the territory she wanted to keep when peace came; she was sure of her gains—she thought no more of war, but only of enjoying in peace and quietness what she had won. The people and the Army were tired of war; Radoslavoff's Government lost ground, agitation against the Government and the war began, at first with the object of giving other parties a chance of feathering their nest. This increased the danger of Entente influence gaining ground in Bulgaria, a danger which was all the greater because the Government had permitted agitation against us. The irritation against us was further increased by the fact that out of consideration for the rate of exchange we did not take enough tobacco from them, and many Bulgarians felt that they were losing money in consequence. The representative of the United States, who sat tight in Sofia, took advantage of these conditions very cleverly, and held out prospects of large profits in good Swiss francs. Many failed to resist this temptation ; they turned again to the Entente with whom at heart they had always been in sympathy.

The only conclusion I could come to about Bulgaria was that she would remain faithful to us as long as all went well with us. But if the prospects of victory diminished, or still worse, if we suffered defeat, then things were bound to turn out just as in fact they have. Why should there be any difference between the character of nations and that of men ? I could believe in the steadfastness of the Bulgarian Army for just so long as I could believe in the faith of the Bulgarian nation.

Turkey was faithful to the alliance, but at the end of her strength; whether through her own fault or that of others was immaterial. Her man-power was greatly reduced, and the Army existed to a certain extent only on paper. Palestine was sure to fall an easy prey to England unless the troops there were reinforced. Turkey's disintegration was bound to produce political results over a wide area and must therefore be prevented, even though the decision of the war might be brought about elsewhere.

In Germany the national spirit appeared to be better than with our allies ; nevertheless, it had sunk very low, and feeling had become worse. I must admit I formed too favourable an estimate of our remaining energy. I hoped that the recruiting question would be settled.

The Army had come victoriously through 1917 ; but it had become apparent that the holding of the Western Front purely by a defensive could no longer be counted on, in view of the enormous quantity of material of all kinds which the Entente had now at their disposal. Even where tactical conditions had been absolutely normal, and by no means so unfavourable as in the struggle for the Wytschaete salient or Laffaux Corner, we had lost ground and suffered heavily. These losses had indeed been greater than we had incurred in well-conducted attacks. The enormous material resources of the enemy had given his attack a considerable preponderance over our defence, and this condition would become more and more apparent as our best men became casualties, our infantry approximated more nearly in character to a militia, and discipline declined.

It was also to be expected that the enemy would learn from past battles ; he would probably attack on a broad front, as in the double battle of the Aisne and Champagne in April and May, 1917, and aim at surprise. This he would be able to do by employing material in vast masses. These attacks would doubtless make far greater demands on us than any that had gone before.

The troops had borne the continuous defensive with extreme difficulty. Skulkers were already numerous. They reappeared as soon as the battle was over, and it had become quite common for divisions which came out of action with desperately low effectives to be considerably stronger after only a few days. Against the weight of the enemy's material the troops no longer displayed their old stubbornness ; they thought with horror of fresh defensive battles and longed for the war of movement. In this the Germans had achieved brilliant success in Rumania, Eastern Galicia, Italy and at Cambrai, and had once more proved their superiority, although their staying power was no longer what it had been in 1914. There had been incidents, too, which indicated that their cohesion was no longer the same. As they were depressed by defence their spirits rose in the offensive. The interests of the Army were best served by the offensive ; in defence it was bound gradually to succumb to the ever increasing hostile superiority in men and material. This feeling was shared by everybody. In the West the Army pined for the offensive, and after Russia's collapse expected it with the most intense relief. Such was the feeling of the troops about attack and defence. It amounted to a definite conviction which obsessed them utterly that nothing but an offensive could win the war. Many Generals, among them the most distinguished, spoke in the same strain. Naturally, I did not allow myself to be influenced by this feeling ; my sense of responsibility was far too great. I alone had to decide ; of that I remained conscious throughout. The wishes of the troops and commanders merely indicated what the Army felt regarding its own strength and weakness.

The condition of our allies and of our Army all called for an offensive that would bring about an early decision. This was only possible on the Western Front. All that had gone before was merely a means to the one end of creating a situation that would make it a feasible operation. Until now this situation had not arisen. We had been able to strike a blow at Italy with six or seven divisions, but for the Western Front that was not a sufficient force. I set aside all idea of attacking in Macedonia or Italy. All that mattered was to get together enough troops for an attack in the West.

For this we needed enormous material resources and strong troops who, with their leaders, had been trained for the attack. If this could be effected in time, we could—indeed, we must— attack. The offensive is the most effective means of making war ; it alone is decisive. Military history proves it on every page. It is the symbol of superiority. Delay could only serve the enemy's purposes, since he was expecting certain reinforcement.

That the attack in the West would be one of the most difficult operations in history I was perfectly sure, and I did not hide the fact. The German nation, too, would have to give all it had. The greater the lack of men, the stronger must be its will, the more energetic the work of the Government in the service of the war. General Headquarters would, as in the days of Tannenberg, have to get together for the decisive moment every man that could be spared from the various theatres. We could never be too strong. On the other hand, it would not do to forget that the European fronts were most intimately connected. A failure in Italy, in Macedonia, or in the East, might check our operations in the West.

It was not necessary to leave German troops on the Italian Front, and preparations were made for their departure about the New Year. We retained only a certain interest in the military resources of the occupied portions of Italy which then passed under Austro-Hungarian administration. From the

543

Russo–Rumanian Front, in spite of the objections of the Bulgarians, we moved Bulgarian troops to Macedonia in order to release a few German formations.

The great transport movement from Galicia and the Bukovina to France and Belgium had been arranged for, and a final decision as to the troops to be removed from the Eastern Front and the Balkan Peninsula became urgently necessary. Before we could decide, we had to obtain a clear idea of our future relations with Russia and Rumania and of the attitude of Bolshevism towards the Entente and the Quadruple Alliance, both from the military and the revolutionary point of view. It was necessary for us to be in a position to do so as soon as possible. There still remained a great amount of transport work to accomplish. The American danger rendered it desirable to strike in the West as early as possible ; the state of training of the Army for attack enabled us to contemplate doing so about the middle of March. At that season, too, horses would find some grazing which, in view of the shortage of forage, was a necessary consideration.

If all went smoothly at Brest Litovsk, if our people there worked with real energy, we could expect to have our forces ready for a successful attack in the West by the time mentioned. No delay could be justified. It will be obvious with what interest we watched the peace negotiations.

II

The negotiations at Brest–Litovsk began on December 22nd, 1917.

Their progress was bound to exercise a determining influence on the military decisions, since we were still at war. The really important matter was whether they were going to be conducted in such a manner that we could attack, and make certain of finishing the titanic struggle in our favour after all, and so save ourselves from the tragedy of being defeated.

For the future of Germany it was all-important that the whole Eastern problem should be solved in a manner which satisfied the interests of Prussia and Germany, and as far as possible removed the danger threatening from Poland. The decisions arrived at on the 18th of December at Kreuznach might yet secure that.

An exceptionally heavy responsibility rested on the negotiators and this was by no means lessened by the feelings of the people at home, which had developed under the influence of hostile propaganda without having been counteracted, as it should have been, by a strong and determined Government. There was a general misunderstanding of the enemy's determination, coupled with the fear of arousing his ill-will and thereby making peace more difficult, and this gave rise to hostile criticism whenever definite action was attempted, regardless of whether the interests of the country, or the prosecution of the war and therefore the ultimate peace, would be hindered thereby.

The German Plenipotentiary at Brest–Litovsk was Secretary of State von Kühlmann ; under him was General Hoffmann, as Special Representative of General Headquarters. Austria-Hungary had sent Count Czernin. The other Powers of the Quadruple Alliance were also represented. Herr von Kühlmann declined the Presidency ; it was allotted to the different Powers in turn.

The Russian plenipotentiaries were conceded equal rights in every respect. They at once made proposals of their own.

On the 25th of December Count Czernin, in the name of the four allies, declared his agreement with the Russian proposal of peace without annexations by force and without indemnities.

On this basis the Entente Powers were also invited to join the general peace negotiations, being given till 10 p.m. on the 4th of January to decide.

Count Czernin, the leading diplomat of the Quadruple Alliance, declares in this connection : " Had the Entente at that time been prepared for a general peace, the principle of no annexations would have been accepted in its entirety."

The right of self-determination was interpreted in a manner that lacked clearness and did not accord with German interests.

Instead of simple and plain demands, a number of points

of view were put forward, the discussion of which was bound to take a very long time. The invitation to the Entente, too, could produce nothing but delay. There was no prospect of its being accepted. Nothing was in accordance with the decisions arrived at under the presidency of His Majesty on the 18th of December. Our future in the East was called in question. How the Letts would now act, one could not tell. The danger of the Lithuanians and White Ruthenes being betrayed to the Poles was immeasurably increased, and the latter, in accordance with Austrian interests, were correspondingly favoured. The necessary military measures for securing the frontiers were not thought of. I spoke to General Hoffmann, regretting the way the negotiations were going. He very rightly said he thought that all that had been settled at Kreuznach on the 18th December. I explained to him that we had received no information, and instructed him, now that the fourteen days' term had been fixed, to press Secretary of State von Kühlmann at least to enforce our views regarding Courland and Lithuania, and make it possible for us to secure a protective belt in Poland, which we had hitherto, in accordance with His Majesty's instructions and with our agreement with the Imperial Chancellor, regarded as demands of the German Empire. On General Hoffmann's representation, Herr von Kühlmann now took up a position with regard to Courland and Lithuania more in accord with the Kreuznach agreements. He thereby no 'doubt placed himself to some extent in opposition to Count Czernin who, in order to support Herr von Kühlmann, threatened in the most incomprehensible manner to conclude a separate peace on behalf of Austria-Hungary. During the whole proceedings the absence of previous agreement between the allies proved a stumbling block.

The speeches of the Bolshevik representatives of Russia showed from the first that the Entente was anxious for the negotiations to be drawn out, and that they themselves still hoped that the Entente would help them to bring about a world revolution. They endeavoured to turn the negotiations at Brest into a great propaganda for their ideas. This was all the more dangerous for our internal conditions, in that the destructive influence of Bolshevism on society was only recognized by a few. Above all, it was misunderstood and underestimated by the Majority Parties in the Reichstag. All they saw in the utterances of the Bolsheviks at Brest was a confirmation of their own pacifist ideals and the beginning of universal brotherhood. I took quite a different view. It was clear to me that, with or without the support of the Entente, Bolshevism was for us an uncommonly dangerous enemy, which would have to be kept out by force of arms, even if we did make peace.

At the end of December the delegates dispersed, without having concluded any special agreements, and went home. They were to reassemble at Brest in January at the end of the fourteen days.

Early in January the Field-Marshal and I also went to Berlin, in order to see Secretary of State von Kühlmann and urge him to hasten the negotiations. I also wanted to see General Hoffmann who was in Berlin.

On the 2nd of January there was a council in the presence of His Majesty. I pointed out that the intended blow in the West necessitated an early peace in the East, since the required transport of troops could not take place until it was in sight. On military grounds any attempt at dragging out the proceedings must be opposed. We were strong enough to prevent it. But Herr von Kühlmann received no special instructions to this effect.

Then the Polish frontier-belt was again dealt with. Count Czernin had utilized his time at Brest to induce Herr von Kühlmann to agree to its being narrowed, in contravention of the decision of the 18th of December. The latter must have agreed to it and obtained the consent of General Hoffmann, who was thereupon ordered to report on the matter to His Majesty. His Majesty, quoting General Hoffmann, adopted the view of the Secretary of State. Naturally it was for the Emperor to decide, but I was pained by the reasons given. I had believed that the Field-Marshal and I were His Majesty's responsible military advisers, and I regarded the striking diminution of the protective belt as a danger to the provinces of East and West Prussia. I considered it my duty again to emphasize my view, and gained the impression that I had aroused the Emperor's disapproval.

On the 4th I discussed my relations with the Emperor with General von Lyncker. From what had occurred, I could only infer that His Majesty no longer gave me the confidence which I must demand to enable me to fulfil my arduous duties. I therefore placed myself at His Majesty's disposal for other employment. General von Lyncker advised me to talk it over with the Field-Marshal, who had returned to Kreuznach on the 3rd. I agreed and did so on the 5th. The Field-Marshal asked me to give up the idea, and said he would take the matter up himself, to which I consented.

Much to my regret, something of this became known in Berlin and was immediately associated with the Brest negotiations. That, however, was inaccurate. Now, as at the time of my petition to resign in 1918, His Majesty was personally taking a part against me. This, coming as it did from my Emperor and Supreme War Lord, was unbearable and irreconcilable with my sense of self-reliance.

To my regret the 2nd of January also made trouble between me and General Hoffmann ; but we settled it later.

In connection with these events the Field-Marshal submitted a memoir to His Majesty on the 7th. He gave prominence to the responsibility resting on himself and me to see that the peace should result in such a strengthening of the German people and such an improvement in our frontiers that our enemies would not dare to let loose another war for a long time to come. The attainment of this object was jeopardized by the Secretary of State departing from His Majesty's instructions of the 18th of December regarding the Polish frontier, supported though he was by His Majesty's later decision.

The memoir also alluded to what had occurred at the conference of the 2nd of January, and to the difficult position in which both the Field-Marshal and I found ourselves in regard to His Majesty. It ended as follows :

" As long as we only discuss matters and no action is taken, the differences (with the Foreign Office) are not so apparent. But when, as now, action is taken against Austria in the matter of the Austro–Polish solution, or against the Russians at Brest, they become painfully evident. This will recur on every occasion, and so will the present situation in consequence.

" It is Your Majesty's exalted right to decide. But Your Majesty will not demand that upright men, who have faithfully served Your Majesty and the country, should lend their authority and their name to acts which, they are profoundly convinced, are dangerous to the Crown and Empire.

" Your Majesty will not expect me to submit proposals for operations which are among the most difficult in history unless they are necessary for the attainment of definite military-political goals.

" Most humbly I beg Your Majesty to decide on the fundamental principle. Personal considerations regarding General Ludendorff and myself cannot be allowed to count in matters touching the needs of the State."

His Majesty handed the memorandum to the Imperial Chancellor for reply. In the middle of January we had an interview with him.

First and foremost, Chancellor Count von Hertling opposed the view that the Field-Marshal and I had a share in the responsibility for the peace-terms. He insisted that the responsibility was his alone. The Field-Marshal did not intend now, any more than he had in the time of Chancellor von Bethmann-Hollweg, to encroach on the functions of the Imperial Chancellor in any way. But in this matter our moral responsibility was involved, of which we were profoundly conscious, and of which no one could relieve us. Further, it was certainly true that in the Army and among the people the Field-Marshal and I were very definitely considered to share the responsibility for the peace. That was the fault of the Government itself, which often enough had proclaimed our agreement with its views, or had shielded itself behind our objection to plans and wishes which it had been unable to satisfy.

Count von Hertling himself had not done so ; he was obviously trying to free himself from the supposed tutelage of G.H.Q. I was, now and again, surprised at the way in which he did so. As late as the middle of January he expressed himself strongly to this effect. Unfortunately, in public, the Government did not state sufficiently clearly and emphatically that it, and not General Ludendorff, was governing.

As a matter of fact, there was no doubt whatever as to the constitutional responsibility of the Imperial Chancellor, and the tacit moral joint responsibility of the Field-Marshal and myself. But the more clearly the Chancellor marked out the dividing line the heavier became his own responsibility.

We now learned also that Count Hertling had expressly approved Count Czernin's Christmas speech at Brest. So he was, as was his right, following his own policy absolutely and did not hold himself bound by any agreement with us. What it was that caused him to change his attitude in this way I cannot understand to this day. We considered His Majesty's decision of the 18th December as binding, and could not but expect that he would inform us of any change. Otherwise grave misunderstanding and personal friction such as had now occurred could not be avoided. They would, however, have been avoided if we had been kept informed. The opinion of the Field-Marshal and myself would have remained the same, but it would have been differently expressed.

Neither the discussions nor the decision which His Majesty gave the Field-Marshal made any difference. In particular, we received no information as to the military-political objects which were being pursued. Up till then Count von Hertling's object in the West had been to prevent Belgium becoming a deployment area for our enemies. That was also the view of G.H.Q.

III

In the meantime the peace delegations re-assembled at Brest. The Entente, of course, had not come. Many people were somewhat curious to see whether the Russians would return. They came under the leadership of Trotsky. They came under compulsion. The dissolution of their army was progressing rapidly; it was in a state of utter disorganization, and wanted peace. Our military position was, therefore, as favourable as could be imagined; it was not even necessary for us to act as the Entente did towards Bulgaria, Austria-Hungary and Germany; we had merely to enforce our simple demands with clearness and decision.

We made extensive concessions to the principle of self-determination. We dropped our contention that the people of the occupied territories, Courland and Lithuania, had already been permitted to avail themselves of this right and allowed the inhabitants to be consulted again. All we demanded was that this should take place during our occupation. Trotsky maintained that we must first of all evacuate the country and that the people would exercise their right afterwards.

To evacuate the country was a military absurdity; we needed it for our existence and had no mind to deliver it up to unscrupulous Bolshevism. We declined to evacuate it on this military ground, quite apart from the fact that no exercise of the right of self-determination was possible under the Bolshevik knout. On both these questions opinions are now probably clearer and people may perhaps understand the view of G.H.Q. If we had left the country the armed forces of the Bolsheviks would long ago have been in Germany. They were not the least interested in the right of self-determination; all they wanted was more power. They were politicians who governed by violence and assumed that the territory evacuated by us would fall into their hands without further parley. They were, moreover, so nationally minded that they looked upon the severance of Courland,

Lithuania and Poland—self-determination notwithstanding—as a measure hostile to Russia.

Austria-Hungary had by far the greatest interest in the exercise of the right of self-determination in Poland at the expense of Russia. The Dual Monarchy hoped to gain political and economic strength from Poland.

The Turks wanted Batum and Kars, both of which had belonged to the Turkish Empire for a very long time. For us these wishes were of subordinate importance; but it was part of our duty as an ally to insist upon them.

Our purely military demands were so insignificant that they hardly counted. The demobilization was already making excellent progress, and we had not demanded the surrender of arms or ships.

We did not ask for Esthonia or Livonia, although we would have been glad to deliver our fellow-Germans and the other inhabitants from Bolshevism. This demand was not made, although it was down for discussion and became a military necessity against Bolshevism. Peace was not delayed by our demands, but merely by the revolutionary aims of the Bolsheviks and by want of resolution in our delegates, as well as by the attitude of Germany and Austria where the people, being ignorant of the world, did not understand the inner meaning of the Russian Revolution. When on one occasion General Hoffmann adopted a more uncompromising attitude in order to cut short the negotiations for military reasons and restrict Trotsky's propagandist activity at the same time, there was a chorus of indignation in a large number of German and Austro-Hungarian papers, and in all those others which, like the propaganda of the Entente, talked incessantly of Peace by understanding. In these circumstances Trotsky would have been a fool to have given in on any point; but he was far too clever and energetic for that. His tone became more and more provoking, although he had no real power behind him; his demands became more and more insistent. He threatened to withdraw the Russian delegates on account of lack of sincerity on the part of the German and Austrian representatives and had the satisfaction of being requested to desist from this intention, which he can never seriously have entertained. Trotsky and the Entente were delighted with the prolongation of the negotiations ; the former took every opportunity of delaying them ; he even suggested transferring them to a neutral locality. He proclaimed his Bolshevik ideas by wireless to all the world, particularly to the German working classes. The intention of the Bolsheviks to revolutionize and destroy Germany became more and more obvious to everyone who was not totally blind.

The negotiations made no progress ; moreover, by the way they were being carried on at Brest we should not only never arrive at peace but would undoubtedly bring about a further decrease in our own fighting capacity. All this time I was at Kreuznach, burning with impatience and urging General Hoffmann to hurry on the negotiations. He was well aware of the military necessity, but his position did not allow him to interfere effectively.

On the 18th January Trotsky went to Petrograd, where the Bolsheviks dispersed the Constituent Assembly. In that way they showed the world their idea of freedom of the people. But the Germans would neither see nor learn.

Trotsky had said he would be away only six days ; he did not return until the 30th.

On the 23rd January, at my request, the Field-Marshal declared, during a consultation at Berlin, that we must have the Eastern situation cleared up. Until it was, it would be necessary to retain there good divisions that were fit for employment in the West. If the Russians delayed matters any further we ought to re-open hostilities. This would bring down the Bolshevik Government and any other that might succeed it would have to make peace.

There were other reasons which made me press for an early conclusion. Count Czernin was right when he spoke ironically of a " spiritual wrestling-match." For him, indeed, at Brest, while the war was rushing on to its greatest decision, there was neither time nor place, nor a suitable opponent. What must the statesmen of the Entente think of our need of peace if we tamely submitted to this sort of treatment by Trotsky and his Bolshevik Government, a Government that had not even been recognized by any other State? They and their people could only gain enormously in strength and resolution by witnessing such a spectacle. How necessary must peace be to Germany when she literally ran after such people and put up with open propaganda against her and her army. This was bound to be the effect in every neutral and enemy country. How could the Entente leaders, above all men like Clemenceau and Lloyd George, be afraid of peace, when we allowed ourselves to be treated thus by unarmed Russian anarchists? They would cease to feel any anxiety and come to the conclusion that they ran no risk from us at all. How that would affect the peace-feeling among such enemies there could be no doubt.

Nor did the soldier at the front understand all this talk that went on for weeks on end, seemed to serve no practical object and produce no tangible result. What he had achieved at the expense of his last ounce of strength and in a thousand forms of distress and danger, he naturally wished to see utilized with energy and to good purpose. And what was here at stake was the first peace, the result of which was awaited with no less interest at the front than it was at home. The time had come at last to take some decisive steps. That alone would clear matters up, both at home and abroad.

In the meantime it had become evident that Trotsky did not represent the whole of Russia, not to mention Rumania. On the 12th January delegates arrived at Brest from the Ukraine, and took up a position completely opposed to the Bolsheviks. They were supported mainly by General Hoffmann and gave the representatives of the Quadruple Alliance an opportunity of opening separate negotiations. These were of a practical nature and were not lost in the mists of fantastic projects which take centuries to work out if they are ever worked out at all.

On the 30th January negotiations with Trotsky were resumed at Brest.

Now began a most curious situation, for everything was ordered in accordance with his ideas.

However, the diplomats themselves now seemed to perceive that discussions with him led to no result. Secretary of State von Kühlmann and Count Czernin proceeded to interrupt the negotiations and were back in Berlin on the 4th February. Discussion with the Ukraine was continued on the basis that it bound itself to supply Austria–Hungary and Germany with large quantities of grain, in return for which it was to receive a favourable frontier against Poland in the disputed area of Cholm. In addition, Austria-Hungary promised to create an Ukrainian Crown-Land in Eastern Galicia.

In order to discuss the situation with Herr von Kühlmann and Count Czernin I had also gone to Berlin early in February. At our interviews on the 4th and 5th I received from the former a promise that he would break with Trotsky twenty-four hours after signing the peace with the Ukraine. From all I heard I was confirmed in my impression that Bolshevik Russia did not really want peace at all. It had set its hopes on the Entente and on the gradual spread of the Revolution in Germany, and did not believe we would take any action. Their hopes must have been confirmed by the strikes which broke out in this connection in Berlin at the end of January, 1918, against the wishes of prominent labour leaders. So close, even then, was the connection between a part of our labour movement and the Bolsheviks.

The men at the head of it, and the most influential section of the Socialist Press, both of whom afterwards opposed the Bolsheviks, had not yet recognized that fact. At that time, it is true, the object was still to combat the common enemy, established Authority, and thus consciously or otherwise to undermine the foundations of the country. When this object was subsequently attained and these people had themselves become the masters, the spark they had started had become a devouring fire.

At the discussion in Berlin Count Czernin explained the reasons which had led him to agree to a peace with the Ukraine which was undoubtedly disadvantageous to the Dual Monarchy and might be expected to arouse strong opposition from Poland.

For this reason he requested us to keep the political settlement more or less secret. He said the food situation in Austria-Hungary was so bad that, owing to the ever-decreasing supply from Rumania, they must starve unless they obtained corn from the Ukraine. The Austrian Director of Supplies, General Landwehr, supplemented this depressing picture with details about the Army and asked me if I could help. As Herr von Waldow thought, in spite of our own very serious situation, we could still help to a limited extent, I could raise no objection. What I then heard appeared to me most serious, and must have made a deep impression on the other gentlemen who had to deal with these matters.

Another matter we discussed was the old Austro-Polish solution. This time I was more of a listener. To my satisfaction the Secretaries of State von Stein and Count von Rödern, as well as several other gentlemen, opposed it on economic grounds. The protective belt played practically no part. The Austro-Hungarian Ambassador, Prince Hohenlohe, for whom I have otherwise a warm regard, became irritated at the course the discussion was taking and reproached me with throwing difficulties in the way of Austria–Hungary. I could only point out that on this occasion it was not I, but the others, who had objected to the Austro–Polish solution. The question of Poland remained in abeyance.

The terms of peace with Rumania were also briefly discussed. In this case also I urged the need for energetic action.

Secretary of State von Kühlmann and Count Czernin returned to Brest after the discussion.

Peace with the Ukraine was signed there on the 9th February. I now requested Herr von Kühlmann to carry out his promise of the 5th and break with Trotsky; but he declined.

On the same day a wireless message from the Russian Government called upon the German Army to refuse obedience to the Supreme War Lord.

At the request of the Field-Marshal the Emperor now instructed Herr von Kühlmann to present an ultimatum to Trotsky requiring acceptance of our former conditions, and further to demand the evacuation of the Baltic littoral. This latter instruction the Secretary of State thought he ought not to carry out in view of the state of feeling at home and in Austria-Hungary. The Emperor agreed and this was dropped.

The Secretary of State now urged Trotsky to bring the negotiations to a conclusion. The latter, however, declined to be bound in any way, but declared at the same time that the war was at an end and that the demobilization of the Russian Army had been ordered.

This of course completed the confusion in the East. We could not possibly leave matters in this condition. At any moment fresh dangers might arise while we were fighting for our lives in the West. The military situation made it imperative clearly to define our future plans. This was to be achieved by a conference at Homburg.

IV

The conference at Homburg took place on the 13th February. It had a decisive influence on the events in the East. The Imperial Chancellor, the Vice-Chancellor, Secretary of State von Kühlmann, the Field-Marshal, the Chief of the Naval Staff and I took part in it. His Majesty the Emperor only attended at intervals.

Before this, G.H.Q. had despatched a number of telegrams to the Imperial Chancellor, asking for the Armistice to be denounced. At the moment the Russian Army was no longer of any account ; but the Entente was on the look-out to strengthen its front, and the Bolshevik leaders were men of action who would work by propaganda and, if they were given time, by arms, even without the Entente.

At any moment, somehow or somewhere, the Russian front might become strong again. Nor would Rumania ever make peace until Russia had shown the way. This would make any attack in the West hopeless. We should thus miss the opportunity of victoriously finishing the World War, a war we were still waging, supported only by weak allies, against enemies

557

superior in numbers. We also wanted the Ukraine as an auxiliary against the Bolsheviks, so it must not on any account be surrendered to them. It had already appealed for help.

Whence were we to obtain the corn which, according to her experts, Austria-Hungary so badly needed ? Germany could not supply it ; but that is what it would have come to in the end. Germany herself was extremely short ; the year before she had anticipated credits by early threshing, and now needed extra supplies herself. Rumania was no longer supplying the anticipated quantity. The prospects would be still worse if the coming harvest were bad with us and our allies, as well as in Rumania, which, as a matter of fact, experienced a complete failure. Left entirely to herself, without any outside help, Germany could not exist, as is proved by the great distress in the winter of 1918–1919. Disaster would certainly have come without help from the Ukraine, even if the destruction of public order had not been a contributing cause.

The peace with the Ukraine rested then, owing to the Bolshevik influence, on a weak foundation. That we should have to assist there with military force in order to get corn, unless the peace was to become a futile farce, was evident to the representatives of the Quadruple Alliance.

In order to prevent the Bolsheviks themselves from forming a new Eastern Front against us, we must inflict on their troops a short but sharp blow, which would in addition bring in a great quantity of stores. For the moment no extensive operation was in contemplation.

In the Ukraine we had to suppress Bolshevism and create such conditions that we could get some military value out of it, and obtain corn and raw materials. In order to do that, it was necessary to penetrate deep into the country ; there was no alternative.

In order to prevent Russia being reinforced by the Entente, which the latter was still attempting, it was necessary to hold up their troops and stores on the Murman coast. Otherwise England would certainly come to Petrograd and work against us from there. We must prevent her from obtaining a footing there and in the Gulf of Finland, and in striking at the Bolshevik troops we must advance through Livonia and Esthonia as far as Narva, in order to be able to act from that place in time, whenever necessary. In Finland, too, which had already called upon us for help, we might find an ally against the Bolsheviks. In this way some effect would be produced against the Murmansk railway and that on Petrograd would be increased. For some time past I had been in communication with a few Finnish gentlemen. First and foremost, I would mention the first Ambassador of the young Finnish State, Herr Hjelt, who served it with ardour. At the very beginning of the war a number of young Finns, who fervently loved their country, had been formed into a Jäger Battalion, which was employed at Mitau. Whether we should actually go so far as to undertake military operations in Finland was at that time doubtful. We supplied them directly with arms.

Our military and food situation required that the Armistice should be denounced, the position in the East definitely cleared up, and rapid action taken.

To me, this fresh employment of military force was undesirable. But it was a military absurdity, or worse, to sit still and watch the enemy increase his strength ; so it was necessary to act. That was demanded by the inexorable law of war. It would then be certain that we should obtain peace. That was all I wanted.

It was in this sense that I expressed myself to the Chancellor and Vice-Chancellor and I pointed out to them the enormous difficulty of our task in the West. I also stated my belief that we should never get an honest peace from the Bolshevik leaders, but that they would, as before, certainly continue to work for a revolution in Germany. This danger it was impossible to exaggerate. We could protect ourselves against Bolshevism only by placing a close cordon beyond our frontiers. It was no doubt a disadvantage to extend the containing line in the direction of the Gulf of Bothnia ; but, owing to the large lakes, the line Dvinsk–Lake Peipus–Gulf of Finland did not require many more troops than that from Dvinsk to the Gulf of Riga.

Any intermediate line would require far more. This was no case of a military operation without visible limits to its possible future extension ; it was a purely local and limited measure. I also laid stress on the satisfaction I naturally felt at going to the assistance of the people of Livonia and Esthonia, especially those of our own German race who were calling to us for help against their Bolshevik oppressors.

At first the Imperial Chancellor and the Vice-Chancellor could not be got to agree to the denunciation of the Armistice. They based their refusal on the grounds of internal politics and the condition of Austria-Hungary. Those arguments also determined the attitude of Herr von Kühlmann. Reasons of foreign policy were of no account. Gradually the first two gentlemen were persuaded and agreed to denounce the Armistice, especially in view of the food situation. Secretary of State von Kühlmann remained obdurate. He declared, however, that not he, but the Imperial Chancellor, was constitutionally responsible, and that since the latter had resolved to denounce the Armistice he would not refuse his further co-operation.

I could only assume that Secretary of State von Kühlmann himself did not think his reasons for refusal very sound, otherwise, constitutional responsibility notwithstanding, he would have been bound to draw the appropriate conclusions as regards his own person. The office of Secretary of State for Foreign Affairs was surely such an exalted one that he dare not allow himself to be overridden in a matter of such grave importance. His conduct could not inspire in me that confidence which I should so much have wished to give the head of the Foreign Office.

Unfortunately this incident also impaired my relations with other gentlemen of the Foreign Office, some of whom, especially among the non-professional diplomats, possessed capabilities of a high order. I regretted these difficulties all the more because I took no count of the individuals themselves and was concerned only with the cause. I was as strongly convinced that this Office needed reform as were the great majority of the German people.

On the report of the Imperial Chancellor His Majesty agreed to the Armistice being denounced, or, as was thought more correct from the point of view of international law, to the publication of the fact that, owing to Trotsky's failure to sign the peace treaty, the Armistice automatically came to an end.

What method they chose was immaterial to me.

V

Accordingly, hostilities recommenced along the whole front of Great Russia on the afternoon of the 18th February and the morning of the 19th. Almost immediately the Bolshevik Government by wireless declared itself ready for peace. Profiting by our recent experiences at Brest, we took care to put the affair on a totally different footing. In concert with our allies and in agreement with G.H.Q. the Government demanded, for our military security, but also in compliance with the right of self-determination, that Russia should recognize the independence of Finland and the Ukraine, and give up Courland, Lithuania, Poland, Batum and Kars. The future position of Esthonia and Livonia was not yet settled; for the present they were to be occupied by us.

The army of Great Russia was to be demobilized and the fleet paid off. Russia was further to refrain from all propaganda in Germany. A number of economic questions, arrangements for exchange of prisoners, etc., were left for later discussion. Our advance was to be continued until these demands were finally agreed to in further negotiations. Trotsky at once declared his readiness to send fresh representatives to Brest; he did not come himself, presumably because he saw there was no possibility of carrying on propaganda from there any longer.

The Russian delegation arrived at Brest on the 28th February. No further negotiations took place. The Russian plenipotentiaries, displaying dignity in the misfortune they had brought upon themselves, declared that their only duty was to sign. At 5.30 p.m. on the 3rd March the signing took place. Thus peace was concluded, and hostilities ceased once more on the Russian front.

The conditions of the peace of Brest were aimed at the Bolsheviks whose revolutionary propaganda made a chronic state of warfare against them inevitable. It was no desire of mine to destroy Russia or to weaken her so that she could no longer exist. I hoped rather that the restoration of the Empire would be the work of the Ukraine, and I should have preferred a Russo-Polish solution of the Polish question to any other. Lithuania and Courland are not of vital importance to Russia, any more than Batum and Kars. The loss of Esthonia and Livonia would be painful; but in this district Russia was to receive every conceivable concession. It was superfluous to discuss whether we could go even further and return these two provinces to an armed Russia; an armed Russia did not exist. I therefore supported, in all sincerity, the formation of a Baltic littoral. Otherwise the peace terms refrained from any interference in the internal politics or economic life of Russia and imposed no conditions that were incompatible with the honour of an independent State or reduced the inhabitants to servitude.

It is instructive to compare the peace which Russia then received with the one she could have obtained, and the latter with the terms which we ourselves have had to accept, although we have never refused any offer of peace. The talk about the Brest " Peace of Violence " will cease in time, although a section of the German people is still confiding enough to repeat this shibboleth, invented by hostile propaganda. If Russia now emerges mutilated from the war after her allies, for whom she has repeatedly pulled the chestnuts out of the fire since 1914, have won, that is another affair.

The majority of the Reichstag approved the peace of Brest; they also admitted that the treaty enabled the right of self-determination to be exercised; the Majority Socialists abstained from voting; only the Independent Socialists voted against it.

Deputy Erzberger had already, on the 27th February, welcomed the peace and declared that the conditions conformed to the Peace Resolution of the 19th July.

Special commendation is due to the remarks of Deputy Gröber on the 22nd March; they displayed complete comprehension of our position. He said:

" It is admitted that we cannot describe this peace as a peace of understanding in the exact sense of that word. But I do not think its acceptance should be made to depend entirely upon that. The question is not : is this a peace of understanding, or is it not ? It is a more practical one. Could a treaty of peace have been concluded in any other way ? I say it could not, and so, in the name of my friends, I declare that we unanimously agree to the treaty.

" Gentlemen, the Russian Delegation at Brest-Litovsk, under Trotsky's leadership, had obviously no serious intention of coming to an understanding about peace; it intended to institute propaganda for its Bolshevik ideas. For this purpose it prolonged the negotiations as much as possible; why, Trotsky even refused to agree to the proposed condition that we should live together in peace and friendship in the future ! Even that was too much for him ! And while the German delegates, with lamblike patience—to use no other expression—strove in the sweat of their brow to push on the negotiations and bring them to a conclusion, we received from Russia, and from those who were in close contact with the Russian Government, inflammatory speeches and wireless messages of the most violent description, which could only be ascribed to Trotsky and his colleagues and which meant nothing but contempt of all endeavours to bring about a real, decent peace. Trotsky was evidently suffering under the delusion that he would succeed in bringing about revolution in the other States, particularly Poland, Germany, and England, and eventually the whole world. In the end it was the Russian Delegation, and not that of Germany, which caused the interruption of the negotiations, and their final rupture, and literally forced Germany to resume the fight.

" If, under such circumstances, when the Russian Government proposed to resume negotiations and conclude another armistice, the German Government and its allies did not agree at once and unconditionally, but put forward demands to be definitely accepted or rejected, and made the grant of an armistice and resumption of negotiations dependent upon their acceptance, such a step was, we are convinced, thoroughly justified and even necessary, and no one has the right to reproach the Government on that ground."

These expressions were a valuable help to me, and I recognized that in this matter the majority of the nation supported the Government. Unfortunately, the Reichstag soon neglected the revolutionary danger which was threatening us from Russia.

In their advance, our troops, the bulk of which were Landwehr, had in a surprisingly short time reached Narva, Pskoff, Polotsk, Orsha, and Mohileff. The Russians had made no resistance. The quantity of stores we captured was extraordinarily great. The populace felt that they were delivered from Bolshevism. The newly-occupied territory was placed under the administration of the Commander-in-Chief in the East. We established a cordon to protect the frontier against Russia in order to exploit the whole of the country economically, which was urgently necessary. At the same time the influx of bolshevik propaganda into the occupied territory, and thence into Germany, had to be prevented. I should never have believed then that it would ultimately make its way into Berlin and Germany with Government sanction and by official channels. G.H.Q. would in that case have seen the futility of its efforts and would probably have save men.

Such measures were therefore put in operation as we and the Commander-in-Chief in the East thought necessary for averting the bolshevik danger.

Simultaneously with our advance into bolshevik Great Russia that into the Ukraine had begun. I was in constant communication with General von Arz in order to arrange common action with him. All of a sudden the Emperor Charles drew back; he wanted to save his people the disappointment of learning that the peace with Russia had, after all, not materialized. Necessity, however, obliged him very soon to give his consent. I was surprised by the attitude of Austria–Hungary; she began by

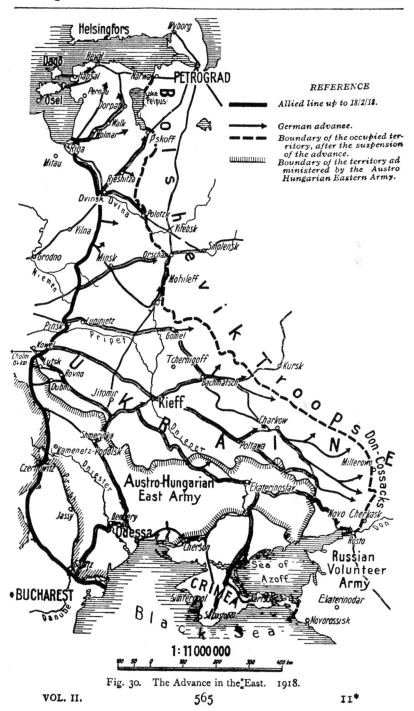

REFERENCE

Allied line up to 18/2/18.

German advance.

Boundary of the occupied territory, after the suspension of the advance.

Boundary of the territory administered by the Austro Hungarian Eastern Army.

1 : 11 000 000

Fig. 30.   The Advance in the East.   1918.

solemnly declaring that the State must conclude an unfavourable peace in order to exist and now did nothing to obtain the means of subsistence which were at her disposal. The final adhesion of Austria–Hungary was a relief to me ; we could not possibly have solved the problem by ourselves.

In the Ukraine also the advance proceeded rapidly. The main weight of our attack was directed on Kieff which we occupied on the 1st March ; that of the Austrians on Odessa. The operations proceeded along the railways ; there were occasional fights between armoured trains ; enormous spaces had to be traversed hurriedly by small forces. The Bolshevik troops offered very little resistance ; the Czecho-Slovak troops—composed of Austro-Hungarian prisoners of war—fought much better, and fierce engagements with them took place. Operations and actual fighting continued into May.

The Commander-in-Chief in the East at once proceeded to form two divisions in Germany from Russian prisoners of war of Ukrainian origin who were selected by the War Ministry ; unfortunately they did not turn out well. As soon as they arrived in the Ukraine they fell a prey to radical influences and had to be disbanded. That was very unpleasant. I had hoped that, just as the Entente had derived some benefit from its prisoners, we should at least obtain some assistance from the sons of the land we had liberated from Bolshevik dominion.

The Turks had also commenced their advance in Armenia at the close of the armistice and meant to continue it to Kars and Batum.

VI

The peace negotiations with Rumania proceeded as unsatisfactorily as those with Bolshevik Russia.

After our experiences at Brest-Litovsk I had considered it imperative, in order to clear up the points of difference with Austria-Hungary, to institute detailed preliminary discussions regarding the negotiations with Rumania, which should at first be confined to the Imperial authorities concerned.

The economic stipulations of the peace with Rumania would have special effect on the conduct of the war, on account of the export of oil and grain for the use of the Army and the nation. Later on these commodities would be of great importance to our economic life. In January I had requested the Quartermaster-General to discuss these points with the Imperial authorities in Berlin and with the Headquarters of Field-Marshal von Mackensen, and to determine what our demands should be. This work provided a foundation for the peace negotiations later on. These negotiations were only in part of a military nature. They were mainly concerned with the economic life of the people.

This preliminary work became all the more important as it was found necessary, in view of the offensive in the West, to hurry on the conclusion of peace with Rumania. Taking our stand on the military situation alone, we could have made a peace such as the Entente has imposed upon us—a peace of violence. But for that there was no reason. In our peace terms we had to consider what the military situation might be up to the time when a general peace would be concluded ; we had no interest in weakening Rumania beyond that period.

It makes all the difference whether a country, which is at war with all the world, makes peace with one only of its opponents, or with all. In the first case its demands must conform far more rigidly to the military situation and to military requirements than after a general cessation of hostilities. It is different when there is an intention, such as is now pursued by the Entente, not only of weakening the enemy for decades to come, but of wiping States off the map and reducing whole nations to a condition of slavery in a way which, up till now, has been peculiar to the barbarous warfare of ancient days.

To allow Bulgaria to absorb the whole Dobrudja, as the Bulgarians wished, was unfavourable for Germany's future. I should have preferred Northern Dobrudja to remain Rumanian ; this was in accordance with the views I had held for the last fifteen months. The rest I had to leave to the diplomats. It was their duty to keep Bulgaria in the Alliance, whilst averting

all difficulties which might arise if the universal traffic route—
Cernavoda–Constanza—fell into Bulgarian hands. Towards
the end I thought of this area as a sort of free port under German
administration.

We objected to extensive annexations by Hungary at
Rumania's expense. For the better defence of the Hungarian
frontier, all that was needed was a slight adjustment at Orsova,
and in the angle of Moldavia south of Kirlibaba. More than
that I did not consider justifiable.

General Headquarters had no objection to Rumania's annex-
ing Bessarabia, nor to sparing her army. The hypothesis was, as
agreed with Secretary of State von Kühlmann and Count Czernin,
that Germany and Austria–Hungary would place a government
in power in Rumania which suited us and consisted mainly of
men who were living at the time in the occupied territory. The
Government, therefore, entered into the closest relations with
those Rumanians who, from honest conviction, wished to side
with Germany.

Another military condition was that, in order to exclude any
chance of surprise by Rumania, the King and the Royal Family
should leave the country until the general conclusion of peace.

The establishment of German political influence in Rumania
was extremely inconvenient to Austria–Hungary. It was feared
just as much as any increase of Germany's economic interest.
Count Czernin opposed both and checkmated us at the end of
January by sending Colonel Randa, the former military attaché
in Rumania, to Jassy, to assure the King of his readiness to
grant Rumania an honourable peace.

I heard of this mission at Kreuznach in a roundabout way, and
was most disagreeably surprised. In our conferences on the
4th and 5th of February I pointed out its dangerous possibilities,
but neither Count Czernin, nor, to my amazement, Herr von
Kühlmann took the matter up ; from which I concluded that the
Secretary of State was not only aware of it, but had given it his
consent. Otherwise, he would have been just as taken aback
by this high-handed action of Count Czernin's as I was when I
heard of it. That landed us in difficulties. Now that we had

commenced to negotiate with the King, and thereby in a sense recognized him once more, we could no longer demand his abdication or his removal from the country. That, in fact, was Count Czernin's object. He needed the King to confirm Austria's position in Rumania ; but Germany, by allowing the Quadruple Alliance to open discussions with the King, struck its most faithful supporters in Rumania a blow in the face, and placed them in an intolerable position, the penalties of which they now have to suffer.

What had very serious consequences was that the diplomats kept on hinting to the Emperor and to General Headquarters that the Rumanians would probably remove their King themselves. This very adversely influenced our military measures. Hoping that the promised change in the Rumanian Government would result in the removal of their King, I omitted to demand the complete disarmament of the Rumanian Army.

These circumstances were responsible for those half-measures in the negotiations with Rumania which afterwards characterized the peace itself.

The conduct of the negotiations was first entrusted to Field-Marshal von Mackensen who very soon found himself everywhere impeded by Austria–Hungary. The military situation demanded that here, too, we should know definitely whether we should have to fight again or would obtain peace. The new Government was formed, but in no way corresponded to our interests, and so all through February the negotiations made no progress. On the 24th of February the diplomats took over the conduct of affairs, and more and more obviously it fell into the hands of Count Czernin. Secretary of State von Kühlmann did not take the prominent place which our prestige, our co-operation in the defeat of Rumania and our military situation warranted. General von Arz might not care whether peace was made to-day or to-morrow ; not so the German General Headquarters. I often requested the Imperial Chancellor to have the proceedings accelerated, and I gave instructions in the same sense to General Hell, Chief of the General Staff at von Mackensen's Headquarters, who also represented General Head-

quarters. To the great detriment of the German cause, Colonel
Hentsch, Chief of the General Staff of the Military Governor of
Rumania, died at this time, and General Hell was not able to
see this matter through. I had expected that, in view of our
extremely strong military position—since we could attack them
from all sides—my insistence would lead to our dealing drastically with the Rumanians. But the Imperial Government
thought fit to reply to my demand by giving way. This simple
fact illustrates the fundamental difference between the ideas of
the Government and my own.

On the 5th of March the preliminary peace of Buftea was
concluded ; its terms were embodied in the Treaty of Bucharest
By the end of March the negotiations were more or less completed.

The Dobrudja difficulty was not settled. The Turks, who
had helped to conquer it, demanded from the Bulgarians, who
wanted the whole of it, a compensation in the form of the return
of the territory west of Adrianople and east of the Maritza
which they had ceded in 1914. I thought the Turkish demand
just and reasonable. In spite of many proposals for mediation
on the part of the diplomats, the two States could not agree.
The southern part, nearly up to the Cernavoda–Constanza
railway, was given to the Bulgarians ; the northern part became
the common property of the Quadruple Alliance. But the
Allies agreed to keep open the Constanza route for Rumanian
commerce. This was proposed by Radoslavoff himself ; what
induced him to do it I do not know. The result of this half-
measure was unfortunate : it embittered the Bulgarians without
satisfying the Turks.

Under pressure from Count Czernin Rumania agreed to considerable cessions of territory to Hungary. General Hell was
repeatedly instructed to oppose them, but could effect nothing.

Rumania was allowed to obtain a firm footing in Bessarabia.

According to the military terms, Rumania was to demobilize
and reduce the army, and hand over a portion of its military
equipment to be guarded by the allies. The French Military
Mission was to be sent away through Russia. But she was left

in possession of Moldavia, even as regards military control, and was allowed to keep a few mobile divisions for the occupation of Bessarabia. Germany and Austria–Hungary retained the right of occupying Wallachia with six divisions of which four were to be German. Field-Marshal von Mackensen remained in Wallachia as administrator until the ratification of peace.

The economic arrangements with Rumania did not secure what I had hoped for. The conditions imposed were not particularly severe.

Besides the supply of oil and grain, the navigation of the Danube was very important. I hoped to secure advantages for the Bavarian Lloyd. The attitude of Austria–Hungary in this respect was again typical ; but so was that of our representatives. It required all the vigilance of the Director of Railways at General Headquarters to obtain even tolerable security for German interests on the Danube.

The question of the dynasty was no more settled than was that of allowing the Ambassadors of the Entente to remain at Jassy. Everything remained as it was. At Jassy the old intrigues against us continued. We had left the Entente a citadel there. Only the Rumanian politicians who were hostile to us were sent to Switzerland, so that they could work against us the more effectively. The Rumanian people were to institute proceedings against Bratiano and Co., the instigators of the war ; that was a farce.

The memory of those Bucharest negotiations is distasteful to me. On the 7th of May the treaty was at last signed. The diplomats allowed us to hope that they would pursue the question of the dynasty further. The peace was never ratified, for the defection of Bulgaria changed the situation in Rumania at a blow and showed how our peace with her was inadequate for this world-war.

That peace was also denounced in Germany as " a peace of violence," so permeated was popular thought by hostile propaganda, so little was our Government able to lead.

*　　*　　*　　*　　*　　*　　*

The situation on the Eastern Front was eased to an extraordinary degree by the Peace of Brest–Litovsk of the 3rd of March, and the preliminary peace of Buftea of the 5th of March. A real peace with Russia had, however, not been arrived at. There was still the danger that a new Eastern Front might be formed, which the Entente and the Bolsheviks, between whom there existed for the time a tacit understanding, were trying to bring about. Only when the Soviet Government discovered that the Entente was its deadly enemy and wished to place another government in power which would be more useful in the war, did it break with the Entente and turn towards Germany, in order to strengthen its position internally and fight Germany, no longer with arms, but by propaganda.

In Rumania the influence of the Entente was not completely broken; the situation there was still obscure.

By our vigorous action against Russia in February and the strong line followed subsequently, no less than by the resolute transfer of troops from East to West, any obvious disadvantages of the prolongation of the negotiations, had been avoided. The Rumanian divisions should, indeed, have arrived on the Western Front earlier, but the attack there could still be carried out. More than forty divisions were transferred. Before the move, their older classes had been replaced by younger, and even the divisions remaining behind were much below strength and subsequently surrendered their younger classes as drafts to the army in the West. What we had in the East was admittedly a strong force; yet all we had achieved there was an armed peace, and many elements of danger remained. During the spring and summer, when conditions had become more stable, the troops in the East were further reduced. The Commander-in-Chief there was repeatedly asked for more, and sent whatever forces were available. General Headquarters knew that it was getting every man that could be spared. But the enormous distances of the East, which cannot be measured by German standards, demanded a certain minimum of troops, without which we could not carry out the tasks required by our military and economic situation.

The four German and two Austro–Hungarian divisions which had been left in Rumania were the very smallest force for the purpose. But even these four German divisions had to send men during the spring. Von Mackensen's group only too willingly gave all it could to secure success in the West.

VII

The training of the army for the offensive was another tremendous task. For this we had to utilize the winter of 1917–18, as the previous one had been devoted to training in defence.

In the same way in which tactical theories had then been summarized in the " Defensive Battle," so now the " Offensive Battle in Position Warfare " came into being. We had to revive in the minds of the fighting forces all those excellent offensive principles which inspired our pre-war regulations. They had to be supplemented by more recent experience in actual battle. Without checking the vigour of the attack, we had to keep down losses as much as possible. The whole line of thought of the Army had to be diverted from trench warfare back to the offensive.

While in the defence the forces in a given sector were more evenly distributed, in the attack the problem was to discover some decisive point and arrange the dispositions accordingly. In defence, high ground had lost much of its value. The Battle of Arras had once more demonstrated that. Positions were held which were completely open to the enemy's view. Often the troops had thought they could not exist without the possession of some height or other ; but if they did not get it they managed to carry on. In the attack in the war of movement, the capture of some high ground brought about the tactical decision. Its possession must therefore be striven for as a matter of principle.

It was necessary to create anew a thorough understanding of the extent of front to be allotted in attack, and to emphasize the principle that men must do the work not with their bodies alone but with their weapons. The fighting line must be kept thin, but must be constantly fed from behind. As in the defence, it was necessary in the attack to adopt loose formations and work out infantry group tactics clearly. We must not copy the enemy's mass tactics, which offer advantages only in the case of untrained troops.

In the infantry company the light machine gun had to become a thoroughly familiar weapon. It was, however, still regarded as an auxiliary weapon. The fact that the light machine gun was now the true " infantryman," while the " infantryman " of yesterday was nothing more than a " rifle carrier," had not yet sunk deep into the mind and conscience of the infantry, let alone the rest of the army. Owing to its power compared with that of a rifle, the light machine gun, as its introduction became more general, was bound to become the main infantry weapon. This did not mean that the rifleman was not to shoot. Quite the contrary. The greatest stress was laid on that part of his training.

The light machine gun and the rifleman formed the infantry group, which had to hang together in trouble and danger and the life and death struggle. Its fire power was further increased by quick-firing weapons of all kinds and various sorts of rifle grenades.

To the heavy machine gun, with its longer range and greater effect, fell the task of facilitating the approach of the groups to the enemy's position by keeping the latter under fire. Of course, it had to accompany the advance of the infantry. Therefore, although itself " infantry," it had already become a sort of " companion" or auxiliary arm to the infantry.

The second auxiliary arm, of special use at short ranges against targets offering more than usual resistance, was the light trench mortar. Originally evolved for trench warfare, it had now to be made mobile and capable of direct fire by means of suitable sights. The light trench mortar was part of the infantry battalion which became more and more the tactical unit of the division, just as the group was the tactical unit within the battalion.

These "auxiliary" arms were not yet effective enough to enable the infantry to advance on their arduous way without excessive losses. Of course, massed artillery prepared the attack. It could, however, only do so in a general way, and left untouched too many of the enemy's strong points, which had to be dealt with later in detail at the shortest ranges. In each division, therefore, field guns were withdrawn from their units for short-range work, and were attached to battalions or regiments* as infantry guns. The formation of special batteries of infantry guns had been started in the meantime, but little progress had been made.

In addition, each division had a company of medium trench mortars which were also to be made as mobile as possible and allotted to battalions as required. Finally, there were the flame projectors, which could be brought into action at the shortest ranges against an enemy in blockhouses, dug-outs and cellars.

We had no tanks. They were merely an offensive weapon, and our attacks succeeded without them. That fact, however, could not release us from the duty of procuring everything that might make life easier for our infantry. I have already explained that our motor industry was already fully occupied in turning out lorries, and that we had not enough of them to enable us to keep our infantry away from the battle area in comfortable billets and yet bring them up in time, as the Entente could do. I mentioned also that for that reason I attached the greatest importance to the provision of lorries. If our rolling-stock situation was unfavourable, it must be improved too. The construction of lorries could not be allowed to suffer. We could not possibly do enough towards supplying lorries for supply work and for carrying infantry. The Army Headquarters were often enough troubled by lack of them. When the Chief of Staff complained to me of the difficulty of bringing up supplies, and particularly ammunition, attributing it to lack of lorries, and I maintained that they were available, I was then told that they had been used for carrying the infantry. General

* At this time the German regiment of three battalions was the exact equivalent of our brigade of three battalions (formerly four). [Tr]

Headquarters was not able to get everything. However, the tank question had been carefully considered.

At Cambrai the tanks were very effective. But there they ran into a position held only lightly, chiefly by older men, and poorly equipped with artillery. In all other cases, although they had been a nuisance, they had achieved no decisive results. I took a much more serious view of " tank fright " than the troops themselves did. In the fighting around Bourlon and in Bourlon Wood our infantry had disposed of tanks at close quarters by multiple grenades.* Our artillery had shot them to pieces. Even the armour-piercing bullets used by our machine guns had been good enough. The best weapons against tanks were good nerves, discipline and intrepidity, which enabled many brave men to climb on to them or destroy them by short-range fire. Not until our infantry lost its discipline and fighting capacity did the employment of massed tanks, combined with artificial smoke, produce a fatal effect on the course of events.

We formed detachments of captured tanks. I had a look at the first one in February, 1918, at an exercise by one of the assault battalions. It did not impress me. Our own tank detachments suffered heavy losses in the fighting which followed without effecting anything.

The Director of Mechanical Transport in the Field had had early orders to start building tanks. The type he showed General Headquarters in the spring of 1917 did not meet requirements. I earnestly requested him to push on their construction energetically. Perhaps I ought to have made greater efforts, and possibly we should in that case have had a few more tanks for the decision in 1918 ; but I do not know what other claim could have been set aside to enable them to be built. We could not release any more workmen, and the people at home could not supply any more. Had any been available, we should have wanted them as recruits. We should never have been able to put masses of tanks into action in 1918—and tanks are only effective in masses.

* The ordinary German stick-grenade with a number of grenade heads attached to it.

Preparations for 1918 Offensive in the West

When, towards the end of the war, the manufacturers were in a position to turn out tanks more rapidly, and in greater numbers, General Headquarters ordered a considerable number from the War Department.

In order to provide aircraft support for the infantry special battle aeroplane flights were formed. As had hitherto been done by individual airmen, they dived down from great heights and flew along at a low level, attacking with machine guns and light bombs the infantry lines, the artillery, and, as the practice extended, the enemy's reserves and transport columns, as well as columns of troops coming up from further in rear. Originally intended to be an " auxiliary " arm to the infantry, these battle-flights were finally given important tactical tasks. Thus the air force gained a new field of activity of the greatest importance. The airmen, in the course of their duties, were not only recon-naissance troops who had to fight ; they were not only bomb-carriers for destructive work far in the enemy's rear, but they had, like infantry, artillery, and all other arms, to take part in the fighting on the ground. Like the other combatant forces, they were a destructive arm in the great battle on land. This, indeed, became their main object and the aerial combat was only a means of attaining it.

For the advance of the infantry in the offensive battle concen-trated preparation by massed artillery was of the utmost import-ance. It was necessary to bring up twenty to thirty batteries, about one hundred guns, to each kilometre (eleven hundred yards) of front to be attacked. No man had ever credited such figures before ; still less had anyone ever thought of the quantities of ammunition hurled on the enemy. These were indeed massed effects ! And yet the battle area was so vast that even these quantities of steel did not destroy all life ; the infantry always found far too much to do.

These masses of guns and ammunition had to be got up close to the foremost lines ; only thus could they engage targets far behind the enemy's front line without having to change position as the battle progressed. At the same time, they had to be covered from view, both from the front and from the air. In these positions in the open it was not intended to fight an artillery duel for days on end ; both guns and ammunition dumps would have been annihilated. Nor was it possible to register, as we used to do ; this would have attracted the enemy's attention, and the artillery action would have started before the battle itself, under conditions unfavourable to us.

We had, therefore, to discover some means of dealing with this situation and ensure an adequate effect without ranging. During the defensive battles we had already endeavoured to do so without constantly checking the barrage. The errors of the day (due to wind and atmospheric density), as well as the gun errors (due to size of chamber caused by wear, and other changes in the bore and carriage), were permanently determined and allowed for when firing. A system was now most carefully elaborated. The Artillery Meteorological Service was regulated on a general plan in combination with the General Commanding the Air Forces. In this way all batteries could be informed of the errors of the day with the least possible delay. All guns were tested for individual errors behind the front. In this way it was possible to determine, by means of simple tables for any gun at any time, how much should be added to, or subtracted from, the normal elevation for any target. It was, of course, a necessary condition that ranges were accurately measured. Faultless maps, trigonometrical and topographical determination of all battery zero points on the ground, and the greatest care in marking targets on the maps, as determined by sound-ranging, flash-spotting and aerial photography—these were the necessary preliminaries, and an enormous work it was. The new procedure was strongly objected to, especially by some of the senior gunners. But it had to be adopted nevertheless, and fulfilled all expectations.

The training and instruction of the troops in the new method was entrusted to Captain Pulkowsky who carried out his duties with great energy and skill.

At the shortest ranges the effect of the artillery was to be supplemented by trench mortars.

General Headquarters intended that after a short artillery

bombardment, lasting only a few hours, the infantry, which was to be held in readiness in the forward positions, should advance to the assault.

This short powerful bombardment was expected to paralyse the enemy's artillery by means of gas which spread over great areas, and keep his infantry in their dug-outs.

At the beginning of the infantry assault, the artillery, while continuing to keep down that of the enemy, was to put down a barrage in front of the infantry and then pave the way for it like a gigantic roller.

The infantry had to keep close up to this wall of projectiles, and did so with admirable determination. The enemy, who came out of his dug-outs when the barrage had passed, was now attacked by our infantry, assisted by auxiliary or " companion " arms, under the protection of our artillery.

It was evident that the closer the infantry could keep to the barrage, the less time the enemy had to leave his dug-outs, and the more chance there was of surprising him in them. Consequently the barrage must not advance faster than the infantry could follow. This pace had to be fixed beforehand, for, in spite of hard thinking and experiments, it had been impossible to discover any means of controlling the barrage. The nature and state of the ground had also to be considered, as regards their effect on the advance of the infantry and the consequent pace of the barrage. Stronger lines required a more prolonged bombardment, and the barrage had to dwell on them longer. So it came about that an advance of one kilometre (eleven hundred yards) required as much as one hour. It was always a great misfortune if the barrage got ahead ; the attack was then held up only too easily. It could not be brought back again without great loss of time, and the infantry suffered losses which it was the duty of all commanders to avoid.

As the range increased the barrage became thinner, as the shorter range guns dropped out, and finally, beyond extreme range, it ceased, and the infantry lost its protection. By this time, some artillery must be already in action in more forward positions, from which to support the further advance. In spite of all auxiliary arms and its " infantry guns," the infantry could not do without it.

What form the fighting would take when the infantry emerged from the protection of the barrage it was quite impossible to foresee. It was necessary to prepare a regular scheme for bringing up a large force of artillery and even larger masses of ammunition. The latter, indeed, was the really important item; often too many guns were pushed up. It was bound to be uncommonly difficult to get many vehicles over our own, and the enemy's system of trenches and wire, as well as shell-holes. It required careful preparation and a great quantity of gear to bridge this belt successfully.

General Headquarters laid great stress on the rule that the attack should be continued for several days on end by the divisions originally in the first line. I opposed the idea that they should be relieved by divisions in the second line on the second or third day. At the beginning of the war we had fought for weeks without relief. That was, indeed, beyond the powers of our present troops. But so frequent a change as many desired was not yet necessary.

The further the attack advanced, the more nearly its character approximated to that of open warfare. In defensive fighting the higher staffs had to keep far behind in order really to conduct the battle; but now their place was nearer the front; the more open the fighting the closer up they must get. The leader now had to make rapid decisions and, if necessary, carry others away by his personal example.

Finally, as our operations progressed, we should come up against a new front which we should not be able to overcome at first, as had happened in Rumania, Eastern Galicia and Italy. Then we should have to return to the defensive and distribute our forces in depth. The right moment for this change was difficult to recognize; only too often we became involved in unnecessary fighting.

Our big attacks had clearly demonstrated the importance of supply, and attention was directed to it as a matter of course. All preparations had to be made to follow the attack across the trench systems with railways, roads and telephone lines, and to connect them up to those in the newly-conquered territory.

In all the theatres of war training was carried out on these principles. To Rumania we sent a specially experienced general to train the troops there on Western principles, so that, in spite of the belated conclusion of peace, they might soon become available for use in France.

In the West we revived courses of instruction for higher commanders and staff officers, as well as for juniors down to group leaders, whose functions were so important a factor to success. Marked activity became apparent throughout the Army. It commenced with recruit-training and ended in exercises by formations of all arms, or on the ranges. The barrage was practised with live ammunition, and the infantry trained to follow close behind it. Now, as ever, all commanders regarded improved discipline as the foundation of our Army and of all success. It was rated the more highly when it was realized that the home influence on the Army was bad. As in peace, special importance was attached to individual training ; exercises were seldom carried out by large forces of all arms.

Just as in the previous year everything had been done to train the Army for defensive fighting, so now it was trained for the attack. The country is indebted to the work of the officers and the well-thought-out scheme of training for the fact that our losses in killed and wounded, though very great, were much less than those of the enemy. According to a rough estimate, England and France have lost far more than two million killed, and Russia as many. Taking half the Russian casualties as having occurred on our front, which is probably too low an estimate, the enemy had far more than three million killed, as compared with two million Germans. I have included those killed on other fronts, both our own and the enemy's. This makes the proportion more favourable to us, and the more we know, the more favourable will it turn out to be. These numbers are terribly high, but they prove that we tried to fulfil our responsibilities towards the troops.

In preparing for attack we did not forget defence, as counter-attacks were to be expected. The principles of defence were retained; we only laid greater stress on anti-tank measures. Both in attack and defence the auxiliary arms served this purpose also. In the artillery, especially in the case of field guns and light trench mortars, training in direct individual fire at tanks was considered of decisive importance. The allotment of special ammunition to the heavy machine guns was increased. Experiments in destroying tanks with multiple grenades were carried out and all experience gained in fighting them was communicated to the troops, whose opinions were called for. Our positions were examined as to their liability to attack by tanks; traps and stops were made, barricades constructed, mines put down and anti-tank guns dug in at many points. Naturally, the extent of these defensive measures largely depended upon the available labour and the views of the troops as to the likelihood of tank attack.

The War Ministry kept us informed of the progress in the manufacture of anti-tank weapons which it pushed on unceasingly.

Once more I spent much time at the front and with the various Army Headquarters in active interchange of ideas on the tactics of offensive fighting, and on the attack itself. Many proposals and counter-proposals, many pros and cons were laid before me. I can still recall the discussions about the barrage and the advanced zone. As was my duty, I had to give the ultimate decision. The tactical principles were considered to be correct and readily accepted by the troops. They left room for individual action in all directions.

I was present at various exercises, and had conversations with many regimental officers. It was evidently not easy for the troops to adopt the open formation which was so necessary. We urgently needed every moment of the time, right up to the middle of March, which was available for training.

VIII

During January and February the divisions in the West that were intended for the attack were taken out of the line ; some of them were replaced by those that had come from other theatres. From this time on they had to devote themselves entirely to training and equipment. We were unable to equip all divisions equally with stores and horses, and had in the beginning to confine ourselves to those which were destined to open the attack. Similar action was taken in regard to the formations not included in the divisions, such as army field artillery, heavy artillery, trench mortars, etc. The horses of the shock divisions were given extra forage rations.

General Headquarters regretted that the distinction between " attack " and " trench " divisions became established in the Army. We tried to eradicate it, without being able to alter the situation which gave rise to it.

In the meantime we had gradually got up everything that could be thought of as required for the attack. Some divisions were still on their way from the East.

We hoped that the forces we were collecting from all quarters would enable us to attack on a continuous front of over thirty miles (fifty kilometres), allotting twenty to thirty batteries, without trench mortars, to each kilometre (eleven hundred yards) of front. By thinning out at suitable places we could extend the front still more. We had at that time twenty-five to thirty divisions more than the enemy on the whole Western Front. But this was not the actual measure of our superiority which was reduced by the numerous specialist arms and territorial troops of the enemy, of which we had not such large numbers. Even so, our superiority was greater than it had ever been, and afforded prospects of success. We thought of carrying out the attack with fifty or sixty divisions. In order to effect this the corresponding weakening of other parts of the Western Front was unavoidable.

General Headquarters had also approached Austria–Hungary. The latter had sent batteries, but unfortunately with so small an amount of ammunition that the actual reinforcement did not amount to much. Austro–Hungarian divisions were not available. Their strengths were too low, and did not increase again until several hundred thousand men returned from captivity in Russia. The removal of German troops from the Italian and Eastern Fronts, where they had held a very considerable portion of the line, made heavier demands on the Austrian troops, in spite of the altered situation.

General Headquarters would very much have liked to bring the Turkish 15th Corps over to the Western Front ; but the poor condition of the Turkish Army induced the Government to send the corps to Turkey. I regretted this afterwards. Enver now had eyes only for the Caucasus and therefore sent it to Batum where it wasted its time doing nothing. It would have been more useful in the West.

Bulgaria wanted her troops on the Macedonian Front ; she could probably, as far as numbers were concerned, have sent troops to the West, but could not appreciate the importance of a common prosecution of the war. In the past she had objected to crossing the Danube, and now only unwillingly released German troops from Macedonia, although it was merely a question of a few battalions of Jäger and some batteries and mountain machine-gun formations. The Bulgarian troops that came to relieve them from the Dobrudja were considerably stronger, but even then we left some German troops behind. The stores belonging to the German formations were left in Bulgaria or replaced by special stocks.

We were well supplied with all stores required for carrying on operations in the West, but our recruiting situation was still very serious. Our representations had had no result. As a matter of fact, in the autumn of 1918, under the influence of recent events, the War Ministry did release men of the Home Army and the garrison troops who could have joined the Field Army sooner. General Headquarters still had a reserve of its own in the Eastern Army and the Army of Occupation in

Rumania. As the situation become more settled, all men under thirty-five were withdrawn from those formations, the strength of which was simultaneously reduced, so that their fighting value was greatly diminished by these measures. The special arms and line of communication troops formed another, though limited, source of reinforcements. I also tried to extend the system of replacing men by women and a female auxiliary telephone corps was to be started.

The recruiting situation need not have been so bad. The loss by desertion was uncommonly high. The number that got into neutral countries—e.g., Holland—ran into tens of thousands, and a far greater number lived happily at home, tacitly tolerated by their fellow-citizens and completely unmolested by the authorities. They and the skrimshankers at the front, of whom there were thousands more, reduced the battle strength of the fighting troops, especially of the infantry, to which most of them belonged, to a vital degree. If these men had been got hold of, the recruiting difficulty would not have been so great. More recruits could have been raised if only the fighting spirit had been stronger at home. It was on this spirit that the ultimate decision depended—but it failed.

War consumes men ; that is its nature. The modern defensive battle is more costly than the attack, one reason more in favour of the latter. The months of August, September and October, 1918, cost us far more than March, April and May of the same year. In the earlier months our losses consisted mainly of slightly wounded men who came back. The prisoners we lost in the defence had to be struck off as lost for good. That the large masses which were led into battle would suffer heavy casualties, in spite of all tactical counter-measures, was unfortunately a matter of course.

The recruiting difficulties were not removed by March, 1918, although a few hundred thousand men were available. They continued to be an uncertain factor in the tremendous contest. England and France had similar difficulties to contend with. In the autumn of 1917 the English divisions still had twelve battalions ; now they were reduced to nine. Since the

Aisne–Champagne battle France had broken up far more than one hundred battalions, as well as territorial and territorial reserve formations. The new American formations, which could not have much fighting value, had not yet arrived. The submarine war had continued to be effective; we could not estimate the amount of tonnage the Entente would set aside for transport work.

The Army had thrown off the depressing effects of the previous year's fighting in the knowledge that it was passing from the defence to the attack. Its *moral* appeared completely restored, but in March, 1918, it could not be denied that secret agitation was making progress here and there. When the 1919 class reached the recruit depots, we began to receive complaints about its general quality and spirit. Moreover, many recruits seemed to have a great deal of money, which must have greatly embittered the older men who had been a long time in the field.

Nothing had been done to strengthen the warlike spirit at home. The abuses in the various departments of war administration had become more flagrant than ever. The generally improved spirit of the Army had a temporary influence on that at home, and blinded us to a good deal. But the large mass of the people was unaffected, caught in the toils of enemy propaganda, wrapped up in its own interests and cares and utterly unconcerned about the doubtful issue of the war. The nation could no longer brace the nerves of the Army; it was already devouring its marrow. How far the secret agitation of the Independent Socialists had extended we were unable to determine. The strikes at the end of January, 1918, had thrown another lurid light on their activities. The party was continually gaining adherents and was firmly controlled by its leaders, whereas the unions were losing influence.

The Government itself, although taking energetic action against the strikes, failed to see the signs of the times in them, as before in the naval mutiny in the autumn of 1917. Everything turned more and more on maintaining order in Germany by resolute action, even at the risk of a temporary falling off in the output of war material. Otherwise, it was to be feared that

586

the revolutionary movement would do even more harm. The Imperial Government was acquainted with this view of General Headquarters. During those days the revolution made definite progress in Germany. It was at that time, as I have just heard, that the first German Soldiers' and Workers' Council was formed at Reinickendorf. Thus a further element of weakness had developed in our own body while we were in the midst of a struggle for our very existence. At that time I did not attach vital significance to these symptoms. My belief in the German people as a whole was then still unshaken.

The commanders and troops in the line shared with General Headquarters the feeling that they would prove equal to the demands that would be made on them in the coming struggle. We hoped for success, even though they were no longer the troops of 1914, but only a kind of militia with much experience of war. The enemy was no better. Wherever we had attacked with similar troops, who were not so well trained for the offensive, we had won. What we should achieve, whether we should break through and start a war of movement, or whether our effort would remain a sortie on a large scale, was uncertain—like everything in war.

In my audience of the Emperor at Homburg on the 13th of February, I had expressed my view of forthcoming events in the West to him and the Imperial Chancellor in the following terms :

" The battle in the West is the greatest military task that has ever been imposed upon an army, and one which England and France have been trying for two years to compass. Yesterday I spoke with the Commander of the 7th Army ; he told me that the more he thought about this task, the more impressed he was with its magnitude. That is how all responsible men in the West think. I believe, too, that I, who have to furnish the Field-Marshal with the foundation on which he bases his request for His Majesty's decision, am more than anyone impressed by the immensity of the undertaking. It can only be successfully accomplished if the authorities who conduct the war are relieved of all intolerable shackles, if the very last man is employed in the decisive conflict, and is animated, not only by love for his

Emperor and his native land, but by confidence in the strength of the military leadership and the greatness of our country. These spiritual forces cannot be underestimated, they are the foundation of the greatest deeds. They must be strengthened by the energy of our action in the East.

" The Army in the West is waiting for the opportunity to act.

" We must not imagine that this offensive will be like those in Galicia or Italy ; it will be an immense struggle that will begin at one point, continue at another, and take a long time ; it is difficult, but it will be victorious. . . ."

The crown of success would be an operation in which we could bring to bear the whole of our superiority. It was our great object. If we did not succeed at the first attack, we should have to do so at the next ; by then, indeed, the situation would have become less favourable—how much less favourable would depend upon the rate of arrival and value of the Americans, and on the losses which both sides sustained. Everything was based on the assumption that we should do well in this respect and although, of course, I expected our own Army to be weakened, I hoped it would be less so than that of the enemy. By continuing to attack we should still retain the initiative. More I could not aim at.

I reported to the Emperor that the Army was assembled and well prepared to undertake the " biggest task in its history."

THE OFFENSIVE IN THE WEST, 1918
(MAP IX.)

I

I T was difficult to decide where to attack, but it was necessary to do so early. It took weeks, and required considerable foresight and the most detailed preliminary work to concentrate the troops in a confined area, bring up by rail the tremendous quantities of ammunition and other stores of all kinds, carry out the work allotted to the troops themselves, such as preparing battery positions, screening roads, constructing anti-aircraft shelters and preparing gear for crossing the trenches, and finally to deploy for battle.

Of course all this increased the danger of discovery. It was therefore necessary to commence dummy works on the fronts remote from the attack, which, as a matter of fact, served as the basis of attack later on. But the bulk of the available labour troops were required on the front of attack at an early date. The preparations on other fronts could not be extensive, but there was some chance of misleading the enemy, and the deception was to be completed by skilfully conducted defensive measures.

I discussed the selection of the front of attack with the Chiefs of Staff of the Army Groups, and with the officers of my Staff, and heard their opinions. Three sectors were considered— Flanders between Ypres and Lens, between Arras and St. Quentin or La Fère, and on both sides of Verdun, leaving out the fortress.   As is always the case, there was a great deal to be said for and against each proposal.

The enemy was in great strength about Ypres and Arras, in front of the Ailette position and further to the east, as far as Verdun ; the weakest part was on both sides of St. Quentin ; north of that town the enemy line had been denser since the battles of Cambrai.

In the north the ground was difficult.   The condition of the Lys valley, west of Lille, across which the main force of the attack would pass, depended to an extraordinary degree upon the season and the weather ; before the middle of April its passability away from the roads was doubtful.   That was very late, in view of the Americans.

In the centre the ground itself presented no difficulties, but further progress would be hampered by the crater-areas of the Somme battle.

The attack at Verdun would lead us into very hilly country.

These two attacks could take place at any time of year.

Tactical conditions, therefore, favoured the centre sector ; here the attack would strike the enemy's weakest point, the ground offered no difficulties, and it was feasible at all seasons.

Strategically the northern attack had the advantage of a great, though limited, objective. `It might enable us to shorten our front if we succeeded in capturing Calais and Boulogne.   The attack on Verdun might also lead to an improvement in our front, though more of a tactical nature.   The centre attack seemed to lack any definite limit.   This could be remedied by directing the main effort on the area between Arras and Péronne, towards the coast.   If this blow succeeded the strategic result might indeed be enormous, as we should separate the bulk of the English Army from the French and crowd it up with its back to the sea.

I favoured the centre attack, but I was influenced by the time factor and by tactical considerations, first among them being the weakness of the enemy.   Whether this weakness would continue I could not know.   Tactics had to be considered before purely strategical objects which it is futile to pursue unless tactical success is possible.   A strategical plan which ignores the

MAP IX

THE GERMAN ATTACK IN THE WEST, 1918

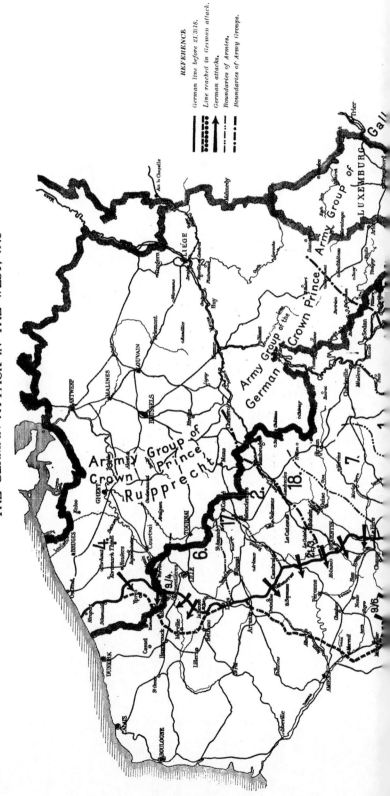

REFERENCE

German line before 21/3/18.
Line reached in German attack.
German attacks.
Boundaries of Armies.
Boundaries of Army Groups.

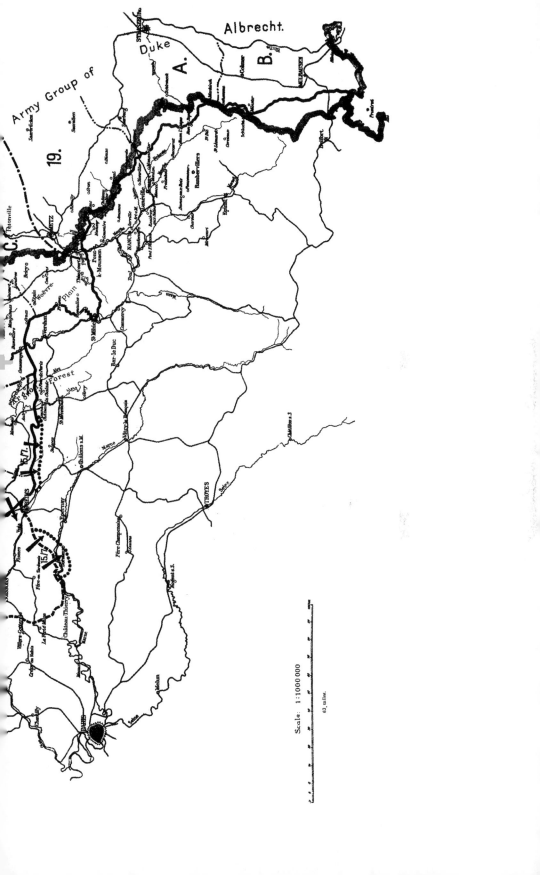

tactical factor is foredoomed to failure. Of this the Entente's attacks during the first three years of the war afford numerou[s] examples.

After selecting the divisions and assembling the material available for the attack, it was decided to strike between Croisilles, south-east of Arras, and Moeuvres, and, omitting the Cambrai re-entrant, between Villers-Guislain and the Oise, south of St. Quentin. It was to be supported on its left by a subsidiary attack from La Fère.

The preliminary work and the conduct of the attack made it necessary to interpolate two Army Headquarters, and new Line of Communication Inspectorates. The 17th Army, formerly the 14th in Italy, under General Otto von Below, Chief of Staff General Krafft von Delmensingen, was put in between the 6th and 2nd opposite Arras, and the 18th, formerly Woyrsch's Group Headquarters, now commanded by General von Hutier, Chief of Staff General von Sauberzweig, between the 2nd and 7th Armies, opposite St. Quentin and La Fère. The boundary between the 17th and 6th was about half-way between Lens and Arras, that between the 17th and 2nd approximately at Moeuvres. The boundary between the 2nd and 18th Armies was formed, roughly, by the Omignon brook, that between the 18th and 7th was just south of La Fère.

The 17th Army, therefore, had to make the attack on the line Croisilles–Moeuvres, the 2nd and 18th that between Villers–Guislain and La Fère. In this operation, the 17th and 2nd were to take the weight off each other in turn, and with their inner wings cut off the enemy holding the Cambrai re-entrant, afterwards pushing through between Croisilles and Péronne. This advance was to be protected on the south flank by the 18th Army, in combination with the extreme left wing of the 2nd. The strength and equipment of these armies were adapted to their tasks.

For the decisive operation the 17th and 2nd Armies were to remain under the orders of the Army Group of Crown Prince Rupprecht. The 18th Army joined that of the German Crown Prince. Remembering the November campaign in Poland in

1914, I meant to exercise a far-reaching influence on the course of the battle. That was difficult if it was being conducted by one Group only ; every intervention was only too apt to become mere interference from above. It was desirable to make the fullest possible use of the resources of the Group of the German Crown Prince and this was facilitated by the organization adopted.

Moreover, it was a personal satisfaction to the Field-Marshal and myself, since the strategical situation required it, that His Imperial Highness the Crown Prince would take part in the first great offensive battle in the West. Dynastic interests did not influence me. Though profoundly loyal to my King, I am an independent man and no courtier.

The possibility of broadening the attack on the north towards Arras, and on the south towards the left bank of the Oise, was anticipated.

Feints and preparations for further attack were made :

Between Ypres and Lens, by the Group of Crown Prince Rupprecht ;

By the German Crown Prince's Group, particularly between Rheims and the Argonne ;

By the newly-formed Group of von Gallwitz, on the old battle-fields of Verdun ;

By the Group of Duke Albrecht, between Saarburg in Lorraine and Ste. Marie-aux-Mines, and also in the Sundgau.

The Group of General von Gallwitz was formed because that of the German Crown Prince had now been extended towards St. Quentin, and could no longer properly attend to affairs at Verdun as well. General von Gallwitz was in immediate command of his own 3rd Army, as well as Army Detachment "C."

The Headquarters of the German Southern Army in Galicia, under General von Bothmer, joined the Army Group of Duke Albrecht, and was put in the line in Lorraine as the 19th Army Headquarters ; the Chief of the Staff was Colonel von Hemmer who had already greatly distinguished himself in a similar position in the East. " A " Army Headquarters took over the sector Saarburg–Ste. Marie-aux-Mines.

All fronts maintained their defensive arrangements in case the enemy should himself attack. In some places it was intended to retire in that case.

Work had been carried on along these lines according to programme and with the greatest devotion from the middle of January. By the beginning of February the attack was fixed to commence on the 21st March, although the situation in the East was still quite obscure. The military situation, however, made a decision imperative. Later on we could always make changes, but we should be unable to make a fresh start.

The work of the Army Headquarters, the Quartermaster-General, the Intendant-General, the Director of Railways and the officers of my immediate Staff all fitted in admirably. I was able to satisfy myself of that when I visited the Front. On these occasions I discussed all relevant questions, adjusted difficulties and helped. The Chiefs of the Staff at the Army and Group Headquarters gave me short verbal reports of the ground, the distribution of the troops, the artillery combat, and the state of the preparations. In my remarks I laid the greatest stress on co-operation between the inner wings of the 17th and 2nd Armies of Crown Prince Rupprecht's Group, so as to ensure the Cambrai re-entrant being cut off, as so much depended upon it, and it seemed to me that the 17th Army was beginning to look to the west a little too soon. We discussed the co-operation of the two Army Groups on the boundary between the 2nd and 18th Armies. Preparations took their intended course. Work was carried on everywhere with confidence and without losing sight of the object. All arrangements fitted in like clock-work. It was certain that the armies would be ready for battle on the day.

I considered it necessary to take advantage of such success as we might obtain in order to strengthen the enemy's inclination to peace by means of propaganda. Colonel von Haeften had drawn up a memoir on the subject which I sent to the Imperial Chancellor, who apparently passed it to the Foreign Office. Nothing of importance was done.

The Imperial Chancellor was perfectly acquainted with our intention of attacking in the West. It was the reason why we insisted on the diplomatic negotiations in the East being accelerated and why we had decided to denounce the armistice with Russia. He knew the enormous importance we attached to this offensive. Further, I had him informed of the date it was to begin. Germany could only make the enemy inclined to peace by fighting. It was first of all necessary to shake the position of Lloyd George and Clemenceau by a military victory. Before that was done peace was not to be thought of. All the world, including the Entente, knew we were going to attack in the West. Clemenceau declared himself, I think on the 6th March, decisively in favour of continuing the war, in spite of events in the East, and in spite of our imminent attack.

At that moment I could not possibly believe in a just peace. Up till now the enemy had invariably rejected a peace by understanding. Should we, in the existing situation, have offered him Alsace-Lorraine, parts of the province of Posen and an indemnity ?

Nor did the Imperial Government mention the possibility of peace. Secretary of State von Kühlmann, who was supposed to be conducting the whole of our foreign policy, was first at Brest and then at Bucharest. Neither he nor the Imperial Chancellor had been able to open up any negotiations which might have led to peace without further fighting. They probably continued their endeavours in that direction, in spite of the Entente's refusal of the invitation to Brest. It was their duty to spare the people and army further fighting, if possible. Count Hertling's declaration of the 25th February, in which he took his stand on President Wilson's four points of the 11th February, had met with no response from the Entente.

Colonel von Haeften had just been visiting foreign countries, in order to discuss questions relating to propaganda. Without my knowledge, he established communication with a subject of one of the enemy countries who was acquainted with the objects and intentions of the authorities in London and Washington, and made me a verbal report on the subject. The terms then demanded of us were so severe that only a defeated Germany could have acceded to them. The Colonel further informed me that the then Reichstag Deputy, Conrad Hauszmann, who has since confirmed this statement, and Herr Max Warburg-Hamburg had also tried to negotiate peace, but without success. The Government never informed me of these events, though it must have known of them. I am all the more surprised that it did not contradict the rumour that a peace would have been arranged in March if I had not insisted on attacking. I personally requested the Imperial Chancellor and the Vice-Chancellor to do so. They both of them refrained, without ever giving me any reason for it.

II

Early in March G.H.Q. left Kreuznach, where it had been for more than a year.

The new headquarters had in the meantime been established at Spa. We got very good accommodation there. The offices were in the Hotel Britannique, in which I had been billeted before, during our invasion of Belgium in the autumn of 1914. Spa was much nearer the Front, and with Verviers could accommodate the whole of G.H.Q. For directing the battle, for operations, it was still too far back. I had therefore proposed to take Avesnes as the quarters of the augmented Operations Branch. From there we could easily reach all parts of the Front by car. I intended to see a great deal for myself, and to send my staff officers to the scenes of important events in order to obtain impressions at first hand.

On the 18th March the Field-Marshal and I went to Avesnes with the augmented Operations Branch. Our offices there were not good, everything was very cramped, but they had to do. We had chosen the place because the 18th Army Headquarters had been there, and the telephone communications only needed slight additions.

Our mess was at first very unpleasant; later on we found more agreeable rooms. We fed the owners and fitted the place up with furniture from Spa. To stay in those rooms and have our meals there was a relaxation we all needed.

His Majesty came the next day. He lived in his Court train, which was side-tracked in a neighbouring station.

On the 20th March, along the whole front of the attack, the guns and trench mortars, with their ammunition, were in position behind, in, and in places even in front of, the foremost trenches. It was a remarkable achievement and at the same time a marvel that the enemy had neither seen anything nor heard any movement at night. At times our batteries were subjected to harassing fire, and ammunition dumps went up here and there. All this must have attracted the enemy's attention. But he observed it all along the Front, and could therefore obtain no certain indication.

The divisions had at first been distributed behind the front of attack, but were now crowded together in anti-aircraft shelters, behind the jumping-off places in our foremost lines. This concentration of 40 or 50 divisions had not been observed by the enemy, nor had it been reported to him by his highly developed secret service. The marches took place at night, but the troops sang as they passed through the villages. Such masses cannot be concealed. But no more did the airmen discover the railway transport that had been taking place behind the front of attack since February. It was heavy behind the whole Front, but the bulk of it was unmistakably going on behind the line Arras–La Fère, as was told us by German airmen sent up to report.

Nor did the enemy discover anything by other means. I must assume this; otherwise his defensive measures would have been more effective, and his reserves would have arrived more quickly. In spite of all efforts to the contrary, the essence of war is uncertainty; that is our experience, and the enemy's too.

On the 18th or 19th March two men deserted from a trench-mortar company. Judging by notes found by us in the enemy's lines, or according to prisoners' statements, they are alleged to have given information of the impending attack.

On the other fronts, particularly near Lille and Verdun, artillery activity had increased.

At noon on the 20th G.H.Q. had to face the great decision whether the attack was to commence on the 21st or be put off.

The Offensive in the West, 1918

Every delay must have increased the difficulties of troops, crowded together close up to the enemy. Already the tension was very hard to bear. The psychological pressure of the mass was urging them forward.

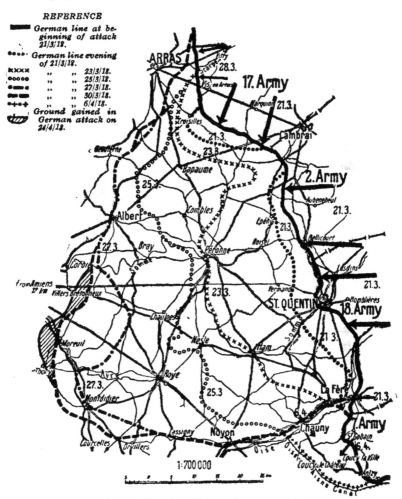

Fig. 31. The Great Battle in France. 1918.

And yet our artillery relied on gas for its effect, and that was dependent on the direction and strength of the wind. I had to rely on the forecast submitted to me at 11 a.m. by my meteorologist, Lieutenant Dr. Schmaus. Up till the morning of the 20th strength and direction were by no means very favourable; indeed, it seemed almost necessary to put off the attack. That would have been very hard to do. So I was very anxious to see what sort of report I should get. It was not strikingly favourable, but it did indicate that the attack was possible. At 12 noon the Army Groups were told that the programme would be carried out. Now it could no longer be stopped. Everything must run its course. G.H.Q., higher commanders and troops had all done their duty. The rest was in the hands of fate; unfavourable wind diminished the effectiveness of the gas, fog impeded and retarded our movements and prevented our superior training and leadership from reaping its full reward. That was the predominant opinion about the fog, but a few thought it an advantage.

On the 21st, just before 4 a.m., the battle began with a tremendous crash on a front of 70 kilometres,* between Croisilles and La Fère. As regards the 2nd and 18th Armies, the hours had been fixed by higher authority for the main operations; the 17th Army, which was fighting by itself, was left more latitude. Within these limits matters were left to the Groups.

For about two hours the whole of our artillery engaged the enemy's batteries, then most of it was switched on to trench bombardment, in which the trench mortars also took part. A little before 9 a.m. most of our fire—only a portion being left on hostile batteries and special points—was concentrated to form a barrage. Our infantry advanced to the assault.

The 17th Army, which had the strongest enemy in front of it, only reached his second line; the barrage had gone far ahead; the infantry had lost touch with it. They remained in this position, lying down, with no artillery support.

In the 2nd Army's attack, the co-operation between the infantry and the artillery was better. The infantry penetrated into the enemy's second position.

With the 18th Army everything proceeded as intended. It was making good progress.

On the 22nd March there was little change on the 17th Army ront, but the 2nd, being firmly in hand and led with energy,

* About 44 miles.

598

defeated the enemy and pressed on. The 18th gained a considerable amount of ground. The 17th appeared to give its various tactical groups too much latitude; but for this the action of the different units was too inter-dependent. G.H.Q. took steps to get the general direction of the fighting under a single control.

The result of the situation on the 17th Army front was that the enemy in the Cambrai re-entrant was not cut off, nor could the opposition to the 2nd Army be indirectly reduced. The latter had been obliged to rely on its own unaided efforts and had, therefore, not got ahead so fast as was desirable from the point of view of assisting the 17th. And so again Crown Prince Rupprecht's Group could not gain ground between Croisilles and Péronne to the extent that had been originally intended.

On the 25th March the 17th and 2nd Armies had passed far beyond the line Bapaume–Combles, fighting hard all the way; the 18th Army had taken Nesle and met with but little resistance. The 17th Army was already exhausted; it had lost too heavily on the 21st and 22nd, apparently because it had fought in too dense formation. The 2nd Army was fresher but was already complaining of the old shell-holes. It could get no farther than Albert. Its left wing had been more delayed by having to cross the Somme than by the enemy. The 18th Army was still full of fight and confidence; on the 27th it took Montdidier. Soon the enemy north of the Somme formed a fresh front, which was sure to be difficult to overcome. In the direction of Amiens the enemy's resistance seemed weaker.

The original idea of the battle had to be modified, and the main weight of the attack vigorously directed on that point. I still hoped we should get through to open warfare and kept it in view in my instructions to the armies. But the 17th Army could not get on; the 2nd and 18th were still gaining ground. I continued my efforts towards reinforcing the left wing of the 2nd Army and directing it and the 18th on Amiens.

The enemy's line was now becoming denser, and in places they were even attacking themselves, while our armies were no longer strong enough to overcome them unaided. The ammunition was not sufficient, and supply became difficult. The repair of roads and railways was taking too long, in spite of all our preparations.

After thoroughly replenishing ammunition the 18th Army attacked between Montdidier and Noyon on the 30th March. On the 4th April the 2nd Army and the right wing of the 18th attacked at Albert and south of the Somme towards Amiens. These actions were indecisive. It was an established fact that the enemy's resistance was beyond our strength. We must not get drawn into a battle of exhaustion. This would accord neither with the strategical nor the tactical situation. In agreement with the commanders concerned, G.H.Q. had to take the extremely difficult decision to abandon the attack on Amiens for good.

The Entente now attacked at Albert and south-east of Amiens in a disconnected sort of way and achieved nothing. On the 24th April, after careful preparation, the 2nd Army made another attempt, with the aid of tanks, to improve its position at Villers-Bretonneux ; it got ahead well, but was unable to hold what it gained.

The front between Albert and Montdidier only settled down gradually. From time to time fighting broke out again, and the situation remained permanently doubtful. The other parts of the new front, towards Arras and Noyon, became inactive much more quickly.

The battle was over by the 4th April. It was a brilliant feat, and will ever be so regarded in history. What the English and French had not succeeded in doing we had accomplished, and that in the fourth year of the war.

Strategically we had not achieved what the events of the 23rd, 24th and 25th had encouraged us to hope for. That we had also failed to take Amiens, which would have rendered communication between the enemy's forces astride the Somme exceedingly difficult, was specially disappointing. Long-range bombardment of the railway establishments of Amiens was by no means an equivalent. However, our troops had beaten the French and English and proved themselves superior. That they did not achieve all the success that was possible was due, not only to their reduced fighting value, but above all, to their not being always under the firm control of their officers. They had been checked by finding food depots, and valuable time had thus been lost.

Generally speaking, our tactics had proved sound. What had happened in the 17th Army did not necessitate any fundamental changes, although some lessons needed more drastic application. Above all, the infantry must be more extended. At many places machine-gun posts had given us an undue amount of trouble and so caused delay. The infantry groups had often been lacking in initiative, and their co-operation with the auxiliary arms had often failed. The troops had found special difficulty in reorganizing themselves for defence at the conclusion of the attack, and particularly in recognizing when no further success was to be gained by continuing the attack. All troops, especially mounted troops, had suffered heavily from bombing by hostile airmen.

It was as yet too early to give a final opinion on the strategical situation ; in itself it was by no means favourable. How G.H.Q. was to deal with it later on could not yet be determined, as we were still in the first stages of the operations. The Avre bridge-head was a special difficulty in the tactical sense. The advisability of giving it up was discussed. But as this would have shown the enemy that we had given up the idea of any further attack on Amiens, we kept it.

The new front had now to be fortified. Some of the played-out divisions were relieved by fresh ones from quiet fronts, the less tired ones were left in the line. Everywhere the greatest attention and care were bestowed on completing the communications in rear. For the main operations it was, however, of the highest importance to take back troops that were no longer required in the new line for rest, training and improving their discipline. We had to collect reserves for further operations and to repel possible counter-attacks which could, however, for the present be only of a local character.

The troops of the 2nd Army were particularly handicapped

by having stuck fast in the western edge of the Somme battle-field. They could find real rest only to the east of our starting line, although in the country they had traversed numerous English hut camps had fallen into our hands undamaged.

Our losses were not inconsiderable ; we had been fighting with large numbers for a long time. The percentage in the 17th Army was too high ; the losses in officers had been heavy throughout. But, besides rich booty, we had taken some 90,000 unwounded prisoners, and in addition the enemy's battle casualties had been heavy. We could expect to get back many of the slightly wounded within a reasonable time. We had been attacking and had come off well, even in the matter of casualties.

The arrangements for dealing with the wounded had not sufficed at all points, although they had been carefully examined by the Director of Medical Services before the battle. The numerous slightly wounded made things more difficult by the stupid and unsatisfactory way in which they hurried to the rear.

The battle cost me a great deal also. My wife's youngest son fell on the 23rd. He was a flying officer, and was at first reported missing. On the battle-field we found a grave with the English inscription : " Here rest two German flying officers." I had the sad task of identifying my son. Now he rests in German soil. The war has spared me nothing.

My journey to the battle-field had taken me through the two trench-systems in which the opponents had faced each other for so long. The impression it made was great ; a strip, many miles in width, bleak and devastated, stretches through France, the mark of the war conjured up by the Entente.

On the enemy the defeat produced an overwhelming im-pression. In spite of my request we did nothing in the diplo-matic sense to utilize it. France trembled. She wanted to be sure of the military support of England and America. Clemen-ceau appealed to the Allies. In England tens of thousands of miners and munition workers were called up for the Army, and yet some ten divisions could not for the time being be brought up to establishment. They disappeared from the

Front, and most of them did not come in again until the autumn. The service age-limit was raised, but the British Government did not yet dare to think of enforcing compulsory service in Ireland. In other respects Lloyd George shrank from nothing. As may be seen by his speeches after the conclusion of the Armistice, he urgently demanded help from Wilson and sent all available shipping—regardless of whether England would suffer or not—to America to fetch the new formations. What did we do? Did we give all? It is good to draw comparisons, so that the lessons of this war may later be taken to heart by the German people. Only the greatest energy is called for in war.

For the sake of victory England and the United States violated the neutral European countries by political and economic pressure, and requisitioned their tonnage in order to reduce the strain on their own. In the long run the submarine war had proved unpleasantly effective after all, and produced a severe transport crisis on land and sea. " In April the German submarines were so successful that England would have been ruined in nine months if the sinking had continued at the same rate." This was the declaration made by an English statesman in the House of Commons in November, 1918. England utilized the shipping taken from neutrals, and whatever else she could make available, for bringing over the American masses, crammed tight in the transports, to France. The men carried only their personal equipment. What they needed in Europe they were given by England and France, but also by the neutral countries, especially Spain. The whole operation was a *tour de force*, uncommonly effective for a short time but impossible to keep up for a long period. Had the war lasted longer a reaction must have followed.

According to the *New York World* of the 8th May, 1918, the President of the Tonnage Committee of the United States Chamber of Commerce, Edward A. Filene, held the following opinion : " At the request of the Allies we are now sending men to France in absolutely senseless numbers. We are sending them without having tonnage enough to keep them supplied. We are literally risking the life of our boys on the assumption that America will be able to provide the minimum tonnage required for their maintenance."

Determination and energy once again brought success.

During the battle we had commenced bombarding Paris from near Laon with a gun having a range of 75 miles. This gun was a marvellous product of technical skill and science, a masterpiece of the firm of Krupp and its director, Rausenberger. The bombardment made a great impression on Paris, and on all France. Part of the population left the capital, and so increased the alarm caused by our successes.

The same effect was intended to be produced by the great activity displayed by our airmen.

III

The operations designed to broaden the front of our attack and improve our strategical position were carried out at the end of March and early in April.

On the 6th April the 7th Army attacked on the left bank of the Oise from Chauny and La Fère in the direction of Coucy la Ville, and also further south. It pushed the French back across the Oise–Aisne Canal, and so gave more security to the long south flank of the 18th Army.

The 17th Army had already attacked in the last days of March in the direction of Arras, making its principal effort on the north bank of the Scarpe. It was to capture the decisive heights east and north of Arras ; the next day the 6th Army was to prolong the attack from about Lens and carry the high ground in that area. I attached the greatest importance to both these attacks. To have the high ground in our possession was bound to be decisive in any fighting in the plain of the Lys.

In spite of employing extraordinary masses of artillery and ammunition, the attack of the 17th Army on both banks of the Scarpe was a failure ; it fought under an unlucky star. Only the 12th Division, under General Lequis, made good progress

REFERENCE

━━━━━ German line before 9/4/18.
●●●●● ,, ,, evening of 9/4/18.
ⅹⅹⅹⅹⅹ ,, ,, 11/4/18.

▬▬▬▬ Final German line.

➤ German attacks.

1:350000

Fig. 32. The Battle of Armentières and Kemmel Hill 1918.

605

south of the stream ; but this was not enough to influence the whole operation. Apparently the artillery had not been sufficiently effective. G.H.Q. now abandoned the attack by the south wing of the 6th Army. It decided to strike in the plain of the Lys between Armentières and La Bassée, as had been proposed by Crown Prince Rupprecht for the main operation. The weather had been dry, and the English had greatly reduced their numbers in the plain of the Lys, as well as in front of Ypres.

The attack was remarkably carefully planned by the 6th Army. General von Quast and his Chief of Staff, Lieutenant-Colonel Lentz, were untiring and had arranged everything in the same manner as had been done for the 21st March. In spite of having but few men available for work everything had progressed so well that the attack could be arranged to begin on the 9th April. I was glad of this. The sooner it could take place the more likely was it to surprise the Portuguese in the plain of the Lys.

I myself visited the 55th Corps Headquarters in the 6th Army as late as the 7th April, and received the impression that we could keep to the time proposed. In order to go over all the preliminary artillery work, Colonel Bruchmüller had been sent to the 6th Army. As early as July, 1917, he had arranged the employment of the artillery in the break-through in East Galicia, and at the time of the attack in March he was Artillery General at the 18th Army Headquarters. His great knowledge and capacity, his devotion to his profession and his arm, and his military enthusiasm marked him out as one of the most prominent soldiers of this war. His suggestions had already formed the groundwork for the employment of the artillery on the 21st March. The artillery of the 18th Army was completely imbued with his spirit. This, added to the fact that it struck the weakest point in the enemy's line, contributed greatly to the fine success of that army. The 17th Army, which certainly had the strongest enemy in front of it, worked on similar principles, but the vitalizing energy which emanated from Colonel Bruchmüller was lacking. This is another instance of the decisive influence of personality on the course of events in war, as in life generally. G.H.Q. had not only to reckon with the enemy, but also with the personal qualities of the men who were striving for the same object with the same devotion.

Colonel Bruchmüller inspected the preliminary arrangements and reported that all was in order. On the morning of the 9th April the attack at first went very well. The reports which came in up till noon were favourable. This was a different birthday to the one I had passed the year before, the day of the heavy defeat at Arras. His Majesty listened to the report on the military situation at Avesnes and stayed to lunch. He remembered me in a few words, and also my two dead sons, and presented me with an iron statuette of himself by Betzner. There were many things which formed a barrier between me and His Majesty; our characters were too different. He was my Imperial Master and I served him, and my country in his person, with the most loyal devotion. The statuette will remain a sacred memento of my Emperor and Supreme Commander who loved his soldiers, desired only the best for his country and his people, and whose whole inmost nature was averse to war—a man whose nature was typical of the German of post-Bismarckian times. The monarch on whom such enormous responsibility lay did not, like his Imperial grandfather, find men like Roon and Bismarck, who were resolved in times of stress to demand from the country everything needed for the prosecution of the war. That is what proved fatal to the Emperor and the country in this war.

In the afternoon the attack seemed to progress more slowly. The ground was still soft in places and this made it very difficult to bridge the enemy's trench-system. The direction of the roads was not favourable to that of our attack, and the detachments of tanks we had employed had proved a hindrance. It took a long time to get up guns and ammunition. The country was close, and this enabled the enemy's machine-gun posts to delay our infantry considerably. In the evening we were advancing towards Armentières, had reached the Lys and were approaching the Lawe. In the direction of Béthune we made little progress. On the left, at Givenchy and Festubert, we were held up. The result was not satisfactory.

On the 10th April the attack continued, but it only gained sufficient ground towards Armentières and across the Lys immediately above Armentières. Towards Estaires we did not penetrate far enough, but stuck fast in the Lys position ; towards the Lawe also, our progress was but slight.

The enemy's machine-guns continued to give our infantry much trouble ; it should have grappled with them more vigorously, as a General Staff Officer told me who had been sent up. But often it wasted time looking for food. The divisions fighting on this front were not " attack divisions " in the same sense as those that had gone into action on the 21st March. But on other battle-fields the trench divisions did as good work as the so-called attack divisions.

On the 11th April we took Armentières. Towards Bailleul the rate of advance was better ; Merville also fell. On the previous day the left wing of the 4th Army had started, and retaken Messines which had been lost on the 7th June the year before.

The objective of the further attack by the 4th and 6th Armies of Crown Prince Rupprecht's Group was the high ground which bounds the Lys valley on the north. Unfortunately we had been unable to hold on to it in the autumn of 1914. It begins at Mount Kemmel, which affords a distant view to the east, and ends at Cassel. The possession of these heights would bring about the evacuation of the Yser position to the north.

After the 12th April the impetus of the 6th Army began to fall off, while the 4th gradually gained more and more ground. The capture of Mount Kemmel on the 25th marked the climax of the fighting. More and more French divisions arrived in front of the 4th Army. Further attacks promised no success.

As the attack on Mount Kemmel progressed, the English, who were east of Ypres were gradually drawn back toward the town. A blow by the 4th Army in the direction of Langemarck was too late.

South of Mount Kemmel Bailleul had also fallen into our hands, but further south the 6th Army had made no more progress.

The Offensive in the West, 1918

The results of the battle of the 21st March had caused General Foch to be appointed Commander-in-Chief of the Entente. In order to hold up the first great penetration the English reserves were concentrated in front of our 17th and 2nd Armies while French divisions from the Aisne–Verdun front opposed the 18th Army. The attacks by the 4th and 6th Armies caused General Foch to move his reserves still further to the north. His attempts to recapture Mount Kemmel were unsuccessful. In view of the enemy's strength G.H.Q. now checked the attack.

As is the case whenever the front becomes stable during the actual progress of fighting, the situation of the 4th and especially the 6th Armies in the plain of the Lys was difficult. The same care was bestowed on strengthening the front lines, completing communications with the rear, withdrawal into rest of all troops that could be spared, perfecting training and discipline, as had been done at the end of the great battle between Croisilles and La Fère.

IV

By the end of April the offensive begun on the 21st March had come to an end. Local attempts at improving our positions and counter-attacks by the enemy prolonged the fighting into May. The main centres were Mount Kemmel and Bailleul, Albert, and the country south of the Somme as far as the Luce.

We had achieved great successes, which we must not allow later events to make us forget. We had defeated the English Army. Only a few British divisions were still intact. Of the 59 English divisions, 53 had been engaged, 25 of them several times. The French had been obliged to engage nearly half their divisions. The enemy had lost large quantities of stores. Italian troops appeared in the Argonne, while the English and French troops that went to Italy the previous autumn stayed there. In Macedonia, English troops were relieved by Greeks.

How much the Americans had got across by April we did not know. In the middle of the month, between St. Mihiel and the

Moselle, the first more important engagements took place against United States troops, who had already been a long time in France. The individual American fought well ; but our success had nevertheless been easy.

There was a lull in the submarine activity, but enterprises by the English Navy against the submarine bases of Ostend and Zeebrugge proved how galling it had been. It was uncommonly difficult to estimate its probable influence on the food supply of England and on the transport of the Americans to France. From our previous experience of the submarine war I expected strong forces of Americans to come. But the rapidity with which they actually did arrive proved surprising. General von Cramon, the German Military Representative at the Austro-Hungarian Headquarters, often called me up, and asked me to insist on the sinking of American troopships ; public opinion in Austria–Hungary demanded it. Admiral von Holtzendorff could only reply that everything was being done to reduce enemy tonnage and to sink troopships. It was not possible to direct the submarines against troopships exclusively. They could approach the coasts of Europe anywhere between the north of England and Gibraltar, a front of some fourteen hundred nautical miles. It was impossible effectively to close this area by means of submarines. We could only have concentrated them on certain routes ; but whether the troopships would choose the same routes at the same time was the question. As soon as the enemy heard of submarines anywhere, he could always send the ships fresh orders by wireless and unload at another port. It was, therefore, not certain that by this method we should meet with a sufficient number of troopships. The destruction of the enemy's freight tonnage would then have been undertaken only spasmodically, and the process would have suffered a distinct set-back. In that way the submarine war would have become diverted from its original object. The submarine war against commerce was therefore continued with all the vigour possible. According to the information available, the enemy's remaining tonnage and his food supply were so reduced that the hope of attaining our object by this means was justified. The shortage of cargo space, at any rate, was established.

The suspension of our offensive had, of course, the most far-reaching results. The enemy recovered at the same time as ourselves. Owing to lack of drafts our losses made themselves unpleasantly felt. In April I again approached the War Ministry with the request that the withdrawal of exempted men from munition work might be carried out more strictly.

The only increase in drafts from home that I received for the future was furnished by prisoners of war returned from Russia. General Headquarters now fell back on its own reserves of men, and prepared its own drafts from the troops of the Eastern Army and Rumania, as well as from among the technical arms and line of communication troops. But these could not suffice unless the Government released the exempted men and took energetic action against deserters and shirkers.

Our troops had fought well; but the fact that certain divisions had obviously failed to show any inclination to attack in the plain of the Lys gave food for thought. However, in that low-lying, intersected country it had been so difficult to arrange proper artillery support that this phenomenon did not cause grave anxiety. On the other hand, the way in which the troops stopped round captured food supplies, while individuals stayed behind to search houses and farms for food, was a serious matter. This impaired our chances of success and showed poor discipline. But it was equally serious that both our young company commanders and our senior officers did not feel strong enough to take disciplinary action, and exercise enough authority to enable them to lead their men forward without delay. The absence of our old peace-trained corps of officers was most severely felt. They had been the repository of the moral strength of the Army. In addition, during the first half of the war the Reichstag had made the penal laws more lenient. The commanders responsible for maintaining discipline were deprived of their most effective punishment, in that a sentence of " close arrest " no longer involved being tied up to a fixed object. No doubt this punishment was extraordinarily severe, and its execution should not be left to the juvenile and inexperienced company commanders, but to abolish it altogether was fatal. The mitigation may have been justifiable at the time, but now it proved disastrous. The frequent declarations of amnesty also had a bad influence on the men. The Entente no doubt achieved more than we did with their considerably more severe punishments. This historic fact is well established.

Other evils in connection with the administration of justice were also due to the long war. The judges had come to regard military offences with a leniency which was often incomprehensible. A contributory cause of this was that the cases which had occurred at the front were not dealt with immediately by the unit, but further in rear in quite different circumstances and after a certain time had elapsed. It should always have been remembered that there were many men in the Army who deserved no mercy whatever; of this the numerous deserters and skrimshankers are a melancholy proof. These people required severe punishment; that was demanded by the distress of our country, but also by consideration for those who were well conducted and brave. Thank God, the latter were always in the vast majority. If one of these men forgot himself, the confirming officer always had it in his power by delaying punishment to make sufficient allowance for a special case. Many offences were committed in order to escape regimental duty and fighting by undergoing punishment. We eventually took to forming punishment companies, which were employed on work in the front trenches. That is a sad chapter! I talked it over with the War Minister. He is responsible for the administration of justice in the Army; General Headquarters had nothing to do with it. Even in dealing with the Army Commanders all I could do was to point out and emphasize that the maintenance of discipline was the first essential. The commanding officers had to be instructed as to the powers and means of dispensing justice at their disposal. All Army Commanders were convinced of the iron necessity of exerting their influence accordingly. With that, all that could be done from outside was done; it now became the duty of the troops to display the strength required to keep their dis-

cipline unimpaired. Here again all depended upon the officer.
And if the discipline in units became slack, the commanders
are partly to blame.

During this time I had many conversations with officers of all
ranks on the training grounds, and they all complained of
the tired and discontented spirit which was being brought
into the Army from home. The leave men had been exposed
to the influence of agitators, and the new drafts had a bad
influence on discipline. All this was lowering the fighting value
of the Army. Among a number of drafts very serious irregu-
larities had occurred, particularly among those from Bavaria and
the East. There were also strong complaints about the spirit
of the men trained at the Belgian training camp of Beverloo.
The units attached all the more importance to getting back,
to the greatest possible extent, men who had already served in
their ranks and who belonged to them territorially. As far as
possible I met their wishes, but could not always get it done.
Afterwards I heard that somebody in an office at home had
been systematically opposing these measures. There were
those who were working to corrupt the Army.

I repeatedly spoke about the spirit of the people at home with
the authorities concerned. In these days I was for the first
time met with the reply that men were also returning from the
Army discontented and tired of the war. They seemed surprised
at this ; but at some time or other the Army was bound to echo
back what was so constantly being shouted at it from home ;
every part of the Army at the front was bearing heavy burdens,
heavier by far than ever the people at home did. The man
who joined the Army after being embittered and worked on by
agitators at home, and then had to suffer great hardships, could
not help causing more ill-feeling when he got home again. But,
in spite of these disintegrating influences, and in spite of the
decay of discipline, the mass of the Army was enthusiastically
confident of victory. It has always been an article of my creed
that Army and people have but one body and one soul, and that
the Army cannot remain sound for ever if the nation is diseased
Really grave symptoms in the Field Army still came to my know

ledge but seldom, as before. As a whole, it was still orderly and disciplined and, after all, it had beaten the enemy. I hoped that the sense of duty and determination of the Army were still strong enough to overcome the numerous adverse influences. The loss of many officers of senior and medium rank during the last actions was bound to make matters worse, as the very young new officers suffered from their natural defects. It was much the same as regards experienced non-commissioned officers. We had reached such a pitch that before an action units detailed a reserve of officers, who did not take part in the fighting, in order that there might be some leaders left at the end of it.

It was necessary to instruct the troops according to the tactical lessons learned in the latest fighting. These were, more extended formations for infantry, greater importance to be attached to storm-troop tactics, better co-operation between groups and companion arms, and between infantry and artillery.

The 28th Division and detachments of the 3rd Jäger Battalion, troops that had had a particularly thorough tactical training, were moved to the neighbourhood of Avesnes. The details were discussed and practised with them, and then demonstrated to a large number of senior officers, including most of the Army Commanders and many Corps Commanders. In this way recent experience was quickly placed within reach of the whole Army.

On all occasions I emphasized the need of not forgetting the necessary formation for defence, and of recognizing the moment when the attack must be stopped and the defence resumed. This must be felt by the systematic hardening of the enemy's resistance.

In arranging for further operations there was no time to lose. The initiative which we had seized on the Western Front must be kept, and the first great blow must be followed by a second as soon as possible.

The movement of the enormous quantities of material employed in attack, the supply of ammunition and formation of dumps, the concentration of the divisions, and, not least, the utilization of the experience gained in the last attack, all these things and many others took time. That was a disadvantage, but with the forces actually available, it could not be altered.

The most favourable operation in itself was to continue the attack on the English Army at Ypres and Bailleul ; but on that front the enemy was now so strong in numbers that it was impossible, even with rested troops. Before we could attack here again the enemy must become weaker, and our communications must be improved. Further south conditions were similar. Besides, the Somme area afforded too little cover for the necessary preliminary work. In front of the 7th and 1st Armies the enemy was weak. Troops had been sent from here to Ypres, and replaced by tired English divisions. The strong positions in the hills certainly looked difficult to attack. But if our own artillery had done its work well, only the difficulties of the ground would remain to be dealt with. They were undoubtedly considerable, but easier to overcome than those we surmounted on the Italian frontier on the 24th of October, 1917. Early in April the Group of the German Crown Prince was directed to submit a plan for an attack between Pinon and Rheims.

At the same time, General Headquarters had to determine what troops were to make this attack. It would be necessary to employ troops that had already taken part in the March attack, but had since then been rested and trained. Before the end of May these divisions would not be fresh and fit to attack ; that was obvious. But the preparations would take as long as that. We dare not risk failure, which would have taken the form of great losses, by undue haste. I could not act according to my wishes and hopes, but must simply deal with the facts as they actually were. It was obvious that all unnecessary loss of time must be avoided. ·

During the discussions with the Group of the German Crown Prince and the 18th, 7th and 1st Armies, the following operations were decided upon, and their feasibility was established :

1. Attack by the 7th and 1st Armies from the line Anizy (south-west of Laon)–south of Berry-au-Bac, in the direction of Soissons–Fismes–Rheims.

2. Prolongation of the attacks, to the right across the Ailette towards the Oise, and to the left as far as Rheims.

3. Attack by the 18th Army west of the Oise, with its principal effort towards Compiègne.

A simultaneous attack on so broad a front was impossible, as a part of the artillery employed in the attack on the 21st of March had to remain for defence with the Group of Crown Prince Rupprecht.

How far the attack would take us could not be foretold. I hoped it would lead to such heavy drain on the reserves of the enemy as would enable us to resume the attack in Flanders.

The Group of Crown Prince Rupprecht was to remain purely on the defensive, although it was also to make preparations for a real attack in Flanders, and, by way of a feint, along its whole front. It was to be expected that in the coming period of rest its divisions, which had suffered and become reduced in the fighting in March and April, would recover and increase again by getting back men who had been wounded, and by the arrival of something in the shape of drafts. Should the enemy be obliged to employ a considerable force against the Group of the German Crown Prince, a continuation of the offensive in Flanders would be the proper operation.

On other parts of the Western Front also, where it was not intended to attack, preparations were to be continued.

It was obvious that all troops who now found themselves in new positions must first of all prepare them for defence.

All armies were specially instructed to devote particular care to men and horses behind the line. Troops in the line could, of course, not be spared as much as I should have wished. Those in the new positions had a hard time ; but the enemy was no better off, although in many places, particularly as regards our troops on the old Somme battle-field, his billets were better than ours. That was unavoidable. But we tried to make up for it by bombarding many places with long-range guns and bombing. On the quiet fronts, from the 7th Army to the Swiss frontier, our units recovered in their positions, and found time to carry out battalion and regimental training in the infantry, and battery training in the artillery. In addition to improvement in discipline, much attention was paid to vigorous training in rear of the whole Army, and in many parts of the actual front.

The equipment of the troops was completed. Each infantry company, which had hitherto had four light machine guns, now received a fifth, as well as improved rifle-grenades. Machine guns were issued to supply columns and transport, as a protection against aircraft, and the equipment of the artillery with them was gradually completed.

The first anti-tank rifles came in ; they were effective, but unfortunately very heavy and took two men to work them ; so that meant the loss of one rifleman.

The men's rations were sufficient, but very inferior to those of the enemy. Grazing turned out to be favourable ; the horses found enough to eat and gained strength, but there was not much corn. Health had so far been good. The first cases of influenza appeared, but the medical officers classified them as slight.

V

During the great events in the West, there had been a lull on the Italian and Macedonian Fronts. They were merely a prolongation of the Western Front and formed the protection of our flanks, the Macedonian Front at the same time protecting the flank of Austria–Hungary. The assistance we received from the Austro–Hungarian artillery in the West was, owing to its exiguous supply of ammunition, insignificant. It returned after it had fired it off.

The situation of the Austro–Hungarian Army in Italy had improved, inasmuch as several hundred thousand prisoners of war had rejoined it from Russia. The Army had thus been strengthened and felt equal to making an attack on the Italians. General von Arz had sent officers to witness our attacks, and was kept informed of our tactical experiences. He intended to assume the offensive in the first half of June, that is to say, soon after our attack on the Chemin des Dames. Thus, at the end of May and in the beginning of June there was to be a great combined effort against the Entente.

It would now have been possible to reinforce the German Army in the West by a few Austro–Hungarian divisions, if the attack in Italy had been given up. But their fighting capacity could not be considered sufficient for employment on the Western Front, and as long as the Austro–Hungarian General Head-quarters at Baden was honestly working for an offensive in Italy, they could not be better employed. A victory in Italy would relieve us just as much as it had done in the autumn of 1917 ; at the best it would draw off a part of the new American formations. This would be of more service than a mere reinforcement of the Western Front by divisions of poor quality. If the attack in Italy should prove unsuccessful, it would still be possible to send a direct reinforcement to the West.

The food situation of Austria and the Austro–Hungarian Army was uncommonly serious. She had received her share of the Rumanian supply in advance and used it up, and was now extracting all she could get hold of from the occupied portions of the Ukraine, needless to say, without any consideration. But even this did not suffice and early in May Austria, being in great need, seized grain belonging to Germany which was being sent to us from Rumania, while it was in transit through the Dual Monarchy. As we had already given help in February, this high-handed action aroused considerable astonishment and indignation. But indignation was no use ; we had to help again, which was the more annoying, as the horses on the Western Front depended for their meagre corn ration on the Rumanian supply.

The Macedonian Front continued inactive. The Bulgarian Army had time for rest and training. But it could not be denied that since about March its spirit had visibly deteriorated, owing to bad food and clothing. The irritation against Germany was cleverly fomented by hostile propaganda and by Bulgarians who favoured the Entente. The peace of Bucharest and the withdrawal of a few German formations to the West added fresh fuel to it. Cases of mutiny showed how far the process of corrosion had gone. General Headquarters and the Group Headquarters of General von Scholtz did all they could to help and to influence the Bulgarians. We gave them food, and the Prussian War Minister provided clothing. We also complied with the wishes of Crown Prince Boris, who had visited the Western Front, and had asked for the removal of sundry batteries to be delayed.

We impressed on the Bulgarian Headquarters the need for holding reserves ready. It had put too many troops in the front line and kept back too few complete formations. Gradually, General Jekoff decided to follow our advice. This was facilitated by transferring the troops in the Dobrudja to the Macedonian Front, which, however, proceeded very slowly. On the enemy's side there now appeared Royal Greek troops, in addition to the Venizelists.

In Palestine the English had, in March, attacked across the Jordan, just north of the Red Sea, with the obvious intention of working round the left wing of the Turkish Army Group posted there, and of driving it off the Damascus railway. The English attack gained ground at first, but ended in defeat, and they were driven back to the west bank of the Jordan. Unfortunately General von Liman, who had in the meantime taken over in Palestine from General von Falkenhayn, had not enough troops to follow up. At the end of April the English repeated their attack, with the same result. After the hot weather, which was now beginning, its continuation was to be expected, but by that time I hoped that the reinforcement of the Palestine Front, promised by Enver, would have been effected. In Mesopotamia English troops were pushing on towards Mosul and obtaining a firm footing in North Persia, replacing the Russians who had dispersed.

In Armenia the Turks had begun their advance at the end of February. By the end of March they had cleared the Russians out of their territory, and by the end of April they had occupied the region of Kars and Batum allotted to them in the peace of Brest. But this was not the limit of their ambition; they contemplated extending their influence in the Caucasus. For this purpose they developed active propaganda among the Mohammedan population of Azerbaian, where Enver's brother Nuri also appeared, in order to raise new formations. At the same time Turkey opened negotiations with the Russian Republics of Georgia, Azerbaian and Armenia, which were in process of formation on the south side of the Caucasus. By order of the German Imperial Government General von Lossow went from Constantinople to attend these negotiations.

In themselves, I was able to assent to any Turkish measures which were of service to the general scheme of the war. But they must not be allowed to divert Turkey from her proper military rôle, nor impede our supply of raw materials from the Caucasus, from which we anticipated very considerable relief. Enver's task was to fight England, in the first place on the Palestine Front, as I pointed out to him repeatedly in clearly-worded telegrams. And now there was an opportunity of striking at the English in North Persia. This was made more favourable by the railway line from Batum via Tiflis to Tabriz. In North Persia it was possible for the Turks to oppose the English with superior numbers. It would have been a real service to have raised the inhabitants of Azerbaian against them ; and I should gladly have supported every effort directed to that end. But Enver and the Turkish Government thought less of fighting England than of their Pan-Islamic aims in the Caucasus. And with these they combined a very material object, namely, the lucrative exploitation of the raw materials to be obtained there. That this would not suit Germany's war industry everyone knew who was acquainted with Turkish business methods. In this way we came in conflict with Turkish policy.

During the negotiations at Batum the representatives of the Georgian Republic had approached General von Lossow with a request for the protection of the German Empire. In 1915 and 1916 we had employed Georgian volunteers in Armenia, though without success. In so doing we had come in contact with influential Georgians. I could only welcome this connection, as also Georgia's request for the protection of the German Empire. We thus acquired a means of securing the raw materials of the Caucasus independently of Turkey, and of getting a hold on the working of the Tiflis railway. The latter was of decisive importance in any fighting in North Persia, and would give better results under a management influenced by

Fig. 33. The Turkish Advance in Armenia.

us than under one in which the Turks shared. Finally, we must endeavour to reinforce ourselves by raising Georgian troops, who might be used against England. Besides, we could never tell what difficulties we might have to meet from the Volunteer Army commanded by General Alexeieff on the north of the Caucasus. I therefore requested that the Imperial Chancellor would take Georgia's application into consideration.

For other reasons also, the Government was inclined to a policy of encouraging Georgia. It was afraid of difficulties that might arise out of Turkey's attitude towards Bolshevik Russia. The Imperial Chancellor strongly condemned the violent measures adopted by the Turks against the Christian Armenians. They were indeed a grave blunder, and nothing could justify them. So when the Georgian representatives came to Berlin with General von Lossow in June, the Government did not give them an uncompromising refusal.

In the Ukraine, the German troops had, after taking Kieff on the 1st March, continued their advance more slowly. Odessa had fallen on the 12th, after a slight resistance. In this operation German troops, which had advanced through Moldavia after the conclusion of the preliminary peace with Rumania on the 7th March, had co-operated. In the succeeding period G.H.Q. had to bear in mind the objects for which the occupation of the Ukraine had been undertaken, and to carry the advance no further than those objects necessitated.

The Ukraine had asked our help. We ourselves, and Austria and her army even more so, needed corn; the country could not therefore be allowed to become a prey, and a source of strength, to Bolshevism. We had to support it sufficiently to enable it to be useful to us.

We had occupied the principal grain district after the capture of Kharkoff on the 8th April. The Commander-in-Chief in the East now found that the railways could not be worked without the coal of the Donetz Basin. So, willy-nilly, we had to agree to occupy this part of the Ukraine as well, and to advance our lines as far as Rostoff which was reached at the beginning of May. In spite of this, we were obliged at first to send very considerable quantities of coal from Germany to the Ukraine; this import, however, decreased when more coal was procurable locally.

Besides the railway, we also needed secure water-transport from the Black Sea ports to Braila. The Russian Black Sea Fleet had caused us difficulties at Odessa, Nicolaieff, and Cherson. Which Government it was under was doubtful; in any event, it did not carry out the conditions of the peace of Brest. In

Sebastopol it would always be a danger to navigation, so at the end of April we occupied the Crimea. Part of the Russian Fleet escaped to Novorossisk. It was intended to make use of the ships captured in Sebastopol so far as we could provide crews for them.

The occupation of this extensive territory had led to fresh conflicts with Bolshevik bands and troops. In most cases they were driven off without trouble. After the advance was stopped the Commander-in-Chief in the East had agreed upon a line of demarcation with the Soviet Government. It was significant of this Government that it often accused our troops of not respecting this line, while we had reports from our Commander-in-Chief that Bolshevik bands had raided the territory which our troops were to protect. Unfortunately the Foreign Office appeared to believe Bolshevik lies sooner than our statements.

After a good deal of discussion with the Austrian Headquarters at Baden our respective spheres of interest in the Ukraine were settled. On this, the Quartermaster-General effected an agreement with Austria-Hungary, and the exploitation of the supplies was regulated. Afterwards, however, in view of the way Austria-Hungary had been seizing our supplies, this agreement had to be modified, so that we undertook the collecting of supplies in the whole of the Ukraine as well as their distribution. This was only an expedient, unfortunately a necessary one, in order to establish a practical working system.

The German military and civil authorities found ample scope for their activities. I followed everything with great attention, since G.H.Q. was principally interested in the result. Field-Marshal von Eichhorn had taken over the Army Group at Kieff; the Government was represented by Ambassador von Mumm. The collection of supplies was in the hands of the Imperial Economic Office. A more confused and motley organization it was impossible to imagine, and it was all due to Berlin's unfortunate attitude towards " Militarism," as well as to its own " Bureaucracy " and hide-bound methods.

As was to be expected, the new Government of the Ukraine had proved incapable either of settling the unrest in the country or of delivering grain to us. This Government disappeared from the scene and Hetman Skropadsky assumed control.

Whilst at the end of April and early in May I was occupied with important work connected with the operations in the West, I received through the Emperor's Military Cabinet a telegram from the Imperial Chancellor to the Emperor, complaining in strong terms of the " Militarist " attitude of the Group Headquarters at Kieff and requesting His Majesty to remedy it. The Military Cabinet had informed the Imperial Chancellor that His Majesty proposed that in the first instance the whole episode should be investigated by means of a joint inquiry by the authorities concerned. I looked forward to this with satisfaction, for I was firmly convinced that by probing the matter to the bottom and eliminating all gossip and prejudice, we should once more find there was nothing in the whole affair. In this case we did not even reach the conference stage, for it was soon made clear that the Field-Marshal and the Ambassador had personally worked well together. So, as it happened, " Militarism " had had nothing to do with it. What actually occurred was that during the course of events a General had dealt somewhat harshly with a former member of the Government, whose conduct had betrayed a highly doubtful attitude towards German interests. But the whole business left a bitter taste behind. I only mention this incident because it was characteristic of the feeling in Berlin. They were always ready there to go against, instead of with, us. It was thought more important to consider certain political interests than practical requirements, even though the latter, like Field-Marshal von Eichhorn's care for agriculture, was of the greatest consequence to our existence. It was particularly regrettable that, without hearing the other side, the War Minister had sided with the Government.

Hetman Skropadsky turned out to be a man with whom it was possible to work well. He was determined to maintain order in the country, and to meet us as far as possible. I made his acquaintance later and formed a very good impression of him. He was never superficial, but got to the bottom of everything.

G.H.Q. could not be otherwise than satisfied with the change of Government at Kieff, as it was favourable to the prosecution of the war. I anticipated being able to increase our armies and our food-supply ; the raising of new Ukrainian formations was actually commenced. This, of course, required time and brought us no immediate relief. The German troops which were in the Ukraine were urgently needed by the Army Group for protection against the Bolsheviks and securing the economic exploitation of the country. Whenever we wanted to reduce them it complained that they were not strong enough.

In the Ukraine the Imperial Economic Office pursued a peace-time policy which anticipated a state of affairs that did not yet exist ; to that no one could object, provided that with the more limited economic policy the purely military motive, for which I pleaded, was not thereby excluded. In her need, Austria-Hungary had taken drastic measures, and, although she did not get anything like what Count Czernin had stated to be necessary early in February, the supplies she drew from the Ukraine, combined with our assistance, undoubtedly saved Austria and her Army from starvation. Only the most urgent needs, however, were satisfied, and even then we did not receive the bread-corn and forage so urgently required to revive the strength of our people at home. Still, the Ukraine did help Germany. In the summer of 1918 it supplied us with meat, and thus the scanty meat-ration we had was made possible without encroaching upon our own live-stock reserves and those of the occupied territories. The Army was also able to get horses in great numbers ; without them warfare would have been altogether impossible, for if Germany had been obliged to raise these horses our own agriculture would have been hard hit. We also obtained raw materials of all kinds from the Ukraine.

The hope that the corn of the Ukraine would prove to be an economic weapon which would improve our position in regard to the neutrals, and would bring us that further economic relief which was so important for maintaining our warlike capacity, had soon to be abandoned.

By occupying the Ukraine we had considerably weakened the

military policy of the Soviet Government. We also established connection with many representatives of nationalistic tendencies of Great Russia, and with the Don Cossacks, whom we could have made use of to combat Bolshevism if the Government had agreed to do so.

On the Great Russian Front of the Commander-in-Chief in the East, from the Pripet to the Gulf of Finland, no change had occurred since the 3rd March.

Finland had risen, and urgently required immediate help. Arms alone were not enough. The Soviet Government made no preparations to withdraw its troops from Finland. The moment when that country would receive assistance from England was approaching.

In order to prevent the formation of another Eastern Front, and to increase our military strength, we complied with Finland's request for troops. General von Mannerheim also supported the dispatch of German troops. He did not want them too soon, nor in too great strength, so that his Finns might have some fighting to do and thereby gain confidence. Those were sound military ideas.

With the consent of the Imperial Government, which we always obtained, we first established an advanced base in the Aaland Islands, because at that time it appeared necessary to land in the Gulf of Bothnia. As only a short time before, Sweden had also landed troops on the Islands, we had to enter into special negotiations with that country which proceeded without difficulty. Later on, Sweden withdrew her troops and we ourselves abandoned the Islands, soon after G.H.Q. had decided to land the expedition at Hangö.

Liaison with General von Mannerheim was maintained by Major Crantz whom I had sent to the Finnish Headquarters, where he settled how the German troops were to be employed. Co-operation with General von Mannerheim was always satisfactory and marked by mutual confidence.

The Baltic Division had been formed at Danzig under General Count von der Goltz ; it consisted of three battalions of Jäger, three regiments of Mounted Rifles, and a few batteries. It

The Offensive in the West, 1918

landed at Hangö early in April while General von Mannerheim with the Finnish White Guards, who had been partly armed by us, was north-west of Tammerfors with his back to Vasa. The Finnish Jäger battalion had been sent to him. Being composed of picked men, it formed an excellent training school for the new Finnish officers.

While General von Mannerheim advanced via Tammerfors, the Baltic Division moved north-east towards Tavastehus. In co-operation with the fleet, it occupied Helsingfors on the

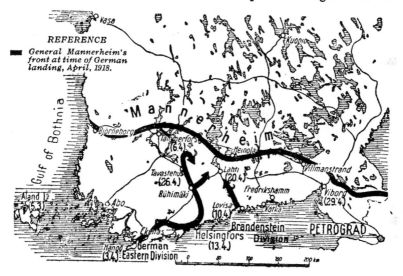

Fig. 34. The Campaign in Finland. 1918.

13th April, with a weak force; the Commander-in-Chief in the East landed a weak detachment under Colonel von Brandenstein at Lovisa and Kotka, east of Helsingfors. This detachment marched north in order to block the retreat of the Red Guards, who were near Tavastehus, at Lahti. In a concentric attack they were completely surrounded after heavy fighting at the end of April and forced to surrender. Finland was thus liberated.

In the meantime Viborg had been occupied from the north by the White Guards; strategically this was a good move; what its actual result would have been, if the decision had not taken place further west, could not be foreseen, owing to the uncertain fighting value of the opposing forces and the support of the Bolsheviks from Russia. The tactical victory and the prompt liberation of Finland were achieved on the field of Lahti-Tavastehus by the splendid collaboration of German and Finnish troops. This concluded operations.

We now held positions at Viborg and Narva which would at any time enable us to advance on Petrograd, in order to overthrow the Bolshevik Government or prevent the English from reaching there from Murmansk. From Finland, moreover, the Murmansk Railway was flanked along its whole length, so that England could not undertake any serious attempt on Petrograd. The English expedition which had occupied the Murman Coast was firmly held there. The diversion of the weak Baltic Division, of which the three Jäger Battalions returned to Germany in August, was well worth while. The Finnish Government at once set about organizing the Finnish Army, assisted by German instructors. That we did not achieve more in Finland is mainly owing to our ever vacillating policy. General Count von der Goltz had won universal confidence, even that of the leading politicians, while the representative of the German Government was not so successful. The want of decision in our foreign policy was unfortunately made evident in this sphere also. The Foreign Office adopted no definite plan, and so made no friends in Finland but only offended Germany's faithful adherents.

The many proofs of warm sympathy which I received from Finland after my resignation prove that gratitude still exists in the world. This sympathy touched me all the more because it was not Finnish but purely German interests that took us there. When in February, 1919, the Swedish Government, for no reasons that I could understand, made difficulties about my staying there, a Finnish delegate suddenly appeared at Hessleholmsgard to offer me an asylum in Finland. I was pleased, but of course refused, as I wanted to return to Germany.

Amid the tremendous overwhelming events of this world-wide war the Ukraine and Finland seem mere incidents. Still, I hope that permanent good may result. Both countries will always afford typical examples of the way in which our Government misunderstood the nature of this war up to the end, and treated every problem merely according to the dictates of party politics. In the military sense both countries afforded us for the time being what we expected of them. The formation of a new Eastern Front was prevented, or at least almost indefinitely postponed. We had broken the blockade in the East and it seemed as if we might regain our strength in that way. The position of the Soviet Government was severely shaken, its continued existence seriously threatened.

When at the end of May the German attack in the West was continued, to be followed in the first half of June by an Austro-Hungarian one in Italy, the situation on all fronts was satisfactory. Only the Palestine Front seemed to be a special danger-point.

VI

The second great German attack in France and the attack of the Austro-Hungarian Army in Italy were, in their main features, carried out according to plan.

In the middle of May we commenced to concentrate the troops which were to break through over the Chemin des Dames. The preliminary work was completed up to time. The artillery was disposed according to Colonel Bruchmüller's suggestions, which were also adopted as regards the preparatory artillery fire.

I frequently visited the Army Commanders concerned and was most favourably impressed.

On the 27th May the attack began between Vauxaillon and Sapigneul. Once more it proved a brilliant success. I had thought we should only succeed in reaching the neighbourhood of Soissons and Fismes. By the second and third days these objectives had in places been left far behind. We had gained ground, especially beyond Fismes ; not so much beyond Soissons. It was most regrettable that one Headquarters did not realize the favourable situation at Soissons, and that we did not push

ahead with the same energy as at Fismes, although it would have
been possible. Otherwise our situation would have been considerably better, not only at Soissons, but on the whole front
of the attack. It would have been more than doubtful whether
the French would have held their positions between the Oise and
the Aisne any longer. This was another case where in a few
moments much might have been achieved which was left undone.
The Commander-in-Chief sits and thinks and can make all
preparations, but the execution of his plans is no longer in his
hands. On the battle-field he must make the best of the *fait
accompli.*

The centre of the 7th Army advanced to the south as far as
the Marne. Its left wing and the right of the 1st Army, which
had, as intended, prolonged the attack on the left towards
Rheims, pushed ahead between the Marne and the Vesle towards
the Forest of the Mountain of Rheims, where they soon encountered resistance too stiff to be overcome. The right wing of
the 7th Army gained ground between the Aisne and the Marne,
south-west of Soissons and as far as the eastern edge of the
forest of Villers–Cotterets, and captured Château Thierry·
General Foch concentrated strong reserves south-west of Rheims
and near Soissons, with which he made fruitless counter-attacks
which subsequently extended as far as Château Thierry.

Early in June we stopped our advance. G.H.Q. did not
intend to attack further except between the Aisne and the
Forest of Villers–Cotterets, south-west of Soissons. We wanted
to gain more ground to the westward, on account of the railway
which leads from the Aisne valley east of Soissons into that
of the Vesle, and be in a position to give tactical support to the
attack of the 18th Army on the line Montdidier–Noyon.

In spite of a few unavoidable temporary crises, our troops
remained masters of the situation both in attack and defence.
They proved themselves superior to both the English and the
French, even when their opponents were assisted by Tanks.
At Château Thierry, Americans who had been a long time in
France had bravely attacked our thinly-held fronts ; but they
were unskilfully led, attacked in dense masses, and failed. Here,

too, our men felt themselves superior. Our tactics had proved sound in every way ; our losses, compared with those of the enemy and the large number of prisoners, though in themselves

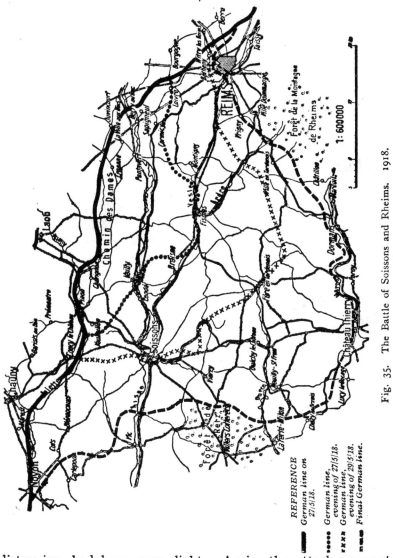

Fig. 35. The Battle of Soissons and Rheims. 1918.

1 : 600000

REFERENCE

German line on 27/5/18.

German line, evening of 27/5/18.

German line, evening of 29/5/18.

Final German line.

distressing, had been very slight. Again, the attack was not broken off early enough at all points. Here and there it was continued where defence was already called for. With a few exceptions the troops had everywhere behaved well and displayed endurance.

On the whole the impression had been very favourable. The group of the German Crown Prince had gained a great tactical victory in the offensive. The enemy had been forced to put in more of his reserves than the troops we had expended. Paris once more received the impression of defeat, and very many inhabitants left the city. In the Session of the Chamber early in June, which I awaited with interest, there was, indeed, no sign of weakening. Clemenceau uttered proud, bold words : " We are now giving ground, but we shall never surrender." " We shall be victorious, if the public authorities are equal to their task." " I fight before Paris, I shall fight in Paris, I shall fight behind Paris." " Remember the fate of Thiers and Gambetta ; I am not longing for the difficult and thankless task of Thiers."

Even after this second great defeat in one year the Entente was not yet ready for peace.

It was a strategical disadvantage to us that we had been unable to take Rheims and get our armies further forward into the hilly country in that region. The supply of the centre of the 7th Army was thereby restricted to the broad gauge railway which leads from the valley of the Aisne, east of Soissons, into that of the Vesle. In order to secure the traffic against all contingencies the construction of a second curve to connect the two valleys further to the eastward was ordered. It was not possible to put in other broad-gauge sections south of the Aisne, as the country was so difficult. From Laon a broad-gauge line ran direct to Soissons via Anizy. The tunnel north of the town, between the Aisne and the Ailette, had been blown up and had to be repaired. One metre-gauge line and sundry light railways led towards the left wing of the 7th Army and the right wing of the 1st, and they afforded great relief ; but they had first to be extended across the two trench systems before they could be connected up to those already in our possession. The unfavourable railway communications threw a great strain on our mechanical transport, which again made the fuel situation serious.

The Offensive in the West, 1918

On the 1st June, as intended, our attack had already been extended to the west as far as the junction of the Ailette and the Aisne. The transfer of the necessary artillery had been carried out smoothly. The fighting took us forward into the trench system which we had abandoned in the Alberic movement of March, 1917.

It was intended that the 18th Army should attack on the 7th June between Montdidier and Noyon, the 7th to attack at the same time south-west of Soissons. At a conference early in June at 18th Army Headquarters I became convinced that

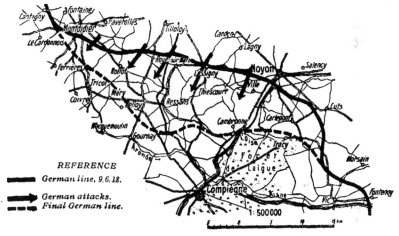

Fig. 36. The Battle of Noyon. June, 1918.

its preliminary artillery work would not be done in time. The arrival of the reinforcing artillery from the 7th Army had been delayed. The attack was, therefore, postponed to the 9th June. This was a drawback, since it thus lost much of its tactical connection with the great action between the Aisne and the Marne, for which a local operation south-west of Soissons could form no complete substitute. The enemy would find the transfer of his reserves facilitated. In spite of these objections I decided for the later date because thorough preparation was essential to success and to keep down casualties.

The attack of the 18th Army began on the 9th and was directed on the right towards Méry, on the left against very strong positions on the high ground just west of the Oise. This time the enemy was prepared but our infantry got through his whole trench system and beyond it, in some places as far as the Aronde.

On the 11th the enemy directed very heavy counter-attacks, particularly against our right at Méry, which gained some ground. They continued throughout the 12th and 13th without result. In consequence of the great accumulation of enemy troops G.H.Q. directed the 18th Army to break off the attack on the 11th, in order to avoid casualties. It was quite evident that the attack commenced in the meantime by the 7th Army south-west of Soissons would not get through.

The action of the 18th Army had not altered the strategical situation brought about by the attack of the 7th Army, nor had it provided any fresh tactical data.

In the middle of June nearly the whole of the new front of the German Crown Prince's group became inactive. Only between the Aisne and the Forest of Villers-Cotterets was there a state of tension, which occasionally broke out into local actions. On both banks of the Ardre, between Rheims and the Marne, the situation was also somewhat unsettled. The captured territory provided us with plentiful resources and eased our food supply.

The attack of the Austro-Hungarian Army in Italy was originally fixed for the 11th June. Owing to the backward state of the preparations it was put off till the 15th. It was to commence with an advance at the Adamello on the West Tyrol Front, so as to distract the attention of the Italian Headquarters in that direction. General von Arz intended to make the main attack between Asiago and the sea in several groups, directed on the Brenta, the Montello, and the lower course of the Piave. In spite of local successes the attack produced no result, and after a few days General von Arz had to make up his mind to withdraw the troops that had pushed across the Piave under General Goiginger. According to the reports I received from Baden the Austro-Hungarian troops had fought well. What causes prevented their success I do not know. I have no means of judging whether it is true that the attack was made on too broad a front, as has been alleged.

The manner in which the failure on the Piave was discussed shortly afterwards in Austria-Hungary, especially in the Hungarian Parliament, was most deplorable. Under very similar circumstances after the Aisne–Champagne battle in 1917, and now in far more difficult ones, the French had maintained a high and dignified demeanour. From Buda-Pest we heard unpleasant speeches, which could only make everyone more depressed. Nobody asked the Hungarian Parliament by what right it uttered this criticism. Had it really done everything to make

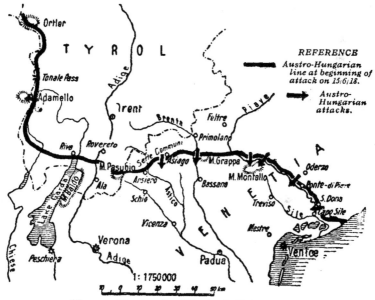

Fig. 37.   The Austrian Offensive in Italy.   1918.

victory possible?   If so it might criticize, but to do so in public and at that time was a mistake. The impression produced by the failure on the Piave was further deepened by events in the Dual Monarchy.

This unsuccessful attack was extremely painful to me. I could no longer hope that relief on the Western Front might be secured in Italy itself. However, in other respects the military situation there remained as before. For the time being the opposing forces balanced each other. A further reinforcement of the Entente Front in France by Italians was not to be feared.

General von Arz was considering the possibility of renewing the attack in the autumn.

I at once proposed to the Allied Headquarters that it should send all its available troops to the Western Front. General von Arz agreed. In this matter he probably had a struggle with his Imperial Master, who disliked sending troops away. After a good deal of pressure the whole reinforcement provided by Austria-Hungary amounted to four divisions. At the outset, only two arrived in July. They were supposed to be good troops, but their condition, particularly as regards ammunition supply, was wretched. They required several weeks' training before they were fit to put in the line in trench-warfare on the Western Front. Late in August and early in September the other two arrived. In the middle of September General von Arz was going to send two more but they had to go to Serbia, as the defection of Bulgaria threatened to lay open Austria's flank, and therefore ours, to the Entente.

Accordingly, the German Army had to continue the battle without anything worth calling help, and with only such resources as G.H.Q. could get together and the home country provide.

On the other portions of the Allied Fronts in Europe there had been practically no fighting, except that west of Lake Ochrida the Austro-Hungarian troops had been driven back north of Berat in June and July.

We now had better hopes of the Bulgarian Army, as its spirit had distinctly improved with the first arrivals of clothing and supplies of food. General von Scholtz fully realized the gravity of the situation, and was always complaining that the Army, ever more deeply involved in party politics, was being played off against Radoslavoff. He would have been glad of more German troops, but as they were needed on the Western Front, he had to do without them in Macedonia. In the event of attack by the enemy, General Headquarters and the Group Headquarters anticipated local retreats. The Bulgarian reserves that had been formed in the meantime were some guarantee against any serious piercing of our line.

The Offensive in the West, 1918

In Palestine local English attacks had failed, and in Mesopotamia those English detachments that had been pushed up to Mosul were again withdrawn ; but, on the other hand, the English appeared to be stronger in Northern Persia and on the southern shore of the Caspian Sea. The Turks were still round Tabriz and close up to Baku.

On the Eastern Front the situation was unchanged, and everything was in suspense.

The contingent that the United States sent to France in April, May and June was, according to the information obtainable, estimated at fifteen divisions. At the moment there might be twenty American divisions in all in France, more than I had believed possible, and not only had our March superiority in the number of the divisions been cancelled, but even the difference in gross numbers was now to our disadvantage, for an American division consists of twelve strong battalions. In those parts of the line where we had hitherto been fighting with divisions which had already been in France some time, we had remained masters of the situation, in spite of our inferiority in numbers.

It was not to be expected that the new formations, which had been hastily brought up and received less training, would fight better than the old divisions. No enemy should be despised, but neither should he be overestimated. How otherwise should we have been able to attack and overcome the Russians in 1914 ? As long as our troops maintained their *moral* they would be able to cope with any enemy, even with the strong American divisions whose nerves were less shaken than those of our men who had been in action continuously for a long time. But the fact that these new American reinforcements could release English and French divisions on quiet sectors weighed heavily in the balance against us   This was of the greatest importance and helps to explain the influence exerted by the American Contingent on the issue of the conflict. It was for this reason that America became the deciding factor in the war.

On June 15th, General Foch had largely spent his reserves, and there was no doubt that no more could be asked of the French Army. From the early summer of 1918 until now, France

637

had disbanded very few battalions. She now drew more deeply on the great reserves of man-power in her colonies than she had done in previous years. It was quite clear that the French would make use of the approaching lull in hostilities to gather up all her strength.

Since the middle of May the English Army had been more or less inactive and its reconstitution must have made great progress, although there is no reason to suppose that it recovered more quickly, even taking the better living conditions into account, than the Army Group of Crown Prince Rupprecht. But the fact that the Entente Armies were far better fed than ours must by no means be left out of account.

Our pro-Flemish propaganda had begun to influence the Belgian Army. Deserters continually came over to us, from whose reports it was clear that, thanks to the Flemish movement, the Belgian Army was becoming more friendly towards us.

Our Army had suffered. Influenza was rampant, and the Army Group of Crown Prince Rupprecht was particularly afflicted. It was a grievous business having to listen every morning to the Chiefs of Staffs' recital of the number of influenza cases, and their complaints about the weakness of their troops if the English attacked again. However, the English were not ready yet. The number of influenza cases diminished, although it often left a greater weakness in its wake than the doctors realized.

The long rest gradually improved the condition of the troops. The battalions of the Crown Prince Rupprecht's Group reached a fairly satisfactory level of strength, not much below the English standard. Only a few divisions remained below strength. The Army Group of the German Crown Prince had, of course, been heavily taxed in the constant fighting; but there were sufficient reserves at hand to make me hopeful that during the lull the battalions might, with few exceptions, be brought up to the French standard.

The battalion strength had been reduced, but was still high enough to allow us to strike one more blow that should make the enemy ready for peace. There was no other way.

The Offensive in the West, 1918

Again and again our thoughts returned to the idea of an offensive in Flanders. Strong English reserves were still assembled here, even after the French divisions had been withdrawn under pressure of the battles with the Army Group of the German Crown Prince. But an offensive at this point still presented too difficult a problem. We had to postpone it.

The bulk of the enemy reserves were on the arc described by the 18th and 7th Armies in the direction of Paris, while the line from Château-Thierry to Verdun was only weakly held. General Headquarters again decided to attack the enemy at his weak point. Accordingly, an attack on both sides of Rheims was planned for the middle of July, whereby the rear communications of the 7th Army between the Aisne and the Marne would be incidentally greatly improved. Immediately following this operation we meant to concentrate artillery, trench mortars and flying squadrons on the Flanders Front, and possibly attack that a fortnight later. There were hopes that if the offensive at Rheims succeeded, there would be a very decisive weakening of the enemy in Flanders.

In order to reduce transport movements to a minimum and accumulate enough artillery for the two offensives, the fifth and sixth guns were in many places reissued to the field artillery from the reserve of guns. For a short time this increased number of guns had to be served by the batteries, although their personnel was not increased for the purpose. Batteries were also transferred from the East.

General Headquarters was in a very difficult position as regards fixing a time for the offensive. By the middle of July the movement of troops and other preparations for the attack on both sides of Rheims would have been completed, but for the sake of the troops I should like to have waited a little longer. At a pinch, however, it would do, and postponement would have been of advantage to the enemy also. So we decided to stand by our time-table, and keep the first days of August in view for the Flanders offensive. The concentration of troops for this purpose necessitated a certain weakening of other fronts, with the result that the 18th Army and the right wing of the 9th, between the Oise and the Aisne, were at times in some danger, while the whole of Crown Prince Rupprecht's Group and the 7th Army, south of the Aisne, were always well supported.

Strong reserves, which had been resting for some time, were behind the Army Group of Crown Prince Rupprecht, while the Army Group of the German Crown Prince was compelled to build up its reserves by withdrawing divisions of the 18th and 7th Armies which were already very tired. The Army Groups of von Gallwitz and Duke Albrecht had to give up rested divisions in exchange for tired ones. It was once more our business to build up the Army and prepare it for the coming offensive. We lived the same life both at and behind the front as we had lived before the offensive of May 27th.

VII

The attack on Rheims was based on sound military principles, and we undertook the operation with the firm conviction that it would succeed. In the recent battles the men of the German Crown Prince's Group fought as well as their militia character led us to expect they would. In all essentials the men had shown themselves superior to the enemy, so long as they were handled carefully and with an eye to their peculiarities and temperament. I gave serious thought to the question whether, in view of the spirit of the Army and the condition of our reserves, it would not be advisable to adopt the defensive. But I finally decided against this policy, because, quite apart from the bad influence it would have on our Allies, I was afraid that the Army would find defensive battles an even greater strain than an offensive, as such a policy would make it easy for the enemy to concentrate his vast resources in war material on any given battle-field. Of the two an offensive makes less demand on the men, and involves no higher losses. The offensive had the incalculable moral advantage that it could not voluntarily be broken off. Further, all weaknesses in an army become much more prominent in the defensive.

The Offensive in the West, 1918

Reports from the Army about the evil influence of the mood prevailing at home and reports from home about the low *moral* of the Army became more frequent. The Army also complained of the effect of enemy propaganda, which was bound to be great, as the men came under its influence even at home. The 4th Army quoted the following instance: The enemy Propaganda had obtained possession of Prince Lichnowsky's pamphlet which, in a manner entirely inexplicable to me, put the whole blame for the outbreak of war on Germany, although His Majesty and the Imperial Chancellor always maintained that the Entente were alone responsible. The Kaiser's words were compared with the corresponding passages of the pamphlet, and denounced as falsehoods. In order to heighten this impression the opinion expressed in a Social Democratic newspaper was appended. That opinion almost coincided with Prince Lichnowsky's, and could be published, to the great injury of the nation, without fear of the consequences. It was no wonder that the man in the trenches did not know what to think, since Prince Lichnowsky was still at large and such views were printed with impunity. I had already begged the Imperial Chancellor, Doctor Michaelis, to take proceedings against Prince Lichnowsky. On the military side Captain von Beerfelde was called to account for disseminating the pamphlet. But as the author remained unmolested, Captain von Beerfelde could not possibly be punished, so I again approached the Imperial Chancellor, and explained to him that legal measures against the Prince had become a matter of military necessity for the sake of our men, who had to be ready to fight, and, if need be, to die for our good cause. I reported in the same sense to His Majesty, but nothing was done. Prince Lichnowsky shares the gruesome distinction of having undermined the discipline of the Army with the Bolshevists and many others.

It was just about this time that Clemenceau spoke the words : " We shall achieve victory if the public authorities are equal to their task."

In France they were equal to it, but how was it with us ? I have given one instance of enemy propaganda which could never have been so effective if public men in our own country had realized the iron necessities of this war.

The Army was literally swamped by enemy propaganda, the serious danger of which was clearly recognized. General Headquarters gave rewards for the surrender of such pamphlets, but this could not prevent them from poisoning the minds of our soldiers before they were delivered up. Unfortunately the enemy propaganda could not be really effectively fought without the help of the Government. Patriotic instruction alone was insufficient.

It was certainly discouraging that our two great attacks had not forced a decision. That they had been victories was obvious. Disillusionment had come ; it was impossible in this world-war to gloss that over. The reason for the falling off in our *moral* was not to be found in that. It lay very much deeper. The evil effect of the disillusionment was doubled by the fact that we could not overcome it in our then state of mind. For the rest, a belief in a favourable issue of the war still prevailed in every quarter.

A decided deterioration in the army's *moral* resulted from the re-enrolment, after long leave, of soldiers returned from captivity in Russia. They introduced a spirit of general insubordination, showing itself particularly in definite refusal to return to the front, thinking that, like the prisoners of war exchanged from England and France, they were under no obligation to fight any longer. In Graudenz it came to very serious disorders.

In Beverloo it was discovered that some hundreds of Alsatians had formed a plot to escape to Holland. The continual drafting of troops from the East compelled me to send the Alsace-Lorrainers back to the West, where they were by no means welcome. Moreover, the greater part of the reserves who were transferred from the special arms showed themselves unwilling to join the infantry. In this many saw themselves confronted with dangers which had been avoided hitherto.

Meanwhile there were very many things affecting the spirit of the troops in the West, already weakened by influenza and depressed by the uniform diet. Stores, captured in our offensives, made it possible for the moment to vary the food rations in some places, but now potatoes began to fail, despite the fact that the preceding year's harvest in Germany had been particularly good.

Among the Bavarian troops the separatist spirit was getting the upper hand. The influence of efforts in this direction, tacitly permitted by the Bavarian Government, made itself felt, and thus increased the success of enemy propaganda. The agitation against the Kaiser and the Crown Prince, and also against the Bavarian royal house, bore its natural fruit. The Bavarian troops gradually came to regard the war as a purely Prussian affair. The Staffs were no longer so eager to employ them as in the earlier years of the war. Only a few divisions fought as well as before.

The homeland itself was completely under the influence of hostile propaganda and of speeches made by enemy statesmen which were directly levelled at us. We still failed to realize the mental attitude of our enemies. All parties represented in the Reichstag Majority, with the exception of the right wing of the Centre, persistently echoed the catch-words of hostile propaganda, and, just as before, rushed forward their proposals for universal reconciliation, understanding and disarmament.

The Secretary of State for Foreign Affairs, who was the very personification of this idea of universal understanding, expressed his opinion that the war could not be decided on the battle-field. He was quite right, if he meant that it should be waged against the enemy home front, and that the conduct of the war should be supported by an active war policy. But he was wrong, if he placed his faith in reconciliation and understanding, as was really the case.

The Secretary of State was only repeating what was in the minds of the majority. And this was the doctrine that was preached everywhere, in the Reichstag, in the Press, to our worn and weary people and to our soldiers, whom the High Command was asking to offer their lives on the battle-field for the sake of the Fatherland.

Was that the kind of influence calculated to restore flagging spirits ? Was it to be expected that neglected youths, who during these past years had been growing up without paternal guidance, amid party strife and general unrest, who had been earning high wages and were now drafted into the ranks after a short period of training, or that men disposed to unruliness because they were no longer exempt, would make soldiers who would fight devotedly for King and country ? Would not it be far more probable that all of them would think only of preserving their own lives ? Was it not to be expected that such ideas must have a pernicious influence on less stable characters, especially in times of stress, when human weaknesses tend to assert themselves ? Was not all this bound to have its reaction at home ?

In addition there was ever increasing evidence of the creeping growth of Bolshevism, only too gladly accepted and disseminated by the Independent Social Democrats, and which had all this time been allowed to establish itself officially in Berlin. We had protested against Joffe being allowed to go to Berlin, and, prompted by the Commander-in-Chief in the East, had proposed to negotiate further with him in any town in occupied territory. We were soon familiar with the working methods of Bolshevism. Warnngs innumerable were given. Members of the General Staff sent ample data to the responsible authorities in Berlin regarding Bolshevik activity in Germany. Unfortunately, further conduct of the affair was out of their hands.

Meanwhile the Army Command in the Marches and myself repeatedly drew the attention of the Imperial Chancellor, the War Ministry and Foreign Office, and also the Home Office, to the revolutionary intrigues of the Russian Embassy in Berlin, with its very large staff and its association with the Independent Social Democrats, as well as to the revolutionary activity of the latter. But it was all in vain. When once more I called the attention of the Foreign Office to Joffe's work and to the danger of his presence in Berlin, I was told that it was better that he should be in Berlin than anywhere else. There they had him under their eyes. Unfortunately, those eyes were blind. Joffe, while Bolshevism showed itself officially obsequious towards Germany, was able to undermine the fighting power of the

The Offensive in the West, 1918

German people in a way that the Entente alone, despite blockade and propaganda, could never have done.

For this purpose he placed ample means at the disposal of the destructive elements in the country, though, of course, the full extent of his revolutionary activities were only revealed at a later date. At Magdeburg, later, the leader of the Independent Socialists announced :

" We have been preparing systematically for this upheaval since January 25th, 1918. We encouraged our people who went to the front to desert the colours. We organized these deserters, furnished them with false papers and supplied them with money and unsigned pamphlets. We dispatched these men in all directions, but chiefly back to the front, to get at the men there and so undermine the front itself. These men incited the soldiers to desert and thus, slowly but surely, the collapse was brought about."

In conjunction with this, revolutionary and Bolshevik influence was brought to bear on the men on leave. The most extensive propaganda was carried on in railway trains. Soldiers going home on leave were urged to refuse to return to the front ; those returning to the front were incited either to offer passive resistance, to desert, or to mutiny. Much that was still imperceptible at the end of June and the beginning of July was, nevertheless, developing silently but progressively.

Whether Radical, Socialist or Bolshevik, the effort to subvert authority was common to all, and had already been at work for decades. Now, in the State's hour of need, it emerged into the light.

I have no wish to refer here to those ambitious members of the Reichstag who deprived the enfeebled Government of all remaining respect, nor to the efforts exerted on all sides to undermine my position and the confidence reposed in me, just because they saw in me the prop of authority. It is my purpose to deal only with the systematic campaign against the officer.

That was a crime for which the Democratic and Majority Socialist parties were responsible ; indeed, in the words of Talleyrand, it was worse than that, it was a blunder. A blunder so short-sighted and productive of such endless calamity that it can never be excused. Instead of seeing in the officer the pillar of law and order of the State, many regarded him only as the representative of " Militarism," without being at all clear as to exactly what the officer had to do with the grievances which they felt called upon to bring forward.

It was all so senseless. In Germany the Corps of Officers has never taken part in politics ; during the war it had long lost that exclusiveness, antagonism to which was considered a duty in pre-war days. The Corps was recruited from all social circles and from all parties—anybody could become an officer. In many respects, unfortunately, it was no longer the old Corps of Officers. Its shortcomings were due to foreign elements, to the decline of public spirit, and to the inexperience of many officers who were commissioned so quickly only because the losses among officers on the battle-fields had been so extraordinarily high.

At some future date the eyes of the credulous German people will be opened to these facts, and in that hour they will realize their ingratitude and their own criminal guilt against the officers, the Army, the Fatherland and themselves. Let us hope that the real culprits will then be discovered.

Complaints against the officers followed one another as if by order.

The officers, it was implied, lived much better than the men, although whilst in the field or in the trenches they had their meals from the same field kitchen. In billets behind the lines, one officer was always served from the field kitchen, while the others messed together. The N.C.O.'s and men were represented on the mess committee, so why were no complaints heard from them ?

The cultivation of *esprit de corps*, the authority of the commanding officer, the influence of the older men on the younger— were these things less important for the officer ? Where could they operate to better effect than in the common life of the regiment ? The hours of duty alone did not suffice, even during the war, to hand on the tradition of the German Corps of Officers to the younger generation. The officer had to live with his men, and he did so. It was not possible to do otherwise in battle or while in the trenches. Finally, he had to keep up the dignity of his position, which must be clearly defined, and he had to maintain his authority, for how else would it have been possible for him to exert any decisive influence over the troops in all emergencies ? All this demanded, among many other requisites, an attitude of official isolation, for otherwise the officer would lose respect.

Were the reasons forgotten which in peace time prompted the removal of the non-commissioned officers from the men's quarters into separate quarters of their own ? But there was no inclination to think of such things ; people were only anxious to undermine authority, to shatter the foundations of the State in order the more easily to further their own wretched interests.

Life in the Corps of Officers was governed by regard for the men, the officer himself, and, lastly, the whole structure of municipal and imperial order which stands and falls with the status of the officer.

The way of life of the higher staff officers was also sharply criticized. Yet is there a man who does not know of the nerve-racking work and colossal burden they bear unceasingly ? The troops were relieved, but the staff remained on duty, day and night. For four years I endured this state of tension without rest or relief. In such circumstances I could not live on field-kitchen rations. Nevertheless, in October, 1918, I declared to the new War Cabinet of Prince Max that Headquarters was willing to live on the fare provided by the field kitchens if the various Secretaries of State and the whole of Berlin would undertake to do likewise ; but until then we should live in such a way as was considered best for the men and ourselves. The Imperial Chancellor, Prince Max, declined to eat field-kitchen fare, and so long as I remained in the field we messed simply, but as before.

The other Higher Staffs were in a similar position. They lived much in the same way as we did. I have never countenanced excesses, and if they have occurred, I disclaim all responsibility. So long as we have any social order at all, authority must exist, and there must be social distinctions. There must still be, as before, a Corps of Officers, in which the individual officer must keep himself distinct from the soldier while continuing to be his true friend.

Then came complaints that the officers were living at the expense of the men—a shameful calumny spread by enemy and home propaganda. Many men of undoubted honesty and intelligence came to me bleating out such general accusations, instead of vigorously assailing them. They had already lost all regard for the morality of the Corps of Officers, so inextricably had they fallen into the snare spread by the circulators of these reports.

It was said that officers of the regular Army hid in good billets. This was the reward of a grateful people to the regular officer for his sacrifice and devotion! There were only a few of them left. The remainder had fallen or had been hopelessly disabled. The Corps of Officers had lost from eighty to ninety per cent. of its full strength. Could they not understand that to fill certain posts on the staffs, on which the fate of the troops depended, officers of exceptional experience and initiative were required? It is obvious that for such duties the regular officer was more fitted than an officer of the reserve, and that eventually it would be impossible to replace the former.

I begged the Military Cabinet to investigate these charges. This exposed their injustice all along the line.

Notwithstanding this, I persistently issued reminders that officers fit for service should be sent from home and from the various staffs to the front, to be replaced by officers fit only for garrison duty. The staffs during the summer of 1918 were such that several divisional commanders complained to me that they had too few fit officers on their staffs to cope with all demands.

I was always opposed to the presence of father and son on the same staff. When I had direct command, as well as when I was Chief of Staff in the East, I set my face against this. Now all I could do was to draw the attention of the Military Cabinet to it.

I heard unfavourable reports concerning the working of canteens. Here, also, the officers were said to be acting to the detriment of the men. I went into the matter. Everything was in order. The canteen commissions, on which the soldiers were represented, controlled the working and the distribution of profits. The sale of goods in the canteens was strictly rationed for officers and men alike at so much per head. Each man might buy only as much as was allowed on the carefully calculated distribution schedule.

The higher staffs, having no canteens of their own, drew on the central stores at the same prices as the canteens did. As these supplied officers and men at a fixed rate and a certain profit, the higher staffs—both officers and men, of course— bought their goods somewhat cheaper than the regiments. This I also stopped.

Then it was asserted that the canteen moneys were unfairly administered. This accusation was as false as the others. It was only the soldier who derived any benefit from the profits, mainly, of course, in kind.

But it was on the lines of communication that the officers were supposed to live in special luxury. There I have seen an enormous amount of loyal work, from which the Army derived incalculable benefit. It was obvious that on the L. of C., officers, as well as men, lived more quietly and comfortably than was the case with the troops who were only in the L. of C. areas on their way to and from the line. Naturally, also, the men felt this, although everything possible was done for them.

Was it such a crime for an officer to buy something in Belgium or anywhere else to send home to his family, in order to brighten their life a little ? Was it not the families of officers who are rarely men of means, who suffered most severely from the increased cost of living at home ? In July, 1916, when I was with the Commander-in-Chief in the East I arranged similar facilities for the men, these facilities being still further developed later. From the West and Rumania parcels were sent home in large numbers by the men.

Any special case of irregularity on the part of an officer which was brought to my notice, even anonymously, was subjected to most searching investigation. The status and way of life of the officers were frequently discussed by the higher staffs. Under the pressure of the continual complaints the Field-Marshal issued an appeal to all officers.

The Corps of Officers has emerged triumphant from this attack on its honour. The man who infringed the code was an exception, and was not one of us. No measures adopted against him could be too severe. The officer who did not emerge from this war with clean hands as an honourable man, who retained property which was not his, even if only to save it from destruction, besmirched the Fatherland, the Army, the Corps of Officers and himself.

The Corps of Officers, as a whole, may be proud of itself, not least because, despite all the work of agitation going on in its rear, it held the Army together for four years, led it so often to victory, and was still able, in co-operation with loyal non-commissioned officers and men, to lead it back over the Rhine— a stupendous achievement, amongst the greatest deeds of the war.

Enemy propaganda did not concern itself with the non-commissioned officers. It was considered that their authority was already impaired, and it was not deemed necessary to pay any particular attention to them. But antagonism between commissioned and non-commissioned officers, which had not existed in the army in peace time, was ingeniously created.

Many signs of disease had been progressively showing themselves in the German people and army. The symptoms of disorder were no longer to be ignored, indeed their presence was recognized by many. The German Crown Prince, who frequently visited me at Avesnes, referred to the matter with increasing anxiety, and also sent in a report to the Kaiser on the subject. I could only acquiesce in this. In cases of mental disease it is exceedingly difficult to know exactly what to do during the initial stages. The existence of the malady is felt. It is only later, however, when the disease comes to a head, that the significance of the preliminary manifestations can be fully realized.

The Offensive in the West, 1918

The process of disintegration at work in many parts of the army, with all its serious consequences, was as incomprehensible to me as the disintegration of the nation, which revealed itself in such a surprising fashion on November 9th, was to millions of Germans.

I communicated my anxiety again and again to those gentlemen who, with me, were called upon to diagnose these symptoms and provide a remedy. But I spoke to deaf ears. The German nation, itself not without guilt, has now to pay the penalty with its very life.

The question of reserves was a constant anxiety to us. I had the opportunity of impressing on His Majesty the gravity of the situation. The desire had been expressed that the so-called Asiatic Corps should be reinforced, so that Jerusalem might be recovered, whereas, in view of our situation with regard to drafts, I had agreed with Enver upon a reduction of the German troops and had prevented the dispatch of more men to Palestine.

G.H.Q. had again approached the Imperial Chancellor with those old demands of the autumns of 1916 and 1917 for an increase in the quota of recruits. I sent Colonel Bauer to the meetings called in Berlin to consider the matter. But we found that we were without the necessary support of the War Ministry. At the end of June discussions on all the above-mentioned questions were resumed at Spa between the Imperial Chancellor, the Field-Marshal, the War Minister and myself. I referred to the conferences in Berlin with Colonel Bauer, and once more emphasized as gravely as I could the necessity of obtaining adequate reserves, of adopting the most severe measures against shirkers and deserters in the homeland, and above all of encouraging the determination of the people, with regard to which I again drew attention to the dangerous influence of a section of our Press, enemy propaganda and Bolshevism.

I spoke my mind on these points far more often than I have recorded in these pages. Once more I was promised a great deal. The situation, however, remained unchanged. I do not know whether those gentlemen thought that my reports were exaggerated or that they were merely the fruit of my " Militarism." Neither would the War Office accede to my request for a general conference of employers and employees, to come to an understanding with regard to the necessity of drawing upon the exempted men.

Meanwhile I tried again to exploit our successes in order to further the peace movement in enemy countries. Another memorandum on this subject was sent to the Imperial Chancellor. On June 19th he sent for Colonel von Haeften. After long consultation the essentials of such propaganda were decided on. Vice-Chancellor von Payer, in particular, showed a lively interest in these questions. During the discussions at Spa I again begged the Imperial Chancellor to appoint a Minister for Propaganda. Beyond this we did not refer to the prospects of peace.

In view of Clemenceau's speeches, we were compelled, in my opinion, to continue the war or submit to humiliation. I must assume that the responsible statesmen held the same view, for even though I always hoped for success, they could have had no doubt of the gravity of my view of the situation.

In May and June Colonel von Haeften, quite in accord with my views, urged the Foreign Office to make a conciliatory declaration concerning Belgium. Secretary of State von Kühlmann, however, declined to take any initiative in the matter. He was well aware of the impossibility of any exchange of ideas with the enemy Governments. He said so openly.

On June 24th, basing his remarks on a speech of Mr. Asquith's on May 16th in favour of peace, he spoke in the Reichstag to the following effect :

" As long as every opening is accepted by the other side as a Peace Offensive, as a trap, as untrustworthy, as calculated to sow dissension between the Allies, and so long as every advance is violently denounced by the opponents of a *rapprochement*, it is impossible to foresee how any exchange of ideas that might lead up to peace is to be brought about."

The Imperial Chancellor adopted the same attitude in his speech of July 12th. He gave expression to our constant readiness for peace, but so long as the enemy's will to destruction persisted we must carry on ; though as soon as the enemy evinced any serious inclination to pave the way to peace we should at once prepare to meet him.

"I may also tell you that this point of view is not confined to myself, but is expressly shared by the General Staff, for they are not carrying on the war for its own sake, but told me : ' So soon as an earnest desire for peace shows itself on the other side, we must not be behindhand.' "

The Imperial Chancellor accurately represented the view of the Field-Marshal and myself.

When I now reflect on the possibility and prospect of a peace move, had it been undertaken by the Government, I am firmly convinced that we should have been granted an armistice and peace only on the conditions that we are now compelled to accept. We should not have taken upon ourselves that responsibility, as indeed we ought not to have done in October, despite the gravity of our situation.

Whether I was right or wrong in my view of the conditions then available, only Clemenceau, Wilson and Lloyd George can decide. England and the United States wished for our economic destruction; England, in addition, wanted to render us powerless, and France to bleed us white. Common to all our antagonists was the desire to inflict the deepest humiliation on their hated enemy before the world, and to impede the development of the German people for all time.

The Entente only pursued ideals for the betterment of the world in so far as they were compatible with a strong national policy. This was the motive of all their actions, all else was but a means to the same end. It was the very reverse with us ; our first ideal was universal happiness, our second the security of the Fatherland. The war once begun, its conclusion did not rest with us alone.

At the beginning of July, Secretary of State von Kühlmann retired from office. His attitude in the Reichstag, and particularly his assertion that the war could hardly be ended by a purely military decision, was going too far for the Imperial Chancellor. We also had felt it our duty to express our opinions.

But what finally turned the scale in favour of the resignation of the Secretary of State von Kühlmann was his personal attitude during these days.

I was in Avesnes and had neither the time nor inclination to interfere in the proceedings at Spa. Secretary of State von Kühlmann was the typical German diplomatist of post-Bis-marckian times.

His name will always be associated with the entry of the Bolsheviks into Berlin, and the tacit acquiescence in the propaganda work of the Russian Embassy.

I was glad to see Secretary of State von Hintze appointed his successor, as I considered him a strong man. I discussed with him my hope of even yet making the Entente ready for peace, pointed out to him the danger of Bolshevism and also drew his attention to the revolutionary activities of Herr Joffe. As regards Bolshevism, he pursued the same course as his prede-cessor, partly because of his own views on the Russian situation, and partly also because he was not really strong enough to master the old tendencies of the Foreign Office.

VIII

In Russia events had developed along lines of their own, illustrative of the lying propensities of the Soviet Government. With the consent of this Government the Entente had formed Czecho–Slovak units out of Austro–Hungarian prisoners. These were intended to be used against us, and were therefore to be conveyed to France by the Siberian railway. All this was sanctioned by a Government with whom we were at peace, and we actually took it lying down ! At the beginning of June I wrote to the Imperial Chancellor specially on the subject, and pointed out the dangers which threatened us from the Soviet Government.

The weapon forged against us was now to be turned against the Soviet Government itself, for the Entente, realizing that they could not work with a Government which looked for support to Germany, took action against Bolshevism, and instead of sending these troops to France, held them up along the Siberian railway on the frontier between Russia and Siberia, in order to fight against the Government in Moscow. They gradually pushed forward to the middle Volga, in the direction of Kazan and Samara. In addition to this, by garrisoning the railway, the Entente prevented the return of our prisoners of war from Siberia. This was unquestionably a serious loss for us.

If the Soviet Government had been really honest in its professions of peaceful intention, the trains which took away the Czecho–Slovaks could have brought back German prisoners of war. But it was not honest. Bolshevism did us all the damage it could.

The situation in Siberia, behind the Czecho–Slovaks, was so confused that the Entente could find no support there. For that reason it was without importance for us also. From the point of view of the war, the only serious thing was that the Siberian railway was in the Entente's possession. The relations between Japan, England and the United States were without interest except in so far as they showed signs of approaching differences between these countries.

The new Entente front in Russia began with the Czecho–Slovaks on the middle Volga.

It was continued north by the Entente troops which were feeling their way forward from the White Sea, up the Dvina, and south from the Murman coast along the railway of the same name.

On the Dvina they were advancing slowly but with no definite aim. As the White Sea freezes in winter, nothing of importance could be undertaken here. The Murman railway was torn up by the Bolsheviks. The Finnish patrols, on reaching the railway, found nothing more to be done. The united German and Finnish troops were now so strong that the Entente gave up their advance.

Up the Volga, and west of its lower course, which was still entirely in Bolshevik hands, the Don Cossacks held the lower Don as far as our own area of occupation. Their Hetman,

General Krasnoff, was decidedly anti-Bolshevik, and was opposing the Soviet troops. He had, however, neither arms nor ammunition. I had got into touch with him in order to prevent his joining the Entente. The situation was complicated by the fact that I could not put difficulties in the way of the Home Government's pro-Bolshevik policy, of which, of course, I was informed, and Krasnoff regarded the Soviet Government, and not the Entente, as his enemy.

At all events, I succeeded in holding him back from openly siding with the Entente and, to a certain extent, in making an ally of him. If we had decided to attack Moscow, he would openly have thrown in his lot with us.

In the wide, fertile Steppes of the Kuban region between the Don Cossacks and the Caucasus, General Alexeieff, with his Volunteer Army, was, as I have already stated, fighting the Bolshevik troops. He was acting under English influence. I think, however, he was too good a Russian not to have joined us if we had been opposing the Soviet Government. Alexeieff's military position was at the moment unfavourable ; he had neither arms nor ammunition. The Bolsheviks, for the time being, had the upper hand. Although the Government in Moscow were prepared to go to any length in their assurance of pacific intentions, at the end of July they sent several thousand men from the region south-west of Azoff, across the Sea of Azoff, and landed them at Taganrog. Here they were very soon annihilated by German troops. From about the beginning of August the position of the Volunteer Army in the Kuban region became more secure. In Novorissisk lay what was left of the Russian ships that had escaped from Sebastopol. It was certainly our military right and a law of necessity to demand or compel their return. Here, again, the Foreign Office prolonged the negotiations out of regard for the Soviet Government, although no better proof of its hostile attitude, or, at any rate, of its inability to prevent hostile conduct by its troops could possibly have been furnished than the landing at Taranrog. At last the Soviet Government consented to the return of the ships to Sebastopol. Only a part of them arrived, the majority being sunk in harbour by the Bolsheviks in an outburst of what was, after all, patriotism. We had stipulated with the Soviet Government that during the war we were to make as much use of the ships as the military situation demanded. We had no need to take advantage of this.

As on the lower Volga, the Bolsheviks in June were masters of the Caspian Sea also. To the Soviet Government this was still of great importance in connection with the oil supply of Great Russia, which had already lost the coal of the Donetz basin and the corn of the Ukraine and the Don and Kuban districts.

The Turks were before Baku. They had also firmly established themselves in Northern Persia, without, however, pressing forward far into that region. English troops were at Enzeli, on the southern shore of the Caspian Sea, in touch with the Kuban district.

This position, coupled with the situation in Finland and the Ukraine, formed the basis of our whole policy in the East. As regards Great Russia, this policy, as carried out by *Ministerial-direktor* Krieg, worked directly in favour of the Bolsheviks. There is no doubt that right through the summer it prevented us from forming a new military front. This I recognized. On general grounds I held such a policy to be short-sighted, as it was bound in the long run to strengthen the whole Bolshevik movement. That could only do us harm ; and I regarded it as the duty of our Government to guard against such an eventuality, not only on military grounds, but also, and indeed more urgently, from the purely political point of view. Dr. Helfferich regarded this as quite possible. The position of the Government was certainly difficult, but they had only themselves to thank for it. They assured me that their policy reflected public opinion in Germany. Here, again, I was compelled to believe that consideration for tendencies of internal politics was impeding the effective prosecution of the war. As for our military position, we could easily have made a rapid attack on Petrograd with the troops we had in the East. With the help of the Don Cossacks we could also have attacked in the direction of Moscow. This would have been far better than merely defending a long line, which absorbed more troops than would have been required for a short advance, besides unnerving the troops, whose *moral* would have been maintained by active operations. We could have deposed the Soviet Government, which was thoroughly hostile to us, and given help to other authorities in Russia, which were not working against us, but indeed anxious to co-operate with us. This would have been a success of great importance to the general conduct of the war. If some other Government were established in Russia, it would almost certainly have been possible to come to some compromise with it over the Peace of Brest, whereas, in dealing with the Bolsheviks, a simple abandonment of the treaty without any idea as to how matters would develop, would have been the same kind of " payment in advance " policy as were all the ideas about a peace of " understanding," so long as the enemy would accept no such peace.

Our Government remained wholly ignorant of the underground activities of the Bolsheviks, whom they regarded, or wished to regard, as honest. They entered into further negotiations with them over those points of the Treaty which had not been cleared up. Nothing, not even the unavenged murder of our ambassador at Moscow, shook their faith. They walked straight into the trap set by the Bolsheviks, while simultaneously showing distrust of all other tendencies in Russia. The Bolshevik Government was very accommodating : it granted the German demands with regard to Esthonia and Livonia, conceded the independence of Georgia, agreed to pay an indemity by instalments, and held out prospects of the delivery of raw materials, including oil, from Baku. What we had to give in return was relatively little. Coal from the Donetz basin, the transport of corn from the Kuban district by means of the railway running northwards from Rostoff on Don (which, I must admit, was hardly feasible, in view of the attitude of the Don Cossacks), and finally the exercise of our influence in persuading Turkey not to take Baku. We further agreed to evacuate, *pari passu* with the payment of the instalments of the indemnity, the Great Russian territory which we had occupied in February on the Beresina and Dvina. Later on, the first instalments were actually paid as agreed, an eventuality I had doubted somewhat.

Our Government's confidence in the Bolsheviks went so far that they actually wanted to supply arms and ammunition to Herr Joffe. The gentleman who brought from the Foreign Office the document dealing with the matter, remarked to me : " This material remains in Germany, and Joffe will use it against us here."

At the conference in Spa, when our Georgian policy was being discussed, the Imperial Chancellor agreed to send Colonel von Kress, who had returned to Germany from the Palestine Front, to Tiflis as his representative, with an escort of one or two companies. It had become essential for us to show a stronger hand in this district—not merely because we hoped to secure some military assistance from that quarter, but also in order to obtain raw materials. That we could not rely on Turkey in the matter had been once again demonstrated by her conduct in Batum, where she claimed the right to retain all the stocks for herself. We could only expect to get oil from Baku if we helped ourselves. The shortage of fuel at home, and the difficulties of our winter lighting, with all their attendant inconveniences, were only too firmly impressed on my memory. After the attack of the 7th Army, the Army's reserves of fuel had also run out, and we felt the shortage keenly. Oil was needed for the Ukraine railways also. The production of oil in Rumania had increased to the limits of the possible, but this could not make good the whole shortage. It now seemed possible to supplement it from Trans-Caucasian sources, and in particular from Baku, if transport facilities could be provided.

The Director of Railways had to solve the problem of tank ships. I was highly disgusted when the Bolsheviks, simply in order to injure us, sank the *Elbruz*, the largest tank steamer in the Black Sea, at Novorossisk. The Batum–Tiflis–Baku railway, which was well supplied with oil trucks, was to be taken in hand by Colonel von Kress in co-operation with the Turks. The crucial question, of course, was how we were to get to Baku. Here, again, consideration for the Soviet Government prevented us from acting firmly or rapidly, and the first event of importance was that the English from Enzeli crossed the Caspian Sea at the beginning of August, and took possession of the town.

Their occupation of Baku, which was only rendered possible by the complete inactivity of the Turks in North Persia, was a serious blow for us. By this move the English also came into closer touch with the Volunteer Army in the Kuban district, but, on the other hand, at Baku they were within our reach. An attack upon them, involving only a small force, seemed possible G.H.Q. set about preparing a blow against them, with the co-operation of Nuri's troops, and sent a brigade of cavalry and a few battalions to Tiflis. The question of the transport of troops had not yet been settled, when Nuri took possession of Baku, and immediately afterwards the situation in Bulgaria compelled us to send the troops to Rumania.

The position in North Persia was not destined to undergo any change. We supplied arms from the Ukraine for the tribes there who wished to join the Turks, but the latter remained absolutely inactive, although they had ample forces round Batum and Kars.

In the East I went only so far as in my view was absolutely demanded by our military position and economic needs. I had no Napoleonic dreams of world conquest. The anxious struggle in which I was so deeply engaged left me no time to pursue fantastic schemes. I wanted no territory in the Ukraine or Caucasus ; my only object was to procure the supplies that were so urgently needed for our bare maintenance and the prosecution of the war. I hoped also, now that we had succeeded in breaking the blockade at this point, to improve our economic position, and thus to raise our physical strength and *moral*. I wished to make what use was possible of the man-power of these districts, partly by direct recruiting, but on a larger scale, and with greater prospect of success, through enlisting labour for employment in Germany, so as to release men for the front. I pursued this course in all parts of the East, and had

hopes even of obtaining direct recruits from the German population there. We did not, however, work quickly enough. The
8th Army, at Riga, complained that the Ministry of War, in spite
of all my persistence, had failed to give any instructions in the
matter.

It was only to protect and foster German *Kultur* that I went
beyond immediate military requirements and thought of the
future. That did not involve any expenditure of military
resources. I wanted to strengthen and consolidate German
national spirit, and thus increase its influence. Some of my
acquaintances had placed a substantial sum of money at my
disposal for this end. I used it to support the German national
Press in Austria. I steadily furthered my pet scheme of settling
the isolated Germans scattered throughout Russia, side by side
with our soldiers, in the Eastern districts. In this matter I
made myself the advocate of Germanism against the Government.
I rejected as fantastic, however, such proposals as the foundation of a German colonial state on the Black Sea.

With regard to the districts lying within the administrative
area of the Commander-in-Chief in the East, I asked the Government on several occasions in the course of the summer to give
a clear definition of their policy, in order that my actions here
should be consistent with the views of the highest authority.
Esthonia and Livonia were, with Courland, united into one
military governmental district, the " Baltic Littoral." Lithuania had retained its former frontiers. I proposed to extend
to Livonia and Esthonia the policy which had hitherto been
employed in Courland. The civilization of the Esthonians and
Livonians was German, and I aimed at uniting them in one state
under German influence without obliterating their racial distinctions. Immediately after the liberation of these countries
in February much could have been done, but our Government
let valuable time slip by. They even asked me to lay down
our policy in Esthonia and Livonia, though nothing could be
expected from that unless we were really supported by Berlin.
However, all Berlin did was to press for the establishment of
the University at Dorpat. In filling the chairs there, the

Esthonians were ignored for some wholly incomprehensible reason, and the whole point of the measure was thus lost.

In Lithuania, too, we made no progress, the negotiations with the Lithuanian Diet coming to a complete standstill. The Poles were becoming more and more active ; the Government was still unable to see the danger from that quarter, and failed to use its influence in Rome in favour of the appointment of a cleric of Lithuanian sympathies to the vacant see of Vilna, an appointment the Lithuanians earnestly desired and which I did my best to secure. It is possible, however, that the Gove rnment did what it could without meeting with any encouragement from the Vatican.

No progress had been made with the solution of the Polish problem. The Emperor Charles' attitude varied from time to time. Baron Burian, the successor of Count Czernin, adhered to the Austro-Polish solution. Our Government was still in the position of not knowing its own mind. It was as uncertain on this point as in the rest of its Eastern policy. A good opportunity to dispose of the Austro-Polish question once and for all was not taken. The Emperor Charles had written the Parma letters. Under pressure from Vienna he had to decide in May to make his " Canossa " pilgrimage to Spa. The position was one of which anything might have been made. The Field-Marshal and myself urged Count von Hertling and Secretary of State von Kühlmann to use this favourable opportunity to get matters put on a clear footing. They, however, lacked the necessary resolution. With great solemnity, some document or other was drawn up and signed, not merely by the leading statesmen, but also by the two monarchs personally. This agreement, however, laid no obligations whatever on Austria-Hungary and was utterly worthless. Our diplomacy had failed and the Dual Monarchy had won. Everything had turned out as we soldiers had prophesied. Baron Burian felt himself, and with good reason, not bound by anything. He continued to aim at the Austro-Polish solution with the persistence which was at once so prominent a feature of his character and so annoying to our diplomats.

IX

The preparations for the third great attack in the West were exactly similar to those for the battles of the 21st March and the 27th May. Colonel Bruchmüller was again available as artillery adviser to the Army Group of the German Crown Prince.

The 7th Army was to cross the Marne east of Château-Thierry, and at the same time to advance on both sides of the river in the direction of Epernay, while the 1st and 3rd Armies were to attack from the east of Rheims as far as Tahure, in order to carry their right wing past the wooded hills of Rheims, and advance also on Epernay, while making Châlons-sur-Marne their principal objective. The attack of the Army Group left untouched the enemy positions between the Ardre and east of Rheims, thus acquiring a considerable breadth, which seemed favourable to success. The junction of the two attacking groups in the neighbourhood of Epernay might lead to very important results. The attack was in the main entrusted to divisions which had carried out the advance over the Chemin des Dames. This was a heavy demand on the troops, but the position required it, and it allowed the divisions of Crown Prince Rupprecht's Army Group all the more rest for their later task of attacking in Flanders.

To relieve the 7th Army Headquarters, the 9th Army Headquarters from Rumania was put in between the Oise and the Ourcq astride the Aisne.

In the attack on both sides of Rheims we reckoned on an enemy counter-offensive between the Aisne and the Marne, with Soissons as its principal objective, and we disposed the 9th Army and the right wing of the 7th accordingly.

Originally the attack of the Army Group of the German Crown Prince was to be carried out on July 12th, but, in order to make thorough preparations possible, it had unfortunately to be postponed until the 15th. On the 11th or 12th, while the preparations were in full swing, a deserter brought news that a big tank offensive from the forest of Villers-Cotterets was imminent, and this report gave us additional reason to re-examine and perfect our defensive measures. At the most critical point, south-west of Soissons, we had placed a division that had fought with special success in the East, and which had always met the demands made upon it in the West. This division had not taken part in the May battles, and had therefore had as much rest as could be given to any division. In this respect, at any rate, we were no worse off than the enemy. Further south, two divisions, not fully rested, and whose battalion strength was not up to the standard required, held that space along the front that was usually allotted to one division only. The other divisions were good trench-divisions,

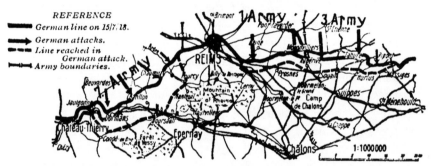

Fig. 38. The German Attacks on the Marne and in Champagne. 1918.

and held normal divisional fronts ; a few were kept behind the lines as reserves. The fortification of our positions was, of course, not far advanced ; high corn obstructed the view in front of, and still more within, them. Influenza was prevalent, but not more so here than anywhere else along the front. The attack that had been announced never took place, and I hoped that the news would have thoroughly roused the men.

The Army Group of the German Crown Prince emphasized the necessity of the organization in depth of all our defensive fronts.

I was always in touch with the Headquarters of the Armies detailed for the attack. Above all, I was anxious to know if in their opinion, or in that of the troops, the enemy had any knowledge of our preparations. They thought not, and only on the Marne was the artillery fire more lively.

The Offensive in the West, 1918

I had especially pointed out that no reconnoitring was to be carried out on the southern bank of the Marne, but in spite of my warning a pioneer officer swam over and was captured. As we found out after the battle, he gave away much information to the enemy. Acting officers of the heavy artillery, who fell into the hands of the enemy on the Ardre, acted in the same way. In some places the Entente made raids and took prisoners, but I do not know what information was gained in this way.

It is also a fact that an attack at Rheims was discussed in the most irresponsible way throughout Germany. To my great regret it was only later that I received many letters from home on the subject. Wireless messages sent out by the enemy after the battle also plainly indicated that they had had early information of our plan. Within the Army itself it was very difficult to keep the secret, as the very concentration of heavy artillery and trench-mortars, which played a part in every attack, revealed our intentions.

In spite of long consideration, we had been unable to think of any other way. We clearly realized how cumbrous was the method of attack, and made all efforts to deceive the enemy as to our intentions ; everything possible was done in this direction. Postal prohibitions were useless ; there were so many channels connecting us with home, and I could not stop leave, which was, after all, the only concession the Army could make to the men. Leave had had to be stopped for a considerable period on account of the railway transport conditions in February and March, and at that time many Army Commanders urgently desired it to be resumed. While the commanders were doing their utmost to keep these secrets, the love of talking and boasting that is inborn in Germans betrayed to the world and to our enemies matters of the greatest weight and significance.

We attacked early on the 15th. Our crossing of the Marne was a remarkable achievement which succeeded, although the enemy were fully prepared for it. The 7th Army, between the Marne and the Ardre, also penetrated the most obstinately defended positions. The Italian Divisions stationed there suffered particularly heavily.

About five kilometres south of the Marne the attacking troops came upon an enemy force so strong that it could only be overcome by bringing a large number of batteries over the river, and so the attack at this point came to a standstill. On the 16th, by hard fighting, we slowly gained ground up the Marne and towards the Ardre.

According to plan, the enemy had withdrawn in front of the 1st and 3rd Armies, to their second position, and held us firmly all along the line.

By noon of the 16th G.H.Q. had given orders for the suspension of the offensive of the 1st and 3rd Armies, and for their organization for defence by withdrawing certain divisions for this purpose. A continuation of the offensive would have cost us too much. We had to content ourselves with the improvement in our position, brought about by regaining possession of the heights we had lost in the spring of 1917, and we had even secured a deep forward zone. The troops that had been withdrawn were at the disposal of the Group of the German Crown Prince, or of G.H.Q. as reserves. I considered it of the greatest importance that they should be available as soon as possible.

Once the difficult decision to suspend the offensive of the 1st and 3rd Armies had been taken, it was useless to attempt to advance further across the Marne, or to leave our troops on the southern bank. It seemed out of the question to withdraw the troops immediately, as the few bridges were under incessant artillery fire, and were constantly bombed or machine-gunned by enemy planes. We had to make arrangements for crossing before the retreat could even begin. On the 17th the retreat was fixed for the night between the 20th and 21st. The troops on the Marne had lived through days of severe trial and behaved like heroes.

G.H.Q. thought that only north of the Marne could the offensive be continued up the Ardre Valley, in order to surround Rheims still more closely, and possibly even to take it. By the 16th the Army Group of the German Crown Prince had received the necessary instructions. On the afternoon of the 17th I was in Rethel at 1st Army Headquarters to discuss the continuance of the attack on Rheims. I urged the necessity for speedy action, so that we might retain the initiative on this battle-field also. From the report of the Chief of Staff I gathered that many days would be needed for the preparations to continue even this purely local attack. I was therefore obliged to resign myself, but I begged the German Crown Prince to build up reserves as quickly as possible, and pointed out the probable immediate necessity of strengthening the 18th Army and the right wing of the 9th.

The other fronts were, in my opinion, sound. For the moment G.H.Q. still clung to the idea of an attack in Flanders by the Army Group of Crown Prince Rupprecht, although the hoped-for weakening of the enemy had not come about. The railway transport of artillery, trench-mortars and planes from the Rheims district had begun according to plan on the 16th.

In the night of the 17th–18th I myself went to the Headquarters of the Army Group of Crown Prince Rupprecht, to review once more the state of their preparations. The attack was intended as a continuation of that which had been suspended at the end of April. It was to be made by the 4th and 6th Armies north of the Lys, its objectives being the possession of the commanding heights between Poperinghe and Bailleul, as well as the high ground round Hazebrouck. During the discussion with the Army Group of Crown Prince Rupprecht on the morning of the 18th I received the first news that, by means of an unexpected tank attack, the French had pierced the line south-west of Soissons. At the same time the Army Group of the German Crown Prince announced that it had sent to the battle-field, partly by motor transport, those divisions (in the first instance the 20th Inf. Div.) which had been intended for the continuation of the offensive up the Ardre.

I immediately ordered the 5th Inf. Div. to proceed by rail, via Laon, to the district just north-east of Soissons, where the tunnel was already complete. This division, which had been held at the disposal of G.H.Q., was quartered north-east of St. Quentin, and all arrangements had been made for its rapid movement by rail to any point.

My War Memories, 1914-1918

I concluded the conference at the Army Group of Crown Prince Rupprecht (naturally in a state of the greatest nervous tension) and then returned to Avesnes. I saw the Crown Prince Rupprecht for the last time on that day, and our relations then, as ever, were cordial.

I reached Avesnes at 2 p.m. and was met at the station by the Field-Marshal. We immediately retired to the office. The position of the left wing of the 9th Army and the right of the 7th had become serious.

On the 17th General Foch had attacked without success on the battle-field of Champagne, in the Forêt de la Montagne de Rheims, between the Ardre and the Marne, and also south of the Marne; and had continued the offensive south-west of Rheims and south of the Marne on the 18th with the same results, but between the Ourcq and the Aisne he had gained considerable ground.

After a short and sharp artillery preparation and a smoke screen, he attacked with massed infantry and a stronger force of tanks than had ever before been concentrated in one place. For the first time, small, low, fast tanks, that allowed the use of machine guns above the corn, were used; our machine guns were hindered by it except when they were mounted on special tripods. Here again the effect of the fire from the tanks was insignificant. Tanks were also observed which were solely used for the transport of men. These passed through our lines, put down their passengers with machine guns behind them, to form machine gun nests, and then promptly returned for reinforcements.

Our infantry had not stood firm at all points, and in particular the division south-west of Soissons that had been considered so reliable had given way. The gap rapidly widened, especially towards Soissons. Further south there were other deep dents in the line. The three divisions in reserve here, although not fresh and thrown into action piecemeal, were able to hold the enemy up on the heights south-west of Soissons and to the west of Parcy-Tigny, as well as at the Savières bottom. Between the Ourcq and the Marne the attacks were repulsed. The situation north of the Ourcq made a withdrawal of the troops fighting

The Offensive in the West, 1918

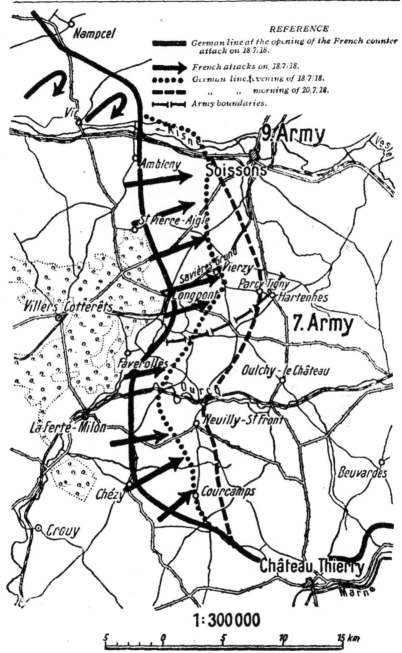

Fig. 39.   The Defensive Battle between Soissons and Rheims.   July, 1918.

on the south bank necessary. They were closely followed up by the enemy.

This was the condition of affairs that was revealed to me in the early hours of the afternoon in Avesnes.

We now had to deal with the heavy counter-offensive by General Foch against our sharp salient between Soissons and Rheims. English divisions were also taking part. The enemy offensive was mainly directed on Soissons and south-west of Rheims down the Ardre. Foch's intention was clearly to cut off this salient. On the Ardre the attack was repulsed, but towards Soissons it made considerable progress. All counter-measures that could be adopted were already under way. At the moment G.H.Q. was unable to give any further help.

The 5th Infantry Div. was being transported north-east of Soissons, but as enemy artillery soon began to shell the railway stations in that area, the troops were compelled to detrain in the Ailette valley. Their arrival was therefore postponed, which was most inconvenient.

The 20th Inf. Div. could be concentrated at its destination by the evening of the 19th. Only the infantry could be brought up by lorries, without any horses or vehicles. Everything else was forced to march, and so the division was completely broken up, the infantry being left with no regular supplies. In the use of these divisions this point had always to be borne in mind. The divisions dispatched by the Army Group of the German Crown Prince could not appear till later. They, too, arrived in lorries.

For the rest we could only await the further development of the situation. The troops on the south bank of the Marne could not be bundled back at a moment's notice. The order to retreat to the north bank on the night of the 20th–21st July was not cancelled, to avoid confusion. It would not do for the troops to be unsettled. For this reason we had to prolong our occupation of the sector west of Château-Thierry for a considerable time, in fact until we had evacuated the south bank of the Marne.

A stand south-west of Soissons and on the Ardre was a necessary consequence A crisis lay before us for the next few days, and until it was over no great strategical decisions could be taken.

The Army Group of Prince Rupprecht continued its preparations for attack. It had to arrange to relinquish certain divisions, but even then an offensive was still possible.

For the time being I shelved my anxiety concerning the 18th Army and the right wing of the 9th. The enemy could not attack everywhere.

The 19th of July was again a critical day, but it passed fairly satisfactorily.

In the neighbourhood of Soissons the enemy made no appreciable progress. Further south, it is true, he crossed the Soissons–Hartennes road, but towards evening he was thrown back by a mighty massed attack of the 20th Infantry Div. This saved the situation there. South-west of Hartennes the enemy gained more ground, but was unable to achieve anything decisive American attacks in the south, in the direction of Château-Thierry, broke down, as on the previous day. Enemy attacks south of the Marne, between the Marne and the Ardre, collapsed again and again. Local fighting took place in Champagne also.

On the whole the situation was much more favourable. Even the remnants of the troops who had allowed themselves to be surprised on the 18th had, generally speaking, recovered and fought well on the 19th.

On the 20th the 5th Inf. Div. would be available south-west of Soissons and new divisions in line on the Ourcq.

I inquired into the reasons for our failure of the 18th. The men had ceased to believe in the possibility of an attack. A Divisional Commander with whom I was acquainted told me that he had been to the front lines on the 17th, and had seen not the slightest sign of activity on the part of the enemy. As a matter of fact, the French troops only received the order to attack a few hours before they came up. Information which was coming through to our lines until immediately before the battle began no longer reached us. The rapid movement of the numerous fast tanks in the high-standing corn increased the effect of the surprise. To all this must be added the diminished strength of the divisions, the result partly of influenza and partly of the monotonous diet. In the sector into which the two weak divisions had been put there had been somewhat of a lull after the earlier battles. All these things helped to heighten the effect of the enemy surprise. When it had worn off on the 19th the troops held well.

The fact that particular divisions were not yet distributed in depth with their artillery was of the greatest significance. Once more they were too intent on following up the attack. This was very laudable in its way, but tactically unsound in their position.

The result of the surprise had been an over-hasty throwing in of reserves.

The battle between the Aisne and the Marne demanded unity of command, so the left wing of the 9th Army, south of the Aisne, was again put under the command of the 7th.

At the points of greatest pressure, south of Soissons and south-west of Rheims, we were, on the whole, successful in repulsing, on the 20th and 21st, strong enemy massed attacks in which tanks were again employed in large numbers.

The withdrawal of the troops south of the Marne to the northern bank took place during the night of the 20th–21st, and was effected in exemplary order. The fact that the French had not attacked here on the 20th helped considerably. Their thrust early on the 21st found everything already evacuated.

Following the withdrawal of the German troops from the south to the north bank of the Marne, we straightened our lines between the Ourcq and the Marne, and between the Marne and the Ardre, to secure local improvements in our positions.

On the 22nd there was a lull in the fighting. The enemy thrust was definitely held up. The crisis had terminated in our favour. G.H.Q. was at this time faced with momentous decisions. The situation of the 7th Army in the Marne salient was grave, not only on account of the unfavourable shape of the front, but also because of its communications. Transport movement between the Aisne and the Vesle valleys had been rendered unsafe. The railway curve east of Soissons was exposed to the effective fire of long range guns. The line in course of construction at high pressure further to the East was not yet ready, and was in any case only a makeshift. The other means of communication were useless for moving troops. Reinforcements for the 7th Army had therefore to be detrained in the Aisne valley or further north, and so were tired even before they reached the front. The necessity for continual relief was as obvious as it had been in the case of the Flanders and Somme battles. We had, in addition to other supplies, to send up immense quantities of ammunition and other war material. The railway communications behind

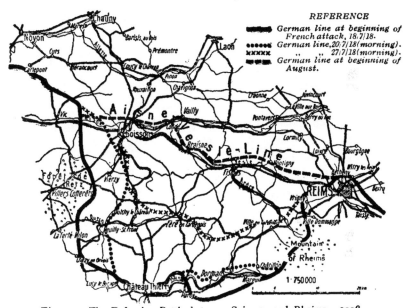

Fig. 40. The Defensive Battle between Soissons and Rheims. 1918.

the lines could not cope with all this. Motor transport and rolling-stock that would have made good this deficiency were not available.

We were thus suffering from a very serious handicap in our struggle with an enemy who had the best imaginable communications at his disposal.

That our strategic position in this salient was a critical one went without saying. Every enemy success at Soissons or on the Ardre would have the most far-reaching consequences. It would not be possible to hold the salient permanently, and a new attack on Rheims seemed hopeless.

I sent officers, among them General von Loszberg, to the fighting front, to report on the position. The commanders and troops at Soissons were obviously under the impression of the battles of the 18th, and the feeding of the troops was everywhere described as very difficult. From a tactical point of view the forward zone system had not proved a success in these battles involving retreats, for its evacuation too easily caused disorder in the main line of resistance immediately behind it.

The descriptions given to G.H.Q. confirmed us in our resolution, to which we had come in the evening of the 22nd, to withdraw the troops on the night of the 26th–27th July from the Marne to the Fère en Tardenois–Ville en Tardenois line. With that end in view I was naturally in constant touch with the Army Group of the German Crown Prince and the 7th Army. Only a short stand was to be made on the line indicated. The enemy would renew his massed attacks. We had to make them very expensive for him. We had in view a withdrawal behind the Vesle, on a straight line between Soissons and Rheims, in the beginning of August, but before this could be carried out, the salient south of the Vesle, and especially the Vesle valley itself, had first to be cleared. The masses of stores accumulated there were absolutely vital to us. Our front contracted as our retreat proceeded. We thereby accumulated reserves, but so did our enemy who could use them for attacks elsewhere.

The serious weakening of the 18th Army and of the right wing of the 9th could now no longer be justified. It had to be made good by reinforcements. These could only be drawn from the Army Group of Crown Prince Rupprecht.

The offensive in Flanders could not bring a rapid and decisive success. According to all indications, the enemy was ready for it. If he avoided the attack, as he had done east of Rheims, we should be unable to force a decision. If he stood firm, his numerous reserves were in a position to hold us up, as they had done on June 11th and 12th in the direction of Compiègne. G.H.Q. therefore decided to abandon this offensive. The Rupprecht

Army Group was to stand on the defensive and to surrender reserves to reinforce the 18th, 9th and 7th Armies; this it was quite capable of doing. The necessary orders were issued. I had as yet no idea how, if at all, we should be able to recover the initiative after taking up the Vesle position. The Army Group of Duke Albrecht was instructed to submit plans for an attack on its front. G.H.Q. suspended its instructions as regards the use of the forward zone on the front of the 7th and 18th Armies, and also for any future retirements.

On the 23rd there was again an extremely vigorous attack which, on the whole, was successfully repulsed along the whole front. During the next few days there were only local attacks which failed everywhere.

In the night of the 26th the withdrawal of the front north of the Marne was accomplished according to plan and in perfect order. In the next few days General Foch made further violent but unsuccessful attacks which cost us the loss of some small strips of high ground, north-west of Fère en Tardenois. According to reports from the troops the enemy had suffered bloody losses. Of course, very heavy demands were made on us too. As had been the case in previous defensive battles, relief by new divisions was continually necessary.

The evacuation of the salient went on steadily, thanks to the splendid organization of the Army Group of the German Crown Prince and of the 1st and 7th Armies. The second railway line was now completed and made the work considerably easier.

In the night of the 1st and 2nd August the front was withdrawn behind the Vesle where troops in hastily prepared positions were ready for the enemy. The enemy followed close on our heels and made a sharp attack on the line of the Vesle. He was everywhere repulsed. Our defensive battle of movement between the Marne and the Vesle was at an end.

The battle was a brilliant achievement on the part of the leaders and men concerned. The shadow cast by the events of July 18th had passed. After that day, in spite of the heavy demands made upon him, the German soldier had fought well and felt himself a better man than his enemy. In some divisions there had certainly been unpleasant revelations. Among other things I subsequently received a report which threw a very grave light on the spirit of one of these divisions ; I sent it to the 7th Army for further inquiry.

As in every other engagement, the losses we had suffered since July 15th had been very heavy. July 18th and the defensive battles arising out of it had in particular been very expensive, although we got our wounded back and did not lose any considerable number of prisoners.

The losses through the battle had been so heavy that we were compelled to break up about ten divisions and use their infantry as reserves for others. The other arms were, generally speaking, not broken up. Those divisions that had been withdrawn from the battle, and other troops, were distributed behind the whole West Front. This was the beginning of a vast railway transport movement. It opened at the end of July, increased considerably at the beginning of August, and from that time onwards hardly ever diminished. The troops, who were very much exhausted, had to be brought up to establishment, rested, and given time to recuperate.

I had not succeeded in getting any clear idea of the enemy's losses since the 15th of July, but considering the massed tactics of the Entente, they must have been high and in no way less heavy than ours.

The armies of the Entente had also suffered ; the battle had cost the enemy as much as it had cost us. The French had sent into action a remarkably large number of Senegalese and Moroccans and had endeavoured to spare their own people. The six American divisions that had taken part in the battle had suffered particularly severely without achieving any success. One division appears to have been broken up in order to bring them up to establishment. Notwithstanding the gallantry of the individual American soldier, the inferior quality of the American troops is proved by the fact that two brave German divisions were able to withstand the main attack made by very superior American forces for several weeks ; and these two divisions, the 4th Ersatz and the 201st, I had up till then considered no better than the average.

The losses sustained by the English and Italian divisions were also heavy.

In the meantime the Group of Crown Prince Rupprecht had prepared for the defensive, by relieving divisions that had been in position for a long period by others that had been intended for attack. Their battalions were fairly strong. Many divisions had not been in action since April. The 18th Army and the right wing of the 9th had also become stronger. Earlier on, the 18th Army had fought in the Avres bridgehead without success. One of the divisions there, which was holding a wide front, had been driven back on the river.

The attempt to make the nations of the Entente inclined to peace before the arrival of the American reinforcements by means of German victories had failed. The impetus of the Army had not sufficed to deal the enemy a decisive blow before the Americans were on the spot in considerable force. It was quite clear to me that our general situation had thus become very serious.

By the beginning of August we had suspended our attack and reverted to the defensive on the whole front. When the divisions that had taken part in the last attack had been rested, we should be able to make fresh decisions. A pause in the operations was nothing extraordinary ; it had occurred after the cessation of the great offensive of the 21st of March, and again after that of the 27th of May. The fighting since the 15th of July had been no less costly than had those attacks. The desire for rest was as legitimate now as it had been then. Whether the enemy would let us have it was the question.

I considered that the enemy might either continue his attack on the Vesle, towards which he was exerting an ever-increasing pressure, or that he might extend it to the area between the Aisne and the Oise, where, in expectation of an attack on our part, he had got together considerable forces. I also thought he might possibly press forward between the Oise and the Somme, perhaps also near Albert and in the plain of the Lys, and finally, in the Sundgau. But I further assumed that these operations would only take the form of isolated local attacks for the enemy was also tired, on the whole not less so than ourselves. The attacks did take place; that they subsequently developed into a great battle on the whole front was mainly due to the considerable successes gained by the enemy on the 8th and 20th of August. These must have demonstrated that our troops were no longer what they had been, and invited him to continue the battle.

Early in August I definitely hoped that we should be able to defeat the imminent local attacks and to deliver counter-strokes, though on a smaller scale than heretofore. Even in extremely critical situations we had hitherto always succeeded in discovering a strategical remedy, and I had no reason to suppose we should not do so again.

In anticipation of these battles a new Group Headquarters was put in to take over the 2nd, 18th and 9th Armies; its commander was General von Boehn, Chief of Staff, General von Loszberg. This organization was to come into force between the 10th and 15th of August. As late as the first days of August I was able to tell General von Boehn that I hoped to hand him over a well-consolidated line. Unfortunately events were to prove me wrong.

If our line held, we should have to co-operate with the Imperial Chancellor, who was kept regularly informed of events at the front, in coming to definite decisions. That I should, in so doing, be obliged to bury many hopes was a fact I could not conceal from myself. It was in this sense that I discussed matters with my Staff; and while still occupied with these thoughts the blow of the 8th of August fell upon me.

Scale, 1:1000000

63 miles

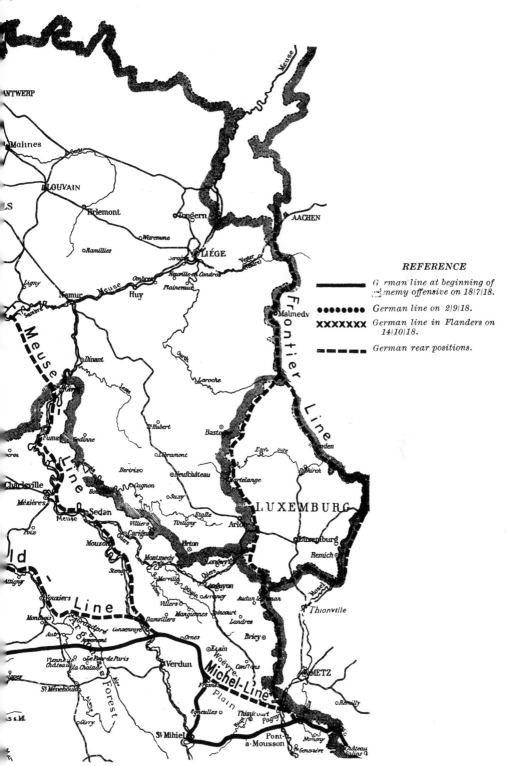

REFERENCE

───────── G rman line at beginning of
　　　　　　enemy offensive on 18|7|18.
●●●●●●●●● German line on 2|9|18.
XXXXXXX German line in Flanders on
　　　　　　14|10|18.
─ ─ ─ ─ ─ German rear positions.

THE LAST PHASE. SUMMER AND AUTUMN, 1918.

(MAPS X. AND VII.)

I

AUGUST 8th was the black day of the German Army in the history of this war. This was the worst experience that I had to go through, except for the events that, from September 15th onwards, took place on the Bulgarian Front and sealed the fate of the Quadruple Alliance.

Knowing that the next measures must be purely defensive, General Headquarters had early in August ordered a gradual withdrawal of our lines in the plain of the Lys, and the evacuation of the bridgeheads on the Ancre and Avre. They were evacuated on the 3rd and 4th of August.

At my special request General von Kuhl proceeded to the 2nd Army, in order to discuss once again the defensive measures on the line Albert–Moreuil. In this area two divisions that had been a long time in line, and seemed specially tired, were relieved by fresh ones. In this storm-centre the divisional fronts were narrow, artillery was plentiful and the trench system was organized in depth. All experience gained on the 18th of July had been acted upon. Only as regards the construction of works, the 2nd Army had not done as much as the 18th, for example, which had captured its positions at a later date.

Early on August 8th, in a dense fog, rendered still thicker by artificial means, the English, mainly with Australian and Canadian divisions, and the French attacked between Albert and Moreuil with strong squadrons of tanks, but otherwise in no great superiority. Between the Somme and the Luce they penetrated deep into our positions. The divisions in line at that point allowed themselves to be completely overwhelmed. Divisional staffs were surprised in their headquarters by enemy tanks. The breach very soon extended across the Luce stream; the troops that were still gallantly resisting at Moreuil were rolled up. To the northward the Somme imposed a halt. Our troops in action north of the river had successfully parried a similar assault. The exhausted divisions that had been relieved a few days earlier and were now resting in the region south-west of Péronne, were immediately warned and set in motion by the commander of the 2nd Army. At the same time he brought forward into the breach all other available troops. The Rupprecht Army Group dispatched reserves thither by train. The 18th Army threw its own reserves directly into the battle from the south-east, and pushed other forces forward in the region north-west of Roye. On an order from me, the 9th Army too, although itself in danger, had to contribute. Days, of course, elapsed before the troops from more distant areas could reach the spot. For their conveyance the most extensive use was made of motor lorries.

By the early hours of the forenoon of August 8th I had already gained a complete impression of the situation. It was a very gloomy one. I immediately dispatched a General Staff officer to the battle-field, in order to obtain an idea of the condition of the troops.

The reserves of the 2nd Army were able to stop the enemy's advance on Péronne at a point south of Bray. In the direction of Roye the enemy had about reached Arvillers; south of the Avre our front had to be bent back from Montdidier.

Six or seven divisions which could certainly be described as battle-worthy had been completely broken. Three or four others, together with the remnants of the battered divisions, were available for closing the broad gap between Bray and Roye.

The situation was uncommonly serious. If the enemy continued to attack with even ordinary vigour, we should no longer

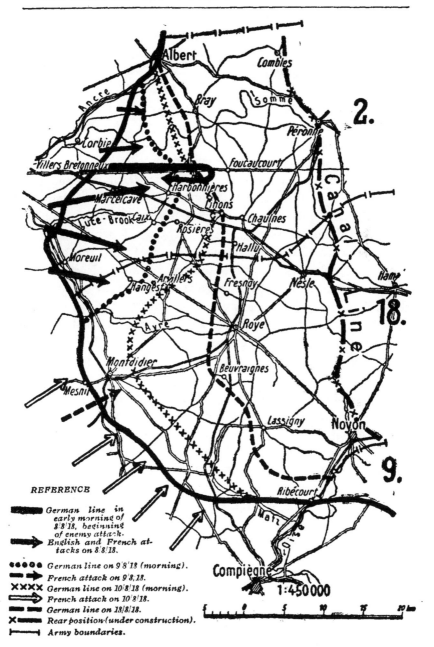

REFERENCE

German line in early morning of 8/8/18, beginning of enemy attack.
English and French attacks on 8/8/18.
••••• German line on 9/8/18 (morning).
■━━▶ French attack on 9/8/18.
××××× German line on 10/8/18 (morning).
⇨ French attack on 10/8/18.
■ ■ ■ German line on 18/8/18.
×━━ Rear position (under construction).
┠───┨ Army boundaries.

Fig. 41. The Battle between the Somme and the Oise. 1918.

be able to maintain ourselves west of the Somme. But the 2nd Army would have to hold on here, while the 18th Army, with its left wing standing fast on the heights along the Matz, swung back its right to Roye.

This movement was fixed for the night of August 9th–10th; should it fail, a great enemy victory was possible.

On August 9th, the enemy, whose attack, fortunately for us, was not pressed with sufficient vigour, gained ground between the Somme and the Avre. North of the Somme, too, the 2nd Army had to fall back a little. South of the river it succeeded in forming a continuous, if thin, line. These troops fought considerably better than the divisions between the Somme and the Luce had done the previous day. The good behaviour of the divisions which had been relieved shortly before the battle on account of exhaustion was particularly notable. North-west of Roye the line held. The 18th Army was able to carry out its difficult manœuvre on the night of the 10th. On the following morning the French vigorously attacked the original positions of that army, which were then evacuated by the rearguards according to plan. Of course, it had to leave a lot of material behind.

The stand made by the 2nd Army, and the withdrawal of their line by the 18th on the night of the 10th, had improved the situation between the Somme and the Oise. Reserves, too, had arrived and strengthened the front of the 2nd Army.

On the 10th and 11th severe but successful fighting took place on our positions south of Albert and between the Somme and the Avre, whilst between the Avre and the Oise the enemy followed up closely and attacked vigorously. Local attacks occurred all along the line during the next few days. Once more our troops stood their ground, but the 2nd Army was thoroughly disorganized, whereas the powers of resistance of the 18th were in no way impaired.

The losses of the 2nd Army had been very heavy. Heavy demands had also been made on its reserves to fill up the gaps. The infantry of some divisions had had to go into action straight off the lorries, whilst their artillery had been sent to some other part of the line. Units were badly mixed up. It could be foreseen that a number of additional divisions would become necessary in order to strengthen the 2nd Army, even if the enemy continued the offensive, and that was not certain. Besides, our losses in prisoners had been so heavy that G.H.Q. was again faced with the necessity of breaking up more divisions to form reserves. Our reserves dwindled. The losses of the enemy, on the other hand, had been extraordinarily small. The balance of numbers had moved heavily against us ; it was bound to become increasingly unfavourable as more American troops came in. There was no hope of materially improving our position by a counter-attack. Our only course, therefore, was to hold on.

We had to resign ourselves now to the prospect of a continuation of the enemy's offensive. Their success had been too easily gained. Their wireless was jubilant, and announced —and with truth—that the *moral* of the German Army was no longer what it had been. The enemy had also captured many documents of inestimable value to them. The Entente must have gained a clear idea of our difficulty in finding reserves, a further reason why they should pursue the offensive without respite.

The report of the Staff Officer I had sent to the battle-field as to the condition of those divisions which had met the first shock of the attack on the 8th, perturbed me deeply. I summoned divisional commanders and officers from the line to Avesnes to discuss events with them in detail. I was told of deeds of glorious valour but also of behaviour which, I openly confess, I should not have thought possible in the German Army ; whole bodies of our men had surrendered to single troopers, or isolated squadrons. Retiring troops, meeting a fresh division going bravely into action, had shouted out things like " Blackleg," and " You're prolonging the war," expressions that were to be heard again later. The officers in many places had lost their influence and allowed themselves to be swept along with the rest. At a meeting of Prince Max's War Cabinet in October, Secretary Scheidemann called my attention to a Divisional

Report on the occurrences of August 8th, which contained similar unhappy stories. I was not acquainted with this report, but was able to verify it from my own knowledge. A battalion commander from the front, who came out with a draft from home shortly before August 8th, attributed this to the spirit of insubordination and the atmosphere which the men brought back with them from home. Everything I had feared, and of which I had so often given warning, had here, in one place, become a reality. Our war machine was no longer efficient. Our fighting power had suffered, even though the great majority of divisions still fought heroically.

The 8th of August put the decline of that fighting power beyond all doubt and in such a situation as regards reserves, I had no hope of finding a strategic expedient whereby to turn the situation to our advantage. On the contrary, I became convinced that we were now without that safe foundation for the plans of G.H.Q., on which I had hitherto been able to build, at least so far as this is possible in war. Leadership now assumed, as I then stated, the character of an irresponsible game of chance, a thing I have always considered fatal. The fate of the German people was for me too high a stake. The war must be ended.

The 8th of August opened the eyes of the staff on both sides ; mine were certainly opened, and so, according to his statement in the *Daily Mail*, were those of General Foch. The Entente began the great offensive, the final battle of the world-war, and carried it through with increasing vigour, as our decline became more apparent.

I considered it possible that the occurrences since July 15th might have shaken the confidence of His Majesty and the Field-Marshal in me. Possibly, also, a fresh mind might be able to judge the situation from an unprejudiced point of view. I therefore earnestly requested the Field-Marshal, as I have previously mentioned, to replace me if he no longer had full confidence in me, or if he considered it advisable for other reasons. He refused. I also discussed my replacement with the Chief of the Military Cabinet in case they had anything against me personally. The Emperor gave me quite special proofs of his confidence in those days. I was deeply moved, but remained anxious as to whether His Majesty really read the whole situation aright. I have since been reassured. The Emperor told me later that, after the failure of the July offensive and after August 8th, he knew the war could no longer be won. The official report of the evening of the 8th announced briefly that the enemy had penetrated our line south of the Somme on a wide front. Early the following morning General von Cramon rang me up from Baden. He informed me that my report had caused great alarm in Vienna. I could not leave him in any doubt as to the serious view I took of the situation. Nevertheless, he begged me to remember how detrimentally the blunt admission of a defeat must affect our Allies who placed all their hopes on Germany. This occurred again on the 2nd of September.

The impression made on our Allies by the failure on the Western Front was great. The Emperor Charles announced his intention of coming to Spa in the middle of August.

Nothing was to be expected from Bulgaria. There the Radoslavoff Cabinet, under the influence of events on the western front and the Treaty of Bucharest, not to mention personal reasons, had been succeeded by Malinoff. Malinoff was no friend of the Alliance; some of his Ministers were openly against it and favourable to the Entente. When the Entente occupied Bulgaria later, although Malinoff was dismissed, they remained in office. The Imperial Chancellor had to pass over the behaviour of Malinoff's Ministry and invoke the assistance of the Tsar to prevent a fresh orientation of policy. The visit of a few Bulgarians to Switzerland also gave food for thought. That, too, we permitted. It was quite obvious that Bulgaria was intent on peace. It was also significant that the Bulgarian Military Representative, General Gantscheff, very seldom visited our G.H.Q.

As soon as I had obtained a grasp of the whole situation brought about by the events of the 8th of August, I decided to arrange conferences as soon as possible with the Imperial Chancellor and the Secretary of State for Foreign Affairs. These took place on August 13th and 14th at Spa.

On the 13th there was a discussion between the Chancellor, the Field-Marshal, Secretary of State von Hintze and myself, in the Field-Marshal's room at the Hotel Britannic. I reviewed the military situation, the condition of the Army and the position of our Allies, and explained that it was no longer possible to force the enemy to sue for peace by an offensive. The defensive alone could hardly achieve that object and so the termination of the war would have to be brought about by diplomacy. At the moment our line on the Western Front was holding, though in view of the element of uncertainty which the insubordination of some of the troops had introduced into our calculations, circumstances might necessitate a withdrawal of the front. I sincerely hoped, however, that the Army in France would stand fast. The state of affairs on the Western Front was naturally bound to make an unfavourable impression on our Allies. In this connection, the *moral* of our Army and people became a matter of even greater importance than before. I laid special emphasis on this. I drew their attention in particular to the damage done by Prince Lichnowsky. I again emphasized the necessity for speeches by our Ministers calculated to make an impression abroad, and the importance of even now inaugurating a propaganda department for educating public opinion.

The Field-Marshal said nothing about the state of feeling at home ; he took a more optimistic view of the military situation than I did. Secretary of State von Hintze drew, from what he had heard, the logical conclusion that peace negotiations were essential and that we should have to bring ourselves to take up a very conciliatory attitude.

The Chancellor spoke briefly of the state of public opinion at home without saying anything worthy of notice. He was very reserved about Prince Lichnowsky's case and referred us to the Supreme Court of Justice.

The following morning there was a conference presided over by His Majesty. The first matter to be discussed was the state of public feeling at home. The Chancellor made a few introductory remarks. I repeated my statement of the previous day about moral endurance. His Majesty then called on Secretary of State von Hintze. Von Hintze offered no opinion about affairs at home but went straight to the military and political situation, adopting the view I had given the previous day, and drawing the same conclusion ; he was manifestly moved ; tears stood in his eyes. The Emperor was very calm. He agreed with Secretary of State von Hintze and instructed him to open up peace negotiations, if possible, through the medium of the Queen of the Netherlands. He also pointed out the desirability of enlightening the people, and the necessity for a united and firm government policy. The Chancellor emphasized the need for upholding authority at home. Diplomatic negotiations must be opened at the right moment. The conference then closed ; deeply moved, I shook hands with Secretary of State von Hintze.

Meanwhile the Emperor Charles had arrived in Spa with Baron Burian and General von Arz. The statesmen are said to have discussed peace questions, as demanded by the situation ; in particular, the step taken by Baron Burian. I was not informed of this at the time but learnt it later from a remark made by von Hintze. Further, the Polish question also came under discussion. Baron Burian adhered to his own conception. We had missed a good opportunity of coming to a definite agreement with Austria. His Majesty meanwhile, supported by the Chancellor, was inclined to favour a solution by which Poland was to have a prince of her own choosing, whilst retaining her economic dependence on Germany. With such divergent views, an agreement with Austria–Hungary was impossible. His Majesty's proposal seemed to me really practical, and indeed corresponded to my personal convictions. I must expressly state here that the Emperor was always against the idea of a personal union with Poland.

The general military situation which had developed was discussed with General von Arz, and also the necessity of reinforcing the Western Front with more Austrian divisions ; so far only two had arrived. General von Arz had not abandoned the idea of an offensive in Italy, but was now of opinion that the Austro–Hungarian Army was no longer in a condition to hold out through the coming winter ; that was my last interview with this General whom I held in the highest esteem both as a man and a soldier.

After the Emperor Charles had left for Vienna the Field-Marshal and I immediately returned to Avesnes. I had thought that the Chancellor would leave Spa as well, in order to acquaint the Secretaries of State and the Reichstag with the situation, in the light of our conference. The education of public opinion was one of his functions. He remained in Spa, however, and left it to Vice-Chancellor von Payer and Secretary of State von Hintze to talk to the party leaders Ebert, Groeber, Stresemann, Count von Westarp and Wiemer. They were requested to attend at the Ministry of the Interior on the 21st. At the conference there, Secretary of State von Hintze explained the military and political situation and arrived at the same conclusion as had been reached at Spa, that the war must be brought to a close as speedily as possible. He announced his intention of taking all steps to procure peace. Gentlemen who were present at this conference told me how they had been very gravely impressed by our military situation. Of course, military considerations and the proposed peace negotiations imposed the necessity for extreme reticence on Secretary of State von Hintze ; it was bound to injure both seriously if, as happened later, our intentions were to be advertised broadcast. With an enemy such as we had to deal with this could only mean the continuation of the war and a peace offer that would completely destroy us. For similar reasons to those which must have actuated Secretary of State von Hintze, I was not in a position to give my views on the peace question to the world in general. I discussed it with a few of the members of my immediate circle. General von Bartenwerffer knew about the conference of the 14th of August through a note from the Secretary of State.

In addition, I discussed the situation with various Ministers. Secretary of State Solf came about this time to Avesnes. A private letter from Weimar informed me of the impressions he had received there. It was said by people standing in close touch with Solf's family, that in Solf's opinion I no longer believed in a victorious issue of the war, whereas the Field-Marshal still had hopes that with God's help it was not beyond attainment.

Vice-Chancellor von Payer came, too, and in the Chancellor's name, placed before me a proposal with regard to the Belgian question which corresponded to the unfavourable turn in the military situation.   I accepted it.   I thought it was to serve as a foundation for the negotiations of the Secretary of State for Foreign Affairs.   Instead of this, Vice-Chancellor von Payer made use of it in September in a speech delivered at Stuttgart ; it caused a sensation because of its attitude towards Belgium.

II

Days of great anxiety were to follow our return to Head-quarters.   Our position on the Western Front became more serious.   When, on the 14th, His Majesty ordered peace negotiations to be opened, the front was still holding though it gave us cause for anxiety.   After August 8th, General von Boehn took over command of his Army Group—the 2nd, 18th and 9th Armies—a few days earlier than had originally been intended. He, with his Chief of Staff, General von Loszberg, did all they could to increase the resisting power of their sector.

The fighting between the Somme and the Oise was still continuing in the middle of August ; the centre of gravity of the enemy's attack lay on both sides of Roye which was held through severe fighting.   A reserve position in rear, which meant that the left wing of the 17th Army would have to swing back, was prepared and consolidated on a line running through Bapaume, west of Péronne, along the Somme, west of Ham, the hills north-east of Noyon.   Where possible, old trench systems were incorporated.   Rupprecht's Army Group had withdrawn the front line of the 6th Army in the Lys Plain a few kilometres.

A further straightening out of the salient, entailing the evacuation of Kemmel Hill, was in preparation. Here, too, reserve lines were established and our former lines evacuated. There was no fighting of any importance. Nothing beyond occasional enemy raids disturbed our peace. About the middle of the month an English attack seemed probable.

The position of the 17th Army was similar. Here, after the 15th, there were indications of an offensive between Arras and the Ancre, especially towards Bapaume. The 17th Army was not to hold its front line but to give battle in a position three to four kilometres in rear; the front line was merely held by outposts who were to fall back on to the main position before the attack. There was thus a possibility of bringing the enemy's first onslaught to naught and getting notice of his intentions in time.

South-east of the battle front between the Somme and the Oise, the 9th, like the 17th Army, had made all preparations to put up a stout resistance. An attack between the Oise and the Aisne was anticipated and might be launched at any time about the middle of August. The reserves surrendered by this Army to the 2nd had been fully replaced and it was now well equipped in every way. Two counter-attack divisions were held in readiness near Cuts and Nouvron, where the enemy's main thrust was expected. The Army Headquarters Staff had thought out and organized everything with the greatest care.

There was less probability of an enemy offensive on the Vesle. There were no indications of an offensive on the sectors held by the German Crown Prince's, von Gallwitz's and Duke Albrecht's Army Groups. The situation might alter very quickly, however, in view of the advanced state of the enemy's preparations on all fronts.

G.H.Q. had to be prepared for the extension of the enemy's offensive to Crown Prince Rupprecht's Army Group (especially between Arras and the Ancre) and to the 9th Army, without neglecting the other sectors. The divisions of the 7th and 1st Armies, which had been withdrawn from the line as late as the end of July and beginning of August, could not be given a long rest. Some of them had already had to be put into support behind Rupprecht's Army Group and this was, of course, very

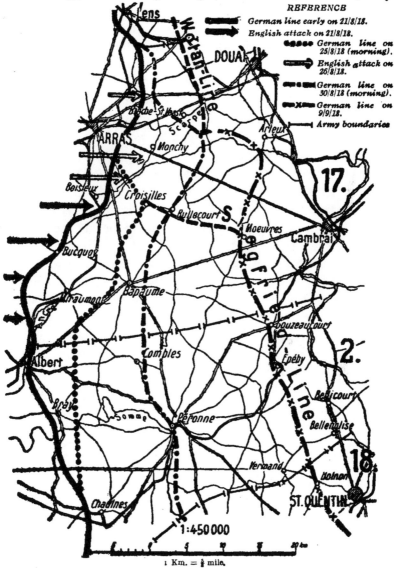

Fig. 42.   The Battle between the Scarpe and the Somme. 1918.

hard on them. An additional strain was thus thrown on the railway communications in the West.

On August 21st the English attacked south of Arras between Boisleux and the Ancre ; this was the first of a series of attacks on Crown Prince Rupprecht's sector which lasted almost uninterruptedly to the end of the war and made the heaviest demands on the Group Headquarters and their armies.

The 17th Army had fallen back in time and the English attack broke down in front of the new line. On the 22nd the 17th Army, by permission of G.H.Q., counter-attacked on its whole front. They were successful, but it would have been better not to attempt it. Immediately afterwards the English offensive spread southwards. On both banks of the Somme there was heavy fighting, the main weight of the attack being directed between Albert and Bray ; the Australians had no success. The first two days had thus gone well for us. I began to hope that here, at least, luck was going to turn. During the following days, however, the English, who had but few fresh reserves at their disposal, gained ground towards Bapaume after very severe fighting. The characteristic of their tactics was narrow but deep penetration by tanks after short but extremely violent artillery preparation, combined with artificial fog. Mass attacks by tanks and artificial fog remained hereafter our most dangerous enemies. This danger increased in proportion as the *moral* of our troops deteriorated and as our divisions grew weaker and more exhausted. The depth of penetration was soon known, but not the length of front to be attacked. Well-timed counter-attacks by reserves generally succeeded in restor ing the situation. There remained the danger, however, of the local command throwing in their troops too hurriedly and piecemeal. As the offensive developed, the enemy succeeded on the north in pushing us back from the Ancre. At this point a Prussian division, known to be a poor one, it is true, and for that reason given a sector covered by the river, had failed badly. This threw the whole line into confusion. The natural difficulties of fighting in the shell-hole area of the Somme battle-field, east of Albert, were increased by the fact that, owing to bad railway communications, it was very hard to get reserves up in this region. The situation there became extremely critical about August 25th. It was certain that the enemy offensive would continue.

South of the Somme, on the Péronne road, only local attacks had been launched. The 18th Army was constantly engaged, but put up a splendid fight. In view of the events east of the Oise the left wing was swung back closer to Noyon ; the handling

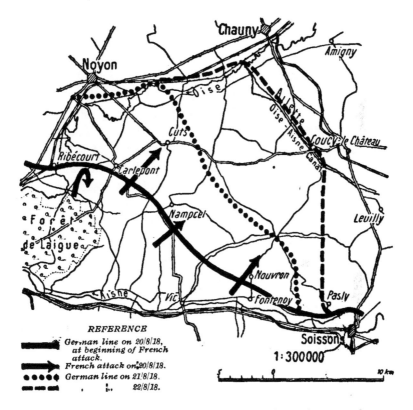

REFERENCE

━━━ German line on 20/8/18, at beginning of French attack.
➡ French attack on 20/8/18.
●●●●● German line on 21/8/18.
▬ ▬ ▬ ,, ,, 22/8/18.

1 : 300 000

10 km

Fig. 43. The Battle between the Oise and the Aisne. August, 1918.

of the 18th Army by General von Hutier was particularly cool, and he was very ably assisted by his Chief of Staff, Lieut.-Colonel Buerckner.

Between the Oise and the Aisne the great French attack had already succeeded on the 20th of August. By the 17th the French had pushed back our advanced troops on to the main line of defence. I found out later that these had offered stronger resistance than they should have done. The fighting strength of several divisions was thereby diminished to an extent that had not entered into my calculations.

The attack on August 20th developed exactly as had been anticipated. The counter-attack divisions stationed near Cuts, however, were not thrown into the fight. A deep salient was made here, rendering the position of the troops, with the Oise in their rear, exceedingly uncomfortable. In the direction of Nouvron, also, the enemy broke into our line but was driven back, although not completely, by counter-attacks delivered by good German Jäger divisions. Even apart from the two points of penetration, we did not succeed in maintaining our main line of resistance intact. The position was now such that it seemed unwise to attempt to maintain our line in front of the Oise and the Ailette. G.H.Q. decided to withdraw the right wing of the 9th Army behind the Oise on the night of the 21st, and on the night of the 22nd, whilst holding the ground to the north-west of Soissons, to withdraw the centre of the Army behind the Ailette. The battle had again taken an unfavourable course, in spite of all our precautions ; the nerves of the Army had suffered. In some places the men would no longer stand the tremendous artillery barrages and tank attacks which had become still more severe. Again we had suffered heavy and irreplaceable losses. August 20th was another black day, literally compelling the enemy to continue the offensive.

I calculated on the continuation of the enemy's attack between the Oise and the Aisne towards Laon ; an advance here would be fruitful of results, rendering untenable the positions of the 18th Army to the north of the Oise, and of the 7th to the north of the Vesle. The enemy was pressing the Soissons–Chauny line strongly. Fierce fighting ensued here, with varying success, and the end could not yet be foreseen.

The 18th Army, which took over the command of the troops on the Oise, was at this point directly and seriously menaced from the south.

As a result of the course of events east of Albert and south of the Oise, the position of the German troops between the Somme and the Oise was by no means so secure as the general military situation demanded. It would have been fatal to run risks at this point.

The Army Groups of the Crown Prince Rupprecht and von Boehn were therefore ordered to retire during the last days of August to the line already reconnoitred, east of Bapaume—in front of Péronne—Somme—in front of Ham—the heights north-east of Noyon. As their reserve line, the Siegfried system was now to be put in order. Von Boehn's Army Group had attached importance to the retention of the left bank of the Somme, in front of Péronne, because from there favourable flanking movements against the area north of Péronne were possible. Between Ham and Noyon a canal, which offered a good obstacle to tanks, determined the position of the line. These movements were carried through about the night of August 26th–27th.

The 17th Army, which had only a short wheel to the rear to perform, and the 18th, carried out the retirement without a hitch and in good order, and held their new positions against enemy attacks. The 2nd Army was less fortunate. North-west of Péronne the new line failed to hold. The division to the south-west of the town let the enemy gain the left bank, thus rendering the situation very difficult for the troops on the northern bank. Once more some divisions failed, putting a terrible strain on other gallant troops.

During this time, Field-Marshal Haig had extended his offensive northwards as far as the Scarpe, in order to get to the rear of the Siegfried position, north of the Croisilles–Moeuvres line. To do so, he had to take our Wotan position, which had been built in 1917, and starting in the north, ran through Biache St. Vaast, and along the Scarpe to the east of Monchy, in the direction of Bullecourt.

On the 26th of August the English offensive against the Arras–Cambrai road opened.

Here again the troops at first fell back according to plan, the early stages of the fighting developing favourably for us. Subsequently the English reached the Wotan system. On September 2nd a strong assault by English tanks over-ran obstacles and trenches in this line and paved a way for their infantry. Shortly after two o'clock in the afternoon General von Kuhl and Lieut.-Colonel von Pavelsz, the Chief of Staff of the 17th Army, reported that it would no longer be wise to form a new line in front of the Arleux–Moeuvres Canal. They requested permission from G.H.Q. to withdraw the 17th Army to that line, whilst holding the position north of the Scarpe. We had to admit the necessity for this measure. In concert with von Boehn's Army Group we had to take another important step in view of the position of the 2nd Army, withdrawing its line and that of the 18th Army to the Siegfried position. It would no doubt have been possible to keep the left wing of the 18th Army in front of the Siegfried line, on the Crozat Canal, but that required more men than the defence of the St. Quentin–La Fère line, with the broad valley of the Oise in front of it. G.H.Q. rejected this idea, and brought the entire 18th Army back into the Siegfried line. The 9th Army, and also the right wing of the 7th, had to conform to this movement, the latter abandoning the Vesle and taking up a position behind the Aisne, whilst the left wing of the same army continued to hold the Vesle to the north-east of Fismes.

Meanwhile the 9th Army had been heavily engaged, battles of tremendous violence developing on several occasions. Thanks to the unflagging skill and foresight of General von Carlowitz and his Chief of Staff, Lieut.-Colonel Faupel, and to the gallantry of several divisions, this Army for the most part maintained its positions. The 1st Guard-Infantry Division, coolly and ably led by Prince Eitel Friedrich, and the well-tried dismounted Guard-Cavalry Division, fought magnificently, quite undaunted by tanks.

It was no easy decision to withdraw the entire front from the Scarpe to the Vesle, but it shortened our line and economized men which, considering our huge wastage, was an advantage worth some sacrifice, notwithstanding that the enemy profited too. Conditions were easier for the troops in and to the east of the Siegfried line, whilst the enemy was compelled to occupy ground rendered desolate by the withdrawal in the spring of 1917.

The centre of the 17th Army was to be withdrawn behind the
Arleux–Moeuvres canal during the night of the 3rd, whilst in

Fig. 44. The Evacuation of the Lys Salient. 1918.

general the retirement was to be undertaken as one movement
the detailed orders being prepared by the Army Groups.

In addition, the long-prepared evacuation of the Lys salient by the 4th and 6th Armies was now carried out in order to save men.

At the same time G.H.Q. gave orders, after consulting the Chiefs of Staff of the Army Groups, for the reconnaissance and strengthening of a new line, the Hermann line, behind the two northern Army Groups. This line was to start on the Dutch frontier east of Bruges, follow the Ecloo Canal southward to the Lys, continue upstream to the east of Courtrai and then along the upper reaches of the Scheldt to south-west of Valenciennes. Further south it was to follow the Solesmes–le Cateau–Guise line. South-west of Marle, the Hermann line joined the Hunding–Brunhild position which, constructed in 1917, passed by Sissonne to the Aisne and continued upstream along that river. To the east of the Aisne the defensive position was continued by the rear lines of Gallwitz's Army Group which terminated in the Michael line. This ran across the Woevre plateau to a point west of the Moselle, near Pagny, flattening out the St. Mihiel salient. The positions which already existed were to be strengthened as much as available labour permitted.

Further, we had a second reserve position reconnoitred, running to the west of the Antwerp–Brussels–Namur line and then upstream along the Meuse; this was called the Antwerp–Meuse line. The fortresses in Alsace–Lorraine were put into a state of defence. Lastly, orders were given that all military material not required for immediate use should be removed from the region west and south of the Hermann–Hunding–Brunhild line, whilst preparations were to be made for the thorough demolition of railways and roads and for putting the coal mines out of working order. Villages were not to be interfered with unless for urgent tactical reasons. Large scale evacuation to Germany was undertaken. Our railway communications were not favourable for this. In the north, they were hemmed in towards Liége by the strip of Dutch territory running south to Maastricht; the line we built near Visé had not proved sufficient to overcome this difficulty. Further south, important railways converged on the Charleville–Montmédy section, and presented a particularly favourable target for enemy air-raids.

The Last Phase. Summer and Autumn, 1918

Supplies from Germany had already been cut down to absolute essentials.

The withdrawal of the front line to the Siegfried position made Avesnes no longer a suitable position for G.H.Q. and we accordingly returned to Spa which we had left in March so full of hope and confidence.

The enemy's strength was heavily taxed as well as ours, as they attacked again and again on various sectors with the same divisions. Their losses, too, must have been heavy, but they were on the offensive and we had to let them rain their blows on us, just as in 1917. Our experiences of those battles were repeated, our troops fighting better in attack than on the defensive. Our relative strength in divisions was more favourable at the beginning of September than it had been in the previous year, but some of our divisions were very weak ; we had, whilst retaining the machine-gun companies, to reduce our battalions from four to three companies. The transport ordinarily needed by four companies was excessive in view of their actual strength ; for example, we did not need four field cookers to a battalion, two or three being amply sufficient. With the breaking-up of a number of our divisions and the arrival of further Americans in the fighting line, the balance of numbers was bound to be still more unfavourable to us.

Shirking at the front became more prevalent, especially among men returning from home leave. Over-staying of leave increased, and the fighting line got thinner and thinner.

The Ministry for War was at last prepared to call up exempted men in greater numbers for the army, with what success remained to be seen. What would be the *moral* of these men ? From the divisions in the East we had long ago extracted every man who could be employed in the fighting divisions of the West. Our position in the East at this time was more satisfactory. The Soviet Government had paid the first, quickly followed by the second, instalment of the Russian indemnity ; relations had been established with the Don Cossacks. We were thus able to dispose of a few divisions of poor fighting quality, consisting of older classes not up to the standard of the Western Front,

Should the peace endeavours of the Government prove unsuccessful, and the war continue over the winter and into the following summer, export from the Ukraine became a vital matter both for ourselves and for Austria. It was as important as ever to maintain the blockade against Bolshevism, and to prevent the Entente forming a new line in the East. For this reason the three German dismounted Cavalry Regiments and the small force of artillery under General Count von der Goltz remained in Finland, faithfully watching the Murman railway and the gates of Petrograd. Our plans against the English garrison in Baku were still being carried out.

The Dual Monarchy could still spare a division or two for the West.

All this, however, was not even numerically, let alone morally, adequate to compensate for the increasing strength and confidence of the enemy in the West. It was quite clear that the distressing manifestations in the German Army would not decrease, but rather multiply, with the constant retreats and the disintegrating influences from home.

It was exceedingly difficult for G.H.Q. to reinforce the Army Groups of Crown Prince Rupprecht and von Boehn. My task would have been easier had G.H.Q. insisted at the end of July on withdrawing the battle-worn or decimated divisions of the 7th Army from the line, and had now taken the same course with all the Armies in action, especially the 2nd.

Our position was now so serious that G.H.Q. could not hope that air-raids on London and Paris would force the enemy to make peace. Permission was therefore refused for the use of a particularly effective incendiary bomb (expressly designed for attacks on the two capitals), sufficient supplies of which were ready in August. The large amount of damage that they were expected to do would no longer have affected the course of the war. Destruction for its own sake had never been permitted. Count Hertling, too, had requested G.H.Q. not to use these new incendiary bombs on account of the reprisals on our own towns that would follow. My views of the general military situation, however, were the real ground for the decision.

The Last Phase. Summer and Autumn, 1918

I retained the policy of ordinary raids on London and Paris, in order to keep enemy anti-aircraft material far from the front, and to prevent the troops noticing the reduction in our strength, but I no longer pressed matters. Only a few more small raids were made on Paris, while London could not at this time be reached, owing to adverse weather conditions.

I was constantly highly exercised in my mind with regard to the *moral* of the army and the people at home. On the visit of the Minister for War to Avesnes in August, I had officers from the front introduced to him with a view to convincing him of the bad influence exercised by the home population on discipline. He and other leading men in the War Ministry had always refused to realize this, or, at least, its full significance. The visit bore no fruit in spite of all my earnest representations to the Minister.

At home our attempt to improve the *moral* of the people by means of propaganda never got beyond the initial stages. After two years of pressure from me, the Chancellor had at last, in August, 1918, decided to create a Central Bureau for Press and propaganda purposes, both at home and abroad. It did not rank above the departments of the Imperial Government, but was attached to the Foreign Office as an unhappy appendage, devoid of real authority. I had to content myself with achieving this much, for I could get nothing else done. My constant proposals and suggestions, repeated time and time again, both verbally and in writing, for the appointment of an Imperial Minister of Propaganda, met with no response ; nobody but a Minister or Secretary of State, who could see the entire military, political and economical situation in its proper perspective could wield the mighty weapon of propaganda in the manner demanded by the war and the hour. He alone would have been able to decide when, where and by what department a public official statement should be made. He would have to work on a carefully-prepared system. Colonel von Haeften, who occupied a leading position in the newly-created Central Bureau, took great pains to get something done. Secretary of State Solf did indeed make one effective speech on his advice.

The Chancellor's speech on his birthday, early in September, was very feeble. The Vice-Chancellor spoke too, but his words were not telling like those of Clemenceau when German troops were within eighty kilometres of Paris. Later, Colonel von Haeften's suggestions to the new Chancellor, Prince Max of Baden, did not result in any more propaganda work being done, although it was particularly necessary in so serious a situation.

III

Tension was high on the Western Front. It had increased since our first peace moves of the middle of August. We still had reason to hope that we would maintain our position ; in Italy and Macedonia our flanks and rear were covered. There was, however, no longer any chance of the pendulum swinging in our favour. On the 3rd September we answered in that sense an inquiry from the Chancellor, which was prompted by his representative at G.H.Q., Count Limburg-Stirum, after he had been informed of our intention to withdraw to the Siegfried line. Count Limburg-Stirum was invariably kept informed of all events. The inquiry rather surprised me, because, ever since the 13th August, the Chancellor must have been fully acquainted with the situation ; the explanation was, however, that Count Limburg-Stirum knew nothing of the discussion of the 13th and 14th August.

G.H.Q. had no news from Secretary von Hintze ; all they knew was that he was to go to Vienna at the beginning of September to confer with Count Burian about peace. I considered that a further discussion with him and the Chancellor was urgently required. It would have to be held in the first days of September, immediately after our return to Spa. Secretary of State von Hintze arranged to attend as soon as he should return from Vienna, but the Chancellor's attendance was impossible in view of his great age.

The conference in Spa with Secretary von Hintze was held on the 8th or 9th September. He informed us that Count

The Last Phase. Summer and Autumn, 1918

Burian intended to dispatch a note to all the belligerents, inviting them to a peace discussion ; he added that, according to accounts received in Vienna, the Austro-Hungarian Army could only hold out until the winter. The need for peace there was growing more urgent. As regards his own efforts, von Hintze said that he confidently hoped for mediation through the Queen of Holland. I could not ascertain from his statements on what ground he based his hope. He had no expectation that the vague move to be taken by Count Burian would lead to any result, and feared that it would make the mediation of the Queen of Holland more difficult ; he considered a definite step, such as he intended to take at The Hague, to be better. On that point I quite agreed with him ; Count Burian's proposal, of which I had only recently heard, was much too indefinite.

It was probably on the Count's advice that the Emperor Charles had recently had certain questions put to the Field-Marshal through General von Cramon, concerning our strategic aims and our views as to the making of a peace proposal. General von Cramon asked me on the telephone to answer him as accurately as possible, as the Emperor Charles attached great importance to it. Of course my replies had to be cautiously worded, because there was a leakage from Vienna to France, as proved by the Emperor Charles's Parma letters. We replied that the German Army would hold its present line in the West, in particular the Siegfried line, but that we were in favour of immediate peace proposals ; we did, however, advise against those of Count Burian. I drafted this reply and it was discussed at our conversation with Secretary von Hintze before being dispatched.

Secretary von Hintze was informed in detail of the military situation. As a result of the discussions of September 9th, he wired from Spa to the Ministry of Foreign Affairs, stating that His Majesty and G.H.Q. agreed to an immediate appeal to the Queen of the Netherlands, and requesting that our Allies should be invited to approve this step and to join in it.

Austria-Hungary did not abandon Count Burian's plan in favour of ours, and his note was published on September 14th.

I do not know whether our proposal appeared to them too indirect, or what other reasons guided the Austro-Hungarian Government. The Emperor Charles explained in a letter to His Majesty that the telegram he had received from G.H.Q had induced him to take early steps for peace. I remarked to Colonel Heye that it was perhaps as well that Count Burian had taken the step he did. It was in accordance with my own views that we did not assume an attitude of opposition to it.

I cannot agree with the diplomatists that Count Burian's peace note rendered mediation by the Queen of the Netherlands impossible. It made it more difficult, but did not exclude it by any means. Above all, I cannot understand why Dutch mediation was not sought before the publication of Count Burian's note, for which there would have been time enough. I do not believe that Secretary von Hintze seriously discussed the matter with the Dutch Ambassador in Berlin.

In those days I no longer concerned myself to any extent with military-political questions. Secretary von Hintze discussed the Polish question with G.H.Q. on lines laid down by the Chancellor. I replied, as my duty dictated, and gave him my views. In a communication dated August 28th, after conferring with a Polish gentleman in Berlin, the Secretary of State placed before us definite proposals for the best constitution for Poland and for defining our relations to that State. He particularly wanted to give Vilna to Poland, as it would always constitute a foreign element in any Lithuanian state ; Poland must certainly undertake to fulfil certain conditions, particularly the military convention, to our complete satisfaction.

G.H.Q. replied on August 30th, signifying their agreement with the Secretary, and calling attention to certain points which had been raised in the previous discussions of which he might be unaware. We laid stress, for example, in the interests of our economic and military policy, on the necessity of a railway convention with Poland, and of ensuring safe communication through Poland with Russia.

I considered it essential, too, that the fulfilment of Poland's obligations should be guaranteed in some way, for I could not overcome my distrust of that country. Vilna had formerly been promised to the Lithuanians by the Chancellor. It was to be feared that they would very naturally regard its cession to Poland as a breach of faith. It was for the Foreign Office to take steps to avoid the trouble to which this might give rise. With regard to Lithuania, even after this serious loss, I was still of the same opinion, and emphasized the necessity of attaching it as a self-governing state to Germany or Prussia through personal union.   Torn from its context, this minute was used in the Reichstag to convict me of muddled political thought. The story of its origin is simple, but it is not clear how it came to be purloined from the Foreign Office. Plans should be followed as long as possible, provided damage does not result in other directions, an eventuality there was no ground to fear in this case.   In this instance the policy of the Foreign Office was sound, and my position quite correct.

From the same point of view we were at that time in favour of the formation of a Baltic state and the settlement of the question of the Finnish throne according to Finland's desires.

Conditions in Rumania were also discussed with Secretary von Hintze.   The obvious military superiority of the Entente had strongly affected the Government in Jassy, which was entirely under the influence of the Entente Ambassador. Their attitude to us became cooler and cooler ; the weakness of the Bucharest peace now made itself felt.   In agreement with Secretary von Hintze, G.H.Q. seriously considered the inauguration of a new campaign against Rumania with the troops that had been released from the East for the West.   General von Arz promised his support, provided the Emperor Charles would agree, but, in spite of the military necessity for this step, the latter refused to sanction any special pressure on Rumania. We therefore renounced the idea of taking military measures and the troops were ordered to their original destination, the West. In the end, however, they had to be sent to Serbia. Later on, Austria-Hungary herself suggested armed intervention in Rumania, but by that time it was too late.

Meanwhile Admiral von Holtzendorff, who had developed

severe heart disease, had resigned and Admiral Scheer became Chief of the Naval Staff. He was an unusually clear thinking man, capable of swift decisions. I got into touch with him as soon as possible in Spa, and talked over with him the situation in the West and the submarine campaign. The evacuation of our submarine base at Bruges might soon become necessary. Admiral Scheer did not think that this would have a decisive influence on the submarine campaign as the vessels already had to travel from Flanders round the north of Scotland, being no longer able to enter the Channel. Of course he did not welcome the necessity of having all our submarine bases on our German coasts.

He thought, too, that submarine construction could be speeded up and better results obtained. He asked me to assist him in the matter, saying he needed more workmen to turn out more submarines. I explained that G.H.Q. was not in a position to supply them, and could only agree to release a certain number of specially trained engineers and skilled hands. This only involved a few men. These discussions lasted into October; the situation had assumed an exceedingly grave aspect, nevertheless I gave instructions for the release of these men. This order also led to considerable public controversy. G.H.Q. could not give in until the sword had been wrested from its hand. There was no need to abandon any desirable political aims, or to forego any useful equipment. In spite of all the difficulties, of which I was only too well aware, I was not the man to throw up the sponge prematurely, and I held firmly to the opinion that the stronger we were in the field the better our position would be in any peace negotiations.

I had introduced a change on my staff. I found in Colonel Heye a former assistant, and placed him in control of several departments that previously had been under my immediate supervision. Their reports went to him, but I reserved to myself decisions of moment. What I had gone through would have left its trace on any man. I had been appointed to G.H.Q., not to make peace, but to win the war, and had thought of nothing else. Like Clemenceau and Lloyd George, I had wanted to call on the whole nation, but I was not a dictator, as men were only too glad to repeat, false though it was. Lloyd George and Clemenceau had the control of their Parliaments, for these were " their " Parliaments. At the same time, they stood at the heads of the entire administrative and executive authorities ; I, on the other hand, had no constitutional power to influence the German Government in order to enforce my views as to the steps necessary for the conduct of the war, and I was frequently confronted with the lack of understanding and energy of the departments concerned. Peace not being obtainable, I had striven to carry the war to the successful issue which alone could save us from the fate we now suffer. I understood now that this successful issue was impossible, and I saw the approach of the disaster which it had been my life's work to prevent.

IV

While these events were proceeding in Spa, the Army Groups of the Crown Prince Rupprecht, von Boehn and of the German Crown Prince had. carried out the withdrawals from Kemmel and the Lys plain behind the Arleux–Moeuvres canal, into the Siegfried system, and on the Vesle. The movement went without a hitch and was completed by the 18th Army, which had furthest to go, by about the 7th September. The armies had not fallen back everywhere to the German trench system. In places they were occupying parts of the old enemy lines. Everywhere the enemy followed close on our heels. They soon resumed their offensive, which developed with special force between Moeuvres and Holnon against the left wing of the 17th, the whole of the 2nd, and the right wing of the 18th Army, and between the Ailette and the Aisne against the left wing of the 9th and the extreme right of the 7th Army. Fighting was very severe, but our line recovered itself, except that in the 2nd Army some weakness still remained. On the 18th and 19th September, particularly heavy attacks were launched on the Moeuvres–Holnon sector ; the left wing of the 2nd Army was pressed back several kilometres on to the Scheldt–Oise canal, north of St. Quentin, the 18th Army being forced to withdraw its extreme right to conform with this retirement. Otherwise, the line was held, severe local fighting continuing up to the 25th and 26th September. The French extended their attack further towards St. Quentin. It goes without saying that these days, too, took heavy toll of the resources of our whole army.

The German Crown Prince's Army Group had taken over command of the 9th Army from von Boehn about the middle of the month. This army and the right wing of the 7th were constantly in action. The Army Group had to find its own reinforcements. Tension was particularly high on both sides of Rheims and, after the 22nd, on both sides of the Argonne also, where on the 26th another great battle was to break out. The construction of the Hermann line behind the two northern Army Groups had begun, and similar work was actively proceeding in the rear of the Crown Prince's Group.

Behind the line between the coast and the Meuse, the work of evacuation was often interrupted by successful enemy air raids. Huge supplies of material had to be moved which were essential for the further prosecution of the war. Many sectors had worked on bad supply systems and the result was now felt.

In front of von Gallwitz's Army Group, between St. Mihiel and the Moselle, much movement had been noticed as early as the end of August. An American offensive seemed probable there. G.H.Q. pushed up reserves. I discussed with the Chief of Staff of the Army Group and of Army Detachment C, which was exposed to the attack, the evacuation of the salient, which had long been planned and prepared. Local commanders were confident in spite of my misgivings. G.H.Q. was reluctant to evacuate the salient, on account of the industrial centres lying behind it, and unfortunately did not order this step until the 8th September. At the same time the southern front of Army Detachment C was to keep the enemy at arm's-length, much as had been the case with the 17th Army in the middle of August. Advanced guards only were to be left in the most forward trenches.

The Last Phase. Summer and Autumn, 1918

The work of evacuation had not been carried very far when, on the 12th September, the attack developed between the Rupt and the Moselle, accompanied by a secondary attack against the northern end of the salient at the Combres heights. The enemy penetrated our line in both places. On the southern sector they broke through a Prussian division and the reserves

Fig. 45. The Battles in the St. Mihiel Salient. 1918.

were not sufficiently close up to restore the position immediately. On the Combres heights there was an Austro-Hungarian division, which might have fought better. As early as noon the local Army Headquarters ordered the evacuation of the salient. I blamed myself, but also the local command. The earlier reports indicated that the evacuation was proceeding satisfactorily, this being facilitated by the enemy not following up. I founded my official communiqué, which turned out later to be too favourable, on these reports.

It has been said that my communiqués were unreliable. They were indisputably truthful and they were framed in accordance with our duty to the army, the people at home and our Allies. The evening communiqué merely described briefly the events of the day. That of midday was founded on the reports which reached G.H.Q. up to the time of my signature—generally 10.30 a.m. I wrote them principally for the army; our soldiers had the right to have their achievements and sufferings reported. The unit, officer or man mentioned in the communiqué was proud of it; was it not uplifting to have one's glory announced to the world? It provided a stimulus of no mean value to the prosecution of the war, and an important psychological spur to achievement. The people at home, too, were rightly proud to have the deeds of their sons recognized. Every word in the official communiqué was carefully weighed; great events were given in detail; only the most important of lesser engagements could be mentioned. In quiet times the communiqués frequently ran: " Nothing particular," or, " No events of importance." From this an intelligent reader gathered that on all parts of the wide front German men stood night and day doing their difficult duty to the Fatherland with loyal devotion. I should certainly have preferred in times of stress to have employed curt phraseology rather than to give full reports, for the events of such times were appropriate to these phrases. But a report on the Flanders battle: " Langemarck is held," or " lost," would have satisfied nobody.

Losses of ground were mentioned, if they affected the general situation, but not until no harm could be done to the troops engaged by doing so. Nobody could expect me to communicate our losses in guns and prisoners to the enemy, not even the German, who thinks so objectively! We were not the iron people about which I was so often told in those very days. The habit of reading enemy communiqués had done damage enough already. Suspicion of the reports from G.H.Q. went at times so far as to cause them to be compared with enemy reports. That was typically German!

Was it not, for example, a great strategic victory for us to have held the line in Flanders in 1917, although we suffered tactical reverses which cost us prisoners and material of war.   If I mentioned in my report that the enemy had reached our artillery lines, one could deduce the loss in prisoners and guns.   Was that not sufficient ?   Did people wish to wallow in misery ?

G.H.Q. had allowed the enemy communiqués to be published, relying on the clear-sightedness of the German people.   I had the impression later that it was a mistake.   The enemy used his communiqués for propaganda and lowered our *moral*.   A belated order forbidding the publication of these reports seemed to me even more questionable.   France knew what she was doing when she forbade the publishing of our communiqués, although ours were never used for propaganda.

I have mentioned that I had also to consider the effect of our official reports on our Allies.   This was important in our case because our Allies placed all their hopes on us.

One thing must be admitted : Wolff's commentaries on my reports, edited in Berlin and intended solely for the neutrals, were not happily worded.   There was good reason for the tone of these telegrams ; but I stopped them, although too late, as soon as I realized the harm they did.

On the Woevre plateau, the evacuation of the salient was carried through, though with heavy losses, and the Michael position was occupied.   The fighting was dying down by the 13th.   According to the reports that reached me, the continuation of the attack against the Michael position seemed probable.

After the 22nd the situation changed in front of von Gallwitz's Army Group.   The likelihood of an attack here diminished and a battle on both sides of the Argonne appeared imminent.

The sector of Duke Albrecht's Army Group was also considered in danger, but that was based rather on the conjectures of my colleagues than on reports.   I, on the other hand, clung to my opinion that the development of the offensive between Rheims and the Meuse was more likely than an attack in Lorraine.

Our troops had suffered severely ; strengths were low and exhaustion was setting in.   The situation grew steadily worse' but the line held with the exception of a few weak places on the 2nd Army sector.

The Austro-Hungarian line held in Italy. There were no indications of an Italian offensive.

Thus matters stood when events in Bulgaria forced us to grave decisions.

On September 15th the armies of the Entente attacked in Macedonia, east of the Vardar, in the mountains between the Vardar and the Cerna, and also with weaker forces near Monastir. On both flanks the attacks broke down. In the centre, where the attack was faced with the greatest obstacles, the Bulgarian 2nd and 3rd Divisions offered no resistance ; they simply surrendered the position. No other explanation exists for the rapid advance of the Entente troops over that wild broken country, eminently suited for defence, with its hilly, or rather mountainous, character. General von Scholtz sought to bring the Bulgarians to a stand on the second line by bringing reserves up in good time, but his hopes were not realized. The 2nd and 3rd Bulgarian Divisions retreated, as if on a definite plan without any show of resistance, behind the Cerna in one direction and behind the Vardar in another. The Bulgarian reserves, equal in strength to three German divisions, did not fight at all.

The German troops, which had recently been reinforced by battalions from Rumania, could not close the gap unaided. The northern descent to the valley of the Vardar in the neighbourhood of Krivolac was open to the Entente.

All further efforts to reorganize and make a stand failed. The Bulgarian Army went home. Only the Bulgarians incorporated in German forces between Lake Prespa and the Cerna behaved better for a time.

On the 16th, or at the latest the 17th, General Lukoff, in command of the troops on the Struma, wired to the Tsar that he must conclude an armistice ; he could not be too quick to desert us publicly and throw himself into the arms of the Entente.

A few days after the 15th, a secret report of the French General Staff fell into my hands which made it evident that the French no longer expected any resistance from the Bulgarian Army.

Entente propaganda and money, and the United States representative who had remained in Sofia, had done their work.   In this
instance again, the Entente had made a thoroughly good job of
it.   Possibly, too, Bolshevik influences from Russia had crept

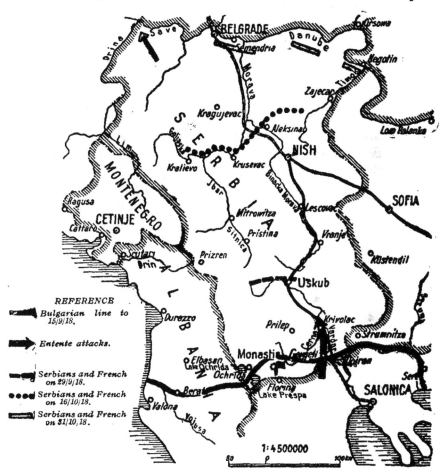

Fig. 46.   The Collapse of Bulgaria.   1918.

in.   Neither the Tsar nor our representative in Sofia knew anything of this.   General Jekoff had merely looked on ; a few
days before the battle, which was known to be imminent, he
developed ear trouble, I understand, and went to a clinic in
Vienna.

General von Scholtz and all the Germans had done their utmost. Where Germans were in command the Bulgarian Army held together. On the mountain sector the Bulgarians refused to have a German command. They even went so far as to leave a divisional general there whom General von Scholtz wished to have removed because he did not trust him ; and they made numerous alterations in personnel in that sector.

The suggestion, put forward by the Bulgarians to cloak their defection, that I was informed that soldiers' councils had been formed among their troops, is untrue. It is equally untrue to say that we had broken a treaty obligation to leave six divisions on the Bulgarian Front, for this obligation was confined to the Serbian campaign of 1915. When I went to G.H.Q. in August, 1916, there was about one division in Macedonia. The obligation must also have lapsed on the formation of the German Supreme Command for the Quadruple Alliance in September, 1916. Nor did this Supreme Command leave anything undone. The forces opposed to each other there were of about equal strength. The Greek troops with the Entente had had no military experience, and their adherence to the enemy was not based on conviction. The Bulgarian Army had had a long rest. They had had the opportunity to strengthen their forces, and ought rather to have helped us in the West than to have sought aid from us. G.H.Q. knew that the Bulgarian Army was, in fact, in a bad state ; but there was ground for the hope that it would be able to withstand the attack which we expected, as, indeed, was the case wherever the men were still willing to fight. We anticipated local failures now as previously, as did the German generals in Bulgaria, but we did not expect the complete collapse of their army. The rumours which had circulated in Sofia, to the effect that the army would not continue fighting after the 15th of September, found only too terrible confirmation. We could not answer every single cry for help. We had to insist that Bulgaria must do something for herself, for otherwise we, too, were lost. It made no difference whether our defeat came in Macedonia or in the West. We were not strong enough to hold our line in the West and at the same time to establish in the Balkans a German front to replace the Bulgarian, as we should have had to do if we were to hold that front in the long run.

The Bulgarian Government did nothing whatever to keep up the *moral* of the troops and the population or to maintain discipline. They gave free rein to enemy influences, and took no steps against any of the anti-German agitations. Entente bribery was the finishing stroke, even the troops that streamed back to Sofia being well supplied with enemy money. These, nothing else, were the true causes of the defection of Bulgaria from the Quadruple Alliance.

There were no illusions about the seriousness of the situation created by the collapse of Bulgaria.

Turkey, too, was now in great difficulties. Her Palestine Front was broken beyond repair. Here, again, the German officers and men had done their duty, and had fought like heroes on the Jordan. They were, however, limited in numbers, and could only keep the Turkish Army together for a time.

The English were gaining ground rapidly northwards along the coast and the railway to Damascus. This, it is true, did not yet amount to a threat to Constantinople, but it had grave effects on the Turks' power to resist. Having regard to the loyalty of Enver and Talaat, this would have not had any decisive effect by itself on the attitude of Turkey ; but the Entente had now substantial free forces in Syria, and were also, as a result of the Bulgarian collapse, able at any time to march on Constantinople across the Maritza. There were only very weak Turkish forces here, the task of protecting this line having been hitherto left to the Bulgarian Army on the Struma. It was, of course, possible to bring reinforcements from the Caucasus, and perhaps also from the Ukraine, but we had never succeeded in arranging transport of troops on any large scale across the Black Sea, the available shipping being insufficient. Reinforcements were, however, moved at once, some battalions from the Ukraine being sent to Constantinople. It was too late, however, to do anything decisive. Constantinople was bound to fall, and whether it fell in November or December made very little difference to the situation as a whole. Once the city fell, it was to be expected that the Entente fleets would establish communication with Rumania through the Black Sea, and send troops through Bulgaria to the Danube. We could not hope to keep Rumania neutral. Sooner or later her hostile attitude would become unmistakable.

It was obvious that the Entente would attempt to liberate Serbia, and to make an attack from there on Hungary, thus giving the *coup de grâce* to the Dual Monarchy. Our Balkan front was unstable, and it was quite uncertain whether we would be able to reconstruct it in Serbia and Bulgaria, or even on the Danube. The position in Sofia at first was far from clear. We could not even tell whether the whole Bulgarian Army was really demoralized. The Serbian Army had fought for years outside its own country, and had shown a brilliant example of true patriotism. The Bulgarians could well have done the same. Of Old Bulgaria, too, not a foot was in enemy occupation.

If the Bulgarian Army fell out altogether, then it would certainly be time for Germany and Austria–Hungary to send substantial forces to the Balkans.

In our situation it was vital to do everything to secure our position in the Balkan peninsula, in order to prevent the Entente moving into Hungary and making a flank attack on Germany and Austria. We sent a German division from Sebastopol through Bulgaria and Rumania to Sofia. General von Arz also dispatched an Austro–Hungarian Division from the Ukraine through Rumania to Serbia. Three German divisions from the East, which had been released for service in the West, and had, in part, already started on their journey thither, were diverted to Serbia. Two divisions from the Italian Front, which had been handed over to us by General von Arz for service in the West, were also sent. Finally, even from the hard-pressed Western Front, G.H.Q. sent the Alpine Corps to Serbia; this corps had just been withdrawn from the line, and still had its mountain equipment which was an essential requirement in the Serbian mountains. The West thus lost six or seven divisions.

While one German division was to be assembled at Sofia,

to support the Tsar's Government, the others were intended to be concentrated at Nish.   Transport was so bad that this could not be completed before the middle of October.

It very soon became clear that nothing more was to be expected from Bulgaria.   The division from Sofia was sent to Nish.   The Tsar abdicated and left the country.   The Government threw itself into the arms of the Entente.   The army dispersed or allowed itself to be disarmed.   The conclusion of the armistice, which would hand the country over completely to the Entente, was to be expected at any moment.

The German troops that had been fighting in the Bulgarian Army maintained their order fully.   While the Entente troops advanced irresistibly up the Vardar towards Uskub, they withdrew in perfect order westwards to Mitrovitza and eastwards to Sofia.   The establishment of our new front in Serbia depended very largely on the resistance of the Austro–Hungarian troops.

The position in Rumania remained in the highest degree obscure and anxious.   We could bring but few troops thither, even including those from the Caucasus.

In the East the Bolsheviks were still hostile.   Our policy in Great Russia had won us no friends who could now help us.

There was the utmost doubt as to whether we could succeed in establishing in Serbia and Rumania a new flank protection for Austria–Hungary and our Western Front, and in retaining the Rumanian oil-fields.

In Italy an attack was sure to come, and it was quite uncertain how the Austro–Hungarian troops there would fight.

The general military position could only become definitely worse ; whether it would move slowly or with terrifying speed could not be foreseen.   It was probable that it would be all over in a relatively short time, as actually happened in the Balkans and on the Austro–Hungarian Front in Italy.

In these circumstances I felt compelled to take on myself the heavy responsibility of hastening the end of the war, and for this purpose to move the Government to decisive action.   Since the 9th of September G.H.Q. had heard nothing of the Peace *démarche* of the Queen of Holland.   Since the middle of August time had passed without anything being achieved. Count Burian's Note had awakened no echo. Our diplomacy, in the face of the enemy's determination to destroy us, had a hopeless task. With all this in mind I came, not suddenly but bit by bit, from the beginning of August onwards and through many hard inward struggles, to the conclusion that I must act, and I called Secretary von Hintze to Spa on the 26th of September.

V

Meanwhile the position in Berlin had become most discouraging, the struggle for power coming ever more prominently into the foreground. The outward and visible sign of this struggle was Erzberger's attack on Count von Hertling, which had raised a fearful storm. The Emperor's appeal of the 14th of August for a united and resolute Government had remained unanswered. I have never fully understood the events of those days. I did not regard the position of the Chancellor as seriously shaken, his great Parliamentary experience having hitherto enabled him to ride every storm. Events in Berlin caused von Hintze to fix his visit for Sunday, the 29th of September. The Chancellor was also invited to Spa by Count Limburg-Stirum. On this occasion I had not asked for his attendance, as early in September his advanced age had been put forward as a reason for his not travelling ; but I was very glad indeed that he was coming, especially as I was growing clearer and clearer in my own mind as to the steps that ought to be taken.

In the meantime tremendous fighting had broken out again in the West. East of Ypres the Entente attacked, and over all the old Flanders battle-field drove us out of our foremost positions, and, in part, also back over the artillery protective line. We were compelled to withdraw the Army to a rear position.

In the direction of Cambrai, on the 27th, a strong enemy attack gained ground beyond the Canal, although every possible step had been taken to resist them. Further south, up to the Vesle, the front held.

In Champagne and on the western bank of the Meuse a big battle had begun on the 26th of September, French and American troops attacking with far-reaching objectives. West of the Argonne we remained masters of the situation, and fought a fine defensive battle. Between the Argonne and the Meuse the Americans had broken into our positions. They had assembled a powerful army in this region, and their part in the campaign became more and more important. We held their thrust, however, the 27th being in the main a day of success for us, while on the 28th, too, we held our lines, apart from certain rectifications of our front which were carried out in accordance with our plans.

The whole Western Front was thus again the scene of tremendous fighting.

On the 29th of September and following days there was further fighting, presenting the normal difficulties, but not compelling us to sudden, momentous decisions. I wish to insist on this fact in what follows, as earnestly as I do upon the fact that since the middle of August the Goverment had done nothing whatever to secure peace. This did not surprise me. Was it for G.H.Q. to wait until Turkey or Austria–Hungary, who were immediately affected, moved in the matter ? That would have been easy, but did not seem to me to accord with my duty.

Were we to hope, after all our writing and pressure, that the Government would at this stage spur the people to further efforts, or would really summon the nation or take a step towards peace through the medium of Holland ? Were there any real prospects of this ? Duty compelled us at last to substitute action for idle time-wasting and empty words. The enemy had to be asked for peace and an armistice. The military position, which would all too probably get worse, demanded this. We were not yet bound to surrender unconditionally. The enemy would have to speak. Would he talk of conciliation or of violence ? In my judgment of Clemenceau and Lloyd George, I feared the worst. Wilson, however, had often stated his terms in the most solemn form imaginable. He, and the great country he represented, must feel themselves bound in honour by these declarations. Besides, the decisive help given in France by the United States, without which the Entente would long before have suffered a military defeat, made it highly likely that Wilson would be able to maintain his views, which he had expressed in the most binding manner, against England and France. We had to see clearly on this matter. If our views of Wilson were right, then we could accept as the basis of negotiations his fourteen points, hard enough, but, at any rate, clear and definite. If, on the other hand, we were disappointed in him, if the enemy imposed too severe conditions, if even their military chiefs refused us the respect to which our brave fight entitled us, the war would have to continue, however hard it might be, and then at last the Government and the people might be brought to heroic measures, when they saw clearly once and for all what was at stake for Germany in this war.

It was for that reason that I simply could not give up hope of a revival of the will to war at home. If the enemy gave the same answer as he did in January, 1917, with any proper leadership a new spirit of determination and unity would surely appear among the people, which could not be without a favourable effect on our *moral*. I cannot doubt that this would have had a powerful effect in encouraging the Army and the whole war industry, and the sooner it came, the more powerful would be the effect We would thus once more have a war-machine through which we could speak with no uncertain voice, if the enemy would not listen to reason. There was nothing unduly optimistic in this view. France, Serbia and Belgium had suffered far more than we had, and had held out. If the war should approach our own territory, if the feeling that he was protecting home and all that the word meant entered into the heart of each man at the front who knew full well what such terms as " theatre of war," " battlefield," even " L. of C.," meant, if the war with all its destructive fury threatened German soil, then I felt that our seventy millions of Germans would stand like one man, determined and ready to sacrifice for their country all the mighty strength that still remained to them.   Whether France herself, bled white and suffering worse than we were, would remain in the field for long after her territory was evacuated, was also doubtful.   In any case, our position was not so bad that we could have justified a capitulation to our people or our descendants; on the other hand we must plainly sue for peace if peace could be had.

I had slowly come to this fateful conclusion, and now felt bound and eager to act upon it, whatever others might say, who were not so well informed as to the military situation as I was.   In all the great decisions of this war, I have followed my own views with a full sense of my own responsibility.   That I should be all the more abused and held responsible for every misfortune I knew well.   Personal hostility could not affect my resolution.

At six o'clock on the afternoon of the 28th of September, I went down to the Field-Marshal's room, which was one floor below mine.   I explained to him my views as to a peace offer and a request for an armistice.   The position could only grow worse, on account of the Balkan situation, even if we held our ground in the West.   Our one task now was to act definitely and firmly, without delay.   The Field-Marshal listened to me with emotion.   He answered that he had intended to say the same to me in the evening, that he had considered the whole situation carefully, and thought the step necessary.   We were also at one in the view that the armistice conditions would have to permit a regular and orderly evacuation of the occupied territory and the resumption of hostilities on our own borders.   From the military point of view, the first was a tremendous concession. We did not consider any abandonment of territory in the East, thinking that the Entente would be fully conscious of the dangers threatening them as well as ourselves from Bolshevism.

The Field-Marshal and I parted with a firm handshake, like men who have buried their dearest hopes, and who are resolved to hold together in the hardest hours of human life as they have held together in success.   Our names were associated with the

721

greatest victories of the world war. We now shared the conviction that it was our duty to sacrifice our names to ensure
the step being taken that we had done everything humanly
possible to avoid.

VI

The lines of the conference to be held with Secretary of State
von Hintze had been settled even in detail at my conversation
with the Field-Marshal on the 28th of September. The discussion took place at ten o'clock in the morning of the 29th,
at the Hotel Britannique, Colonel Heye being present.

' After a short greeting, the Secretary began at once to explain
the political situation at home, without referring to international
affairs. He described the position of Count von Hertling as
so shaken that he could not remain any longer in office, and
even his own position, he stated, was by no means secure. The
domestic situation was such that a complete change of system,
and the formation of a Parliamentary Ministry in Berlin, was
essential. He even spoke of the possibility of a revolution.
Up to this moment I had assumed that G.H.Q. would have to
discuss the further steps that it thought necessary with the
existing Chancellor and Secretary for Foreign Affairs. A change
in these offices at this moment would of necessity bring delay,
confusion and harm. With such great changes a Government
is bound to lose continuity and the grip of business for a time.
To whatever conclusion His Majesty might come, of course, the
Government would remain the Government to G.H.Q., however changed it might be in form or personnel. The incoming
Ministers would be fully conscious of the responsibility they
would bear if they took office in the existing situation. G.H.Q.
would have to urge its views upon the new Government just
as it would have done on the old, and would have to ensure,
if an honourable armistice were really obtainable, that the
Army did not suffer by reason of the change of Government.

In spite of my objections, von Hintze regarded a change of
our whole system of government as essential. He did not

think it would be difficult to carry out. I was unable to form any view as to this, as I was not *au courant* of affairs in Berlin.

The Secretary further informed us that the proposal to approach the Queen of Holland had not been carried out, and that no other steps had been taken towards securing peace. Nothing positive had thus been done.

After this explanation, the Field-Marshal and I reviewed the military position and our views as to the armistice conditions. Von Hintze thought the best course was to approach President Wilson with a proposal for an armistice and peace. The Swiss Ambassador in Washington had again spoken to our Government of Wilson's high ideals. It was clear, of course, that communications with Paris and London via Washington were bound to work slowly, and that an armistice could not be secured by such means at a moment's notice, but only after a lapse of time. The Field-Marshal and I were quite in agreement with what von Hintze said, and we fully agreed with his proposal, although we suggested that an identical Note with that to Wilson should be sent, for information, to the English and French.

After the discussion we went at once to His Majesty who had come from Cassel to Spa. Von Hintze gave the same explanation of the internal situation, adding his proposals as to the offer to President Wilson for an armistice and peace. The Field-Marshal then described the military situation, which I shortly confirmed. His Majesty was unusually calm. He expressed his concurrence with the proposal to approach President Wilson. In the afternoon, at von Hintze's suggestion, an Imperial Proclamation was sent to the Chancellor, who had arrived in the meantime, for the introduction of the parliamentary system in Germany. G.H.Q. did not know of this proclamation until after its publication. Count Hertling thought himself unable to carry it out, and resigned. The search now began in Berlin for the new Parliamentary Chancellor. It was a curious proceeding, in which the Sovereign abandoned all initiative.

To my inquiry, when the new Government would be formed and in a position to come to decisions, and when the Note would be agreed with our allies and ready for dispatch, von Hintze answered Tuesday, the 1st of October.

At first I worked strictly to that date.

At the request of Secretary of State Count von Roedern, who had also come to Spa and with the Vice-Chancellor was to carry on the negotiations with the parliamentary leaders, G.H.Q. sent Major Freiherr von dem Busche to Berlin on the evening of the 29th. He was to explain the military position to the Reichstag if the Government thought it advisable.

Later, at my request, the Field-Marshal decided to accompany His Majesty to Berlin on the evening of the 30th, in order to represent G.H.Q. in Berlin. I was unfortunately indispensable at Spa, owing to the position in the field.

Already, on the evening of the 30th, Major Freiherr von dem Busche had had a short conversation, in the presence of Vice-Chancellor von Payer, with Prince Max who had meanwhile come to Berlin, and had expressed himself to the Prince in the same sense as he was to address the party leaders of the Reichstag on the following morning. He also gave explanations privately to von Payer to the same effect.

We thought it better to refuse a suggestion of Count von Roedern, that von dem Busche should also address the Prussian Upper Chamber, as I suspected that some influence was intended thereby to be brought to bear on Prussian domestic politics, the Upper Chamber being compelled by this direct pressure to abandon the attitude hitherto taken by it to the question of the Prussian Constitution.

At nine o'clock in the morning of the 2nd of October, Vice-Chancellor von Payer introduced Major Freiherr von dem Busche to the assembled Reichstag party leaders, and remained present while the Major spoke. The Major knew my views and intentions and had committed them to writing before making his speech. His speech was quite to the point. He described the position in the Balkans, as resulting from the defection of Bulgaria, perhaps a little too favourably, and the position on the Western Front with all confidence, praising the troops. As was his duty, he stated that the question of reinforcements was very serious, and that we were no longer able to cover wastage. Battalion strength had been reduced to five hundred and forty men, and even this could only be maintained by breaking up twenty-two divisions—*i.e.*, sixty-six regiments of infantry. The *moral* of our reinforcements was bad.

Major Freiherr von dem Busche concluded thus :

" We can carry on the war for a substantial further period, we can cause the enemy heavy losses, we can lay waste his country as we retire, but we cannot win the war.

" Realizing this fact, and in view of the course of events in general, the Field-Marshal and General Ludendorff have resolved to propose to His Majesty that we bring the fighting to a close, in order to avoid further sacrifices on the part of the German people and their allies.

" Just as our great offensive was stopped on the 15th of July, immediately it was seen that its continuation would involve undue sacrifice of life, so now we must make up our minds to abandon the further prosecution of the war as hopeless. There is still time for this. The German Army has yet the strength to keep the enemy at bay for months, to achieve local successes, and to cause further losses to the Entente. But each new day brings the enemy nearer to his goal, and makes him the less ready to conclude a reasonable peace with us.

" We must accordingly lose no time. Every twenty-four hours that pass may make our position worse, and give the enemy a clearer view of our present weakness.

" That might have the most disastrous consequences both for the prospects of peace and for the military position.

" Neither the Army nor the people should do anything that might betray weakness. While the peace offer is being made, you at home must show a firm front, to prove that you have the unbreakable will to continue the fight if the enemy refuse us peace or offer only humiliating conditions.

" If this should prove to be the case, the Army's power to resist will depend on the bold attitude of the home country, and on the spirit which the nation can breathe into the Army."

In this speech, Major Freiherr von dem Busche expressed both my programme and my views, and this not only for the members of the Reichstag, but also for the new Government that was to be formed from their ranks. The soldier who has had to fight heavy battles for four years with insufficient weapons becomes hardened to dangers, but the man is in a very different case who suddenly has such difficulties, of immeasurable greatness, placed vividly before him.

I had been writing to the Government for two years on end with reference to the shortage of reinforcements. The auxiliary service law, my efforts to have it amended, and to bring women more and more into service, my suggestions for rounding-up shirkers and deserters at home, were all fully justified, not only by the Hindenburg programme, but also by the need of man-power at the front. All my suggestions for raising *moral* at home constituted questions of infinite importance in the conduct of the war, for the solution of which the Chancellor was responsible to the whole people. All these problems were interdependent. If *moral* was good, the shirkers and deserters would be kept at the front, the exempted men at home would be more readily released for service ; there would be less difficulty about reserves, and the moral effects of the fighting would be better overcome. The Chancellor never put these considerations before the repre-sentative of the people, the Reichstag, although he was expressly requested by G.H.Q. so to do. Indeed, all this must have been actually withheld from the Reichstag, just as also my view as to the military situation and the need for peace since the 8th of August. Only thus can one understand the misconception of the whole position that existed in Berlin.

I was so surprised by the effect of Major Freiherr von dem Busche's speech, that I questioned him on his return as to whether he had said anything different from what we had discussed. He gave me the draft of his speech, to which he had kept word for word. This draft lies before me now as I write. I do not know whether the manner in which the Major spoke, or the seriousness of his personality, heightened the effect of his words on his hearers, but such an explanation is humanly possible. The Major himself noticed the great shock his words produced.

His fittingly serious peroration as to what was needed of the people was lost. I think that, in their great excitement, his hearers did not really understand them. It is inexcusable that the speech immediately became public, and that, too, in a manner calculated to do us the very greatest harm. There was no better means of informing the enemy of our weakness.

It was highly regrettable that the out-going Government did not inform the Major that there was a Pole among his hearers. They must have known that this individual would immediately publish at home and abroad everything that he heard.

On the assumption that the new Government would be formed by the 1st October, and in my views as to my duty to the Army, I held conversations in Spa on the 30th September and the 1st October with representatives of the Chancellor and of the Foreign Office, and also instructed Major Freiherr von dem Busche to co-operate with the Field-Marshal in pressing urgently for the despatch of the Note on the 1st October, or at the latest at noon on the 2nd.

My principal motive was to avoid further loss of life, but I also attached great weight to the view that the earlier we began the more favourable would our position be at the commencement of the negotiations. If it could not at this time be described as threatening, it might within two or three weeks become of the greatest importance whether the Army was to have an armistice, or (if it had to fight on) a moral impetus from home, twenty-four hours sooner or later. In this position, any delay in the formation of the new Government beyond the time regarded by von Hintze as essential was inexcusable. I spoke often with my Staff to this effect, and always acted on this view. In general, I took my stand on what von Hintze had said, and on the speech of Major Freiherr von dem Busche. These present a complete picture. I am unable to understand how the idea ever arose that I had said that the front would break if we did not have an armistice within twenty-four hours. Between my discussion of the 29th September and the Major's speech on the 2nd October, which are wholly consistent with one another, there was no particular military event that could have led to any modification of my views.

I had repeatedly begged von Hintze to retain his Secretaryship, if the new Chancellor should be willing, in order to secure a certain degree of continuity. This was in vain, however. In the night of the 1st–2nd October the General Staff had simplified communications between His Majesty and the Grand Duke of Baden by laying down a trunk telephone line, in order to hasten the appointment of Prince Max. I acted all the time from the same point of view, that, once the decision was taken, we should get to work at once. We should not allow days to be wasted, let alone, as so often before, the whole thing come to nothing. I repeat that it was no question of obtaining an armistice in twenty-four hours, but simply of initiating communications with the enemy in some way or other. That this was not equivalent to getting an armistice, no one knew better than I, who had a better judgment of the enemy's views than the new Government. In my quiet but anxious thought, I was completely mystified by the events in Berlin, and could find no explanation thereof, save this, that the members of the Reichstag, not having been properly informed of anything at the right time, had now, in their anxiety and excitement, greatly increased by surprise, misunderstood what Major Freiherr von dem Busche had said, and that even Prince Max and the new Government were not sufficiently well informed to understand the position properly.

Late in the night of the 1st October, and in the course of the 2nd, Colonel von Haeften rang me up repeatedly, and described to me the difficulties which were delaying the formation of the new Government and therefore the despatch of the Note. I had informed him on the 30th September of the events at Spa, and had instructed him to urge the Government to act quickly and energetically ; he was not to " hustle " them, but to make clear the grave disadvantages that would follow every day of hesitation and inactivity. To Colonel von Haeften also von Hintze had explained on the afternoon of the 30th September that the new Government would be formed at the latest by the afternoon of the 1st October, so that the peace offer could be despatched on the evening of the same day.

After the discussion with Colonel von Haeften on the evening of the 1st, I understood the situation, and appreciated that von Hintze's expectation would not be realized.   I instructed von Haeften to see that no unnecessary delay occurred, but in view of the position in Berlin I resigned myself to a postponement of the despatch of the Note.

On the 3rd October the new Cabinet had a meeting, the Field-Marshal being present to represent G.H.Q.; he spoke in the same sense as we had done to von Hintze on the 29th September, and set out again, for the benefit of the Chancellor, in my opinion with absolute accuracy, the views of G.H.Q. in a statement running as follows :

" G.H.Q. holds to the demand made by it on Monday, the 29th September of this year, for an immediate offer of peace to the enemy.

" As a result of the collapse of the Macedonian front, and of the weakening of our reserves in the West, which this has necessitated, and in view of the impossibility of making good the very heavy losses of the last few days, there appears to be now no possibility, to the best of human judgment, of winning peace from our enemies by force of arms.

" The enemy, on the other hand, is continually throwing new and fresh reserves into the fight.

" The German Army still holds firmly together, and beats off all the enemy's attacks victoriously, but the position grows more acute day by day, and may at any time compel us to take very serious measures.

" In these circumstances the only right course is to bring the war to a close, in order to spare the German people and their allies useless sacrifices.   Every day wasted costs the lives of thousands of brave German soldiers.

(Signed) " VON HINDENBURG."

The Field-Marshal had added in his own handwriting that the sole motive of the above-mentioned demand for peace of the

729

29th September was to pave the way to the achievement of an honourable peace.

On the 4th October the Field-Marshal returned to Spa, and on the 5th the first Note to Wilson was despatched.

G.H.Q. had no further influence in the drafting of the Note or on the course of the political negotiations. I regarded the Note as somewhat weak in tone, and proposed a more manly wording, but no attention was paid to my demands. It was unfortunately inevitable that we should base ourselves on Wilson's fourteen points. They were not dissimilar in their general lines to the social-democratic views that had come forward in Germany, and so far as number goes they corresponded with the Austro-Hungarian Note to Serbia of the end of July, 1914.

In a telegram on the 2nd October I emphasized " that the fourteen points of the Wilson Note were to serve as the basis for the discussion of peace terms, but were not to be regarded as conditions imposed on us by the enemy." The Field-Marshal had taken the same standpoint in Berlin, but had met with no support from the Secretaries of State, Vice-Chancellor von Payer alone agreeing with him. I was later given the following explanation, that all the Secretaries of State were of the opinion that, although the Alsace-Lorraine and Polish questions had now become international, that did not necessarily involve the abandonment of Alsace-Lorraine and of large territories in the East.

A commission was assembled at Spa to work out the armistice conditions. General von Gündell presided, and the Chancellor was represented by von Hintze. The other members were General von Winterfeldt, Major Brinckmann, and Naval Captain Vanselow.

Efforts were made, by explanations to the Army, to counteract any weakening effects of the request for an armistice and peace.

Subsequently to the 29th September I discussed the offer with many of the Chiefs of Staff. Those who knew the whole situation agreed that it was the right step, while those remote from the fronts could not see the necessity for it. I had the satisfaction that their confidence in myself was not impaired.

VII

In his first important Reichstag speech, on the 5th October, dealing with the necessity for continuing the struggle in the event of the conditions being unacceptable, Prince Max took the same point of view as the Field-Marshal and myself.

The Prince said :

" With stout hearts and full of confidence in our strength, we are resolved, if it be inevitable, to make yet further sacrifices for our honour, our freedom, and the happiness of our descendants."

And again :

" Whatever the result of our offer of peace, I know that it will find the country firm and united in its readiness either for an honourable peace or for a life and death struggle to the last, on which our people are determined, if it be unavoidable. I am not afraid when I contemplate the possibility of this second alternative, for I know the spirit of the powerful forces which are still to be found among our people, and I know too that the clear conviction that each man is fighting for his life will double those forces."

The President of the Reichstag spoke to the same effect :

" Every German at home is ready, like every soldier at the front, to sacrifice everything for his country, if need be."

These were fine and stimulating words, which convinced me that the Chancellor, the Reichstag, and G.H.Q. were fully agreed as to continuing the fight if the worst came to the worst. But it seemed that the Chancellor and the Reichstag failed to realize that every German had been engaged since 1914 in a fight for his life, and that this fight demanded every sacrifice from us all.

731

The clear consciousness of this had been lost among the thousands of catchwords with which both from inside and outside the soul of the German people was poisoned. It was not until May, 1919, when the incredible peace terms were published, that this fact really penetrated the people and the National Assembly. Again the self-same President spoke, using noble and moving words, which seemed like a call to instant action; but the official report did not dare to repeat them. This time, too, however, the words remained bare words. The situation had arisen in which the country should have answered the call.

In those days I went quietly forward on my difficult way. When it became quite clear to me, later, after the receipt of the second Wilson Note, that Wilson could not or did not wish to prevail, but that Clemenceau and Lloyd George would have their way, and that we were to be enslaved, then I certainly thought it was time to translate words to deeds and not to rest content with empty speeches. I expected from Prince Max and his Government a fulfilment of their professions, once they and the country realized that they stood at the grave of all their hopes of a peace by understanding.

Perhaps it would have been better and wiser if I had definitely put to the Government at the beginning of October the question which it would have ultimately to decide : will the people fight on for honour's sake, and will the Government call up the last man and stir the people again to a real and sacred enthusiasm ? I still believe to-day that an appeal to the people at that time would not have met with sufficient success. After four years of war, as appeared from the speeches of the 5th October, there was still no perception of what the war meant, and neither Government nor people had realized the terrible seriousness of the position. The enemy had not then clearly disclosed his determination to destroy Germany, which he made plain for all to read in the second Wilson Note.

Prince Max was of the opinion that it would have been more advantageous to have sent the Note off about a week later, after first publishing a detailed programme of our war aims, making clear to the world our agreement with the principles of President

Wilson, and our readiness to make heavy sacrifices of our national interests to these principles.

We had already adopted Wilson's principles on the 5th October. What else was to be done later ?

The fact that I, without coming into the public eye, succeeded in moving the Chancellor to swift and energetic action, after all the time since the middle of August had elapsed without anything being done, did nothing to injure the general position. On the other hand, the open mention of the fact that G.H.Q. had desired the armistice and had pressed for it did as much damage, if not more, than the distorted reports of Major Freiherr von dem Busche's speech.

Do Prince Max and his supporters really believe that if the step had been taken in the middle of October it would have been regarded as due solely to motives of noble humanity, and as such would have received a friendly welcome from the Entente ? The enemy's point of view was altogether too material and self-interested for this. They were also much too clever. They had as good a view of the military position as our G.H.Q. They knew the conditions in the German Army and in Germany as well as they knew the weakness of the Austro-Hungarian Army in Italy and the position in Austria-Hungary itself. From the statements of the numerous German prisoners they took, who often said far too much, they must have had a clear indication of the low strength of our battalions and of the number of divisions that we had had to break up. Nor can they have been ignorant of the poor *moral* of the troops and people. From Berlin they heard everything. They anticipated our internal collapse with the same certainty as they had anticipated the downfall of Bulgaria. No doubt they saw more clearly than we did ourselves that the way in which the Emperor's edict of the 29th September was issued to Count Hertling was paving the way to the revolution of the 9th November.

Any offer of peace without an offer of armistice would also have had no effect whatever on the enemy determination to destroy us. That is made plain by the fate of our earlier offers, which were treated by the Entente as insincere and dishonourable, and by the result of Count Burian's step. In view of the attitude of the enemy, an offer of armistice alone could convince them of our real desire for peace. An offer of peace alone pre-supposed an enemy ready to meet us half way, and the possibility of concluding negotiations within a reasonable time. Had people forgotten the length of the negotiations in Brest and Bucharest? Now everything was more complicated. The negotiations were bound to last for an indefinite time. Was the Army to suffer and bleed all this time, perhaps to no purpose, and without support from home? And if during all these long negotiations our military position became worse, would not that in its turn have a serious effect on the terms of peace?

Only an offer of armistice would enable us to see at once whether those were right who maintained that we could obtain an honourable peace, which I would have heartily welcomed, or whether we should be faced by the offer of a peace of violence, which would have spurred us to new action. There was no time to be lost, for the Army was in urgent need of reinforcement from home.

The Entente had to show their colours, and we had to act accordingly. At the present day no more doubt is possible as to the intentions of the enemy. Will those who have been talking continually of reconciliation and of the peace by understanding, now at last confess frankly that they have misjudged the enemy, and, after the events of the revolution, that they have misjudged mankind in general, and that the world is not yet ripe for such lessons.

Are we still to believe that Labour in the Entente countries is at one with the holders of the theory of the reconciliation of mankind in a peace of understanding?

The truth was slowly dawning on the German people. On the 5th February, 1919, after the victory of the Government troops in Bremen, *Vorwärts* wrote:

" As Social Democrats we regret deeply that the application of force was necessary. It goes without saying that we are opponents of the use of force. But opposition to force does not mean that we must suffer without resistance every act of violence on the part of our opponents. The love of peace can only be maintained when it is met by similar sentiments. Whoever from a revulsion in principle to the use of force cannot make up his mind to oppose force to force is in the long run strengthening the rule of violence, that is, the rule of his opponents."

Vorwärts thus got back to its standpoint of 1914. It upheld the view that I have upheld all my life. The use of force, abroad or at home, brings joy to no man. In 1914, we had to have recourse to arms, to oppose the rule of violence under which we now suffer.

Theory and practice are not the same thing.

VIII

President Wilson's answer to our offer of the 5th October reached Berlin by wireless on the 9th. From the military standpoint, it demanded as a condition precedent to the conclusion of any armistice the evacuation of the occupied territory in the West. We were quite prepared for this. The Note left the way open for further discussion.

At the request of Prince Max, I went to Berlin, and had a longish conversation in private with him. I knew the Prince already, he having visited G.H.Q. twice; and we had conversed for a considerable time and heard each other's views with interest. We had not much in common. Vice-Chancellor von Payer had now pointed to him as the only possible Chancellor. I was not disposed to differ. I regarded Prince Max, both as Prince and officer, as suitable to introduce the new régime. I thought that he would yield, but act as a brake at the same time. After all, he came of an old princely stock that had a real feeling for the greatness of Germany, and there was hope that he might be of use to the country in its anxious hours. The hope was not, however, fulfilled.

With a view to this discussion, the Prince had had a *questionnaire* placed before me, which was so detailed that it was impossible to answer, but was quite characteristic as showing how

735

little the gentlemen in Berlin knew what the war meant. I answered it as best I could, in accordance with my views of the situation. I saw no reason to depart from my previous standpoint. Wilson's Note still allowed us to hope that we should obtain a peace that would not amount to destruction.

Prince Max begged me in confidence to cut myself off from General von Bartenwerffer, Colonel Bauer, and Lieut.-Colonel Nicolai. I asked what was the accusation against these men. He replied that he did not clearly know and was merely repeating what had been said to him. I thereupon begged him to let me have definite information, and I would have it carefully examined in the interests of these officers. Nothing was ever received. If any definite complaint had been made, I would have investigated it, as my duty was, but I could not get rid of conscientious and loyal men on malicious gossip or unsupported suggestions. The request made a very painful impression on me. That was the sort of work a German Government in Berlin found to do in such an anxious time.

The Prince also wanted to hear the views of other high officers on the situation. Only G.H.Q., however, had a view of the whole position. The conditions were different with each army. It was impossible to generalize for the whole front from one army. I refused his request. The Field-Marshal and I had alone to bear the responsibility. His Majesty could demand explanations at any moment, but not the Chancellor. The Army was still subject to the Emperor as War Lord. At the beginning of November, after I had left office, two Army Commanders gave their opinion to the War Cabinet, and their view of the whole situation practically coincided with mine. The discrepancies were explained by the fact that an Army Commander can only have a partial grasp of the whole situation.

As is always the case after the defeat of an army, criticisms have been expressed or published, which may be correct so long as they avoid all conclusions that the critic is not himself in a position to check. Conditions in the whole Army, and on our extended front, were too varied to admit of generalizations, which personal experiences at one point are apt to tempt men to make. Such generalizations are as dangerous as the empty catchwords which have poisoned the whole of our political life. In science they rank as the most pronounced symptom of the half-informed.

Officers who think that they foresaw everything, would have done better to go honestly to G.H.Q., in which they had confidence, and there to explain what was in their minds. I received but few letters from such men, and if there was anything new in their letters I summoned them to discuss the matter. For example, I saw in this manner Captain Bakhaus, of the 78th Field Artillery Regiment, who gave me information of considerable value.

It was now time, at last, to ascertain definitely whether the German people would fight on, if the negotiations with the enemy did not lead to an acceptable peace. Preparations had to be made. The Press had given us a favourable view of the possibility of continuing the fight. Prince Max had so far done nothing since his speech of the 5th October to carry out the intentions he then stated. I therefore put the necessary question. I had also to ascertain the attitude of the new Government to the Eastern question, in order to adjust the necessary military preparations at G.H.Q.

The sequence of affairs in Russia was quite unknown to the new Cabinet, Vice-Chancellor von Payer being alone acquainted with it. I did not know whether the problem was still the same as it had been in February. In view of the extraordinary importance of the question, I thought a discussion necessary. I questioned the Prince on the Government's views as to the Bolshevik danger, and as to whether the Ukraine was a necessity to us in the future from the point of view of supply. For the settlement of the last question considerable inquiries, and also discussions with Austria-Hungary, were necessary.

On the same day I was present at a meeting of the War Cabinet.

The *questionnaire* was discussed. I, too, put my questions. Everything was gone over, as above described. No particular resolutions were come to. Walther Rathenau's article in the *Vossische Zeitung* on the Levée en Masse was also discussed.

Such catchwords mean little to me. The position was quite different from that of 1870–71. Strength and energy, however, were in truth available among our people, and had to be thrown into the fight. There were thus some who agreed with my view that the German people, in spite of all that they had done, could still do more. The pity of it was that they had not come forward before. It seemed to be particularly characteristic, and filled me with new hope, that men who held views opposed to mine should be arguing for the continuation of the struggle.

At the end of the Cabinet meeting Prince Max thanked me for coming. With the approval of the Field-Marshal, I stated expressly in a short answering speech that we would loyally support the new Government.

The Cabinet was too large. It was called a War Cabinet, but had no resemblance to the War Cabinets of our enemies.

In the evening various leading men in public life came to see me, and asked me whether G.H.Q. had really brought about the offer of peace and armistice. I answered most emphatically that this was correct. I had already let this be known to the public by the Press interview of the 9th October, when there was no longer any military damage to be feared from the disclosure. I owed such a declaration to Prince Max's Government It was not my function to explain to these gentlemen any further what I thought and felt on the matter.

The Government and G.H.Q. were quite in agreement over the answer to Wilson's first Note. I managed to have inserted in this answer a question as to whether France and England also took their stand on the fourteen points. G.H.Q. had nothing to do with the matters of internal politics discussed, nor could we approve the tone of the Note. It seemed to show an undignified haste to jettison everything which had hitherto been sacred to us. Our enemies must have marked with satisfaction the way in which we brought ourselves ever nearer to our own ruin.

All over the world the talk of a peace of reconciliation, with its idealistic catchwords, died down suddenly. That was after all not surprising, for the Press of the world was following the hints of the enemy propaganda, which needed the word no longer. The Entente had achieved its object by the use of the word, and could now throw off the mask and work for a peace of force. In Germany, too, the word took a more modest place. The men who had hitherto preached the doctrine, and had represented a peace of justice and conciliation as perfectly possible and easy of achievement, had not now the moral courage to confess that they were mistaken as to the enemy's intentions, that they had led the people astray and brought them to their ruin. They were, or some of them were, ready to speak in thoroughly un-German language of Wilson's fourteen points as a peace of justice. So far had we trodden the path of disgrace already. They began a strong agitation against myself, alleging that I had now, by undue haste in the armistice offer, brought the people to new misfortunes, after previously making all peace impossible by the extravagance of my demands. Thus did they direct the anger of the people and the Army against me. If all those who had previously talked of the peace of reconciliation had spoken of the war and the terrors of defeat and if they had seconded my efforts to make our last ounce of strength available and keep our people morally capable of victory, I should never have needed to ask for an armistice. The time will come when this is clearly seen.

On the 12th October the second Note to America was despatched.

IX

The battle which had broken out on the Western Front at the end of September had meanwhile continued to rage. It took the form of a powerful attempt on the part of the enemy to break through the army groups of the Crown Prince Rupprecht and von Boehn in the direction of Ghent and Maubeuge, and through those of the German Crown Prince and von Gallwitz on their inner flanks on either side of the Argonne in the direction of Charleville–Sedan. The same idea had been at the root of every offensive operation of the Entente since the autumn of 1915. Up to the present they had failed through the exhaustion of the enemy and our power of resistance. Now we were weaker and one division failed after another. The number of shirkers behind the front increased alarmingly. The information posts, established to direct stragglers to their positions, were no longer equal to their task. The men who fought in the front line were heroes, but there were not enough of them for the long line. They felt themselves isolated. The men looked to their officers, who bore the brunt of the fighting. These officers, with their loyal men, achieved miracles of bravery. Regimental, brigade, and even divisional commanders, with officers and a few soldiers, often with their clerks and servants, personally restored the position, and prevented our line from being broken through by the vastly superior but no longer enthusiastic enemy troops. We may be proud of the men who fought these heroic fights. Our losses, however, were heavy. Our best men lay on the bloody battle-field. Many of our battalions could only muster two companies. Leave was stopped by G.H.Q. On account of difficulties of transport, men on leave at home had to remain there for a time. They stayed longer than was good for them. In the critical November days there should have been very few men on leave in Germany. Unfortunately it was otherwise.

The periods allowed to divisions for rest and repair of their equipment and clothing became ever shorter. Good divisions had more work thrown on them than the less reliable. That, too, had undesirable consequences. The men could not understand why they were so often thrown into the gaps, and they became less and less willing to fight. The strain grew ever greater, and our strength wasted away. It was uncommonly difficult to restore the situation and to reinforce the weak spots. Cases increased where second line divisions had to be thrown in hurriedly, and units replaced wholesale.

The strain on the nerves of the leaders at the front increased without cease, and they had a heavy task ; but they never lost their proud courage or their clear perception of their country's needs. Nothing could break them.

The Last Phase. Summer and Autumn, 1918

While its right wing held firm on the Yser, below Dixmude, and its left wing held round Armentières, the main body of the 4th Army was forced back on Roulers and Menin in continual fighting in the early part of October. It developed into a series of local engagements which remained without results. On the 14th October the enemy renewed their attack. In the direction of Roulers they gained ground beyond the town. Kortemarck, too, we lost. On the other hand, they could not advance much towards Menin. Near Wervicq we beat them off. Local successes also attended the enemy on the 15th, causing our Army to fall back to the line Dixmude–Thourout–Ingelmunster–Courtrai. The divisions of the 4th Army were numerically weak, and the only explanation of the enemy not obtaining greater successes against them, apart from the admirable leadership of the Army, lies in the fact that the enemy had no longer much stomach for the fight. The 4th Army was still under the command of General Sixt von Arnim, whose Chief of Staff was now Major Humser, a gifted soldier.

The 4th Army was by this time in such a difficult position that G.H.Q. had to decide that it must break contact with the enemy and shorten its line. The Army was ordered to retire on the Hermann line, behind the canal at Eecloo and the Lys. This involved the abandonment of the Flanders coast. The submarine station had meanwhile been removed. These movements of the 4th Army were undertaken on the 17th October, on which day I travelled to Berlin again, to attend a discussion of the second Wilson Note, which had by this time arrived.

At the same time, the 17th Army had had a difficult time since the enemy break-through at Cambrai on the 27th September. Up to the 8th October there were violent battles with varying fortunes on both sides of Cambrai, and we succeeded in holding the town. The 2nd Army was not so successful, being pressed further and further back towards Le Catelet in the early days of October. Towards Bohain the enemy gained ground. The right wing of the 18th Army, which was also engaged in heavy fighting, was affected by this loss. On the 8th, it suffered another heavy blow at and south of Le

Catelet and was once more driven back. In the night of the 9th October we were compelled to withdraw the 2nd Army into the Hermann line, as there were no reserves to aid it. To conform with this movement the 17th Army had to move its left wing and its centre back to a line half-way from Cambrai to Valenciennes, the right wing for the present being stationed immediately to the west of Douai. The 18th Army had, like the 2nd, to fall back to the Hermann line. Its left wing remained at La Fère.

The decision that the 2nd and 18th Armies should occupy the Hermann line, whose construction was but little advanced, was a great disappointment to us. I had hoped that the Siegfried line would have held for much longer. Already in the fighting at the beginning of October to the north of St. Quentin, we had been gradually forced back at many points, but we had, generally speaking, kept the line. We had not even completed the evacuation of the ground in front of the Hermann line.

The retirements were carried out smoothly. On the 10th the enemy attacked the new positions and was beaten off. On the 11th, to the north-east of Cambrai, he had a small success against the 17th Army, but this was localized. During the days following up to the 17th, there was further fighting on the front of the 2nd and 18th Armies, which on the whole was successful for us.

As a result of the withdrawal of the 4th Army behind the Lys, we were now compelled to withdraw the 6th and 17th Armies behind the Scheldt into the Hermann line. On the 17th, the 6th Army still stood to the west of Lille, and was to evacuate the town on the night of the 18th. Further to the south the right wing of the 17th, and later the whole of that army, had to conform to this movement.

It had been decided that in the event of the occupation of the Hermann line Boehn's Army Group was to be eliminated. It had now become too small. The 2nd Army was assigned to Rupprecht's Army Group, and the 18th to that of the German Crown Prince. In this group, the 9th Army was taken over by the 7th. Here, too, especially having regard to the arrangement of rear communications, there was no longer room for a separate army. General von Carlowitz took the command of the 2nd Army, and General von Marwitz received that of the 5th Army near Verdun. His Chief of Staff was Lieut.-Colonel Wetzell, my former colleague. A special group was established for General von Gallwitz. In this case, too, it had proved undesirable to burden a group H.Q. with the command of an army.

The necessity to economize forces had led, at the end of September, to the German Crown Prince's Army Group abandoning the Laffaux salient, which had caused us heavy losses, and withdrawing to the position behind the Oise-Aisne Canal, which we had occupied after the disastrous engagement of the 22nd October, 1917.

On the 2nd October, as had been arranged, the left wing of the 7th and the right wing of the 1st Army fell back to the position from which the attack of the 27th May, 1918, had started. Unfortunately, before this movement was carried out, one division was, quite unexpectedly, badly mauled on the heights north-east of Fismes. The centre of the 7th Army held the Chemin des Dames firmly, in the face of many enemy attacks.

The defensive battle in Champagne and on the Meuse, on either side of the Argonne, had followed a favourable course, in spite of the absolutely overwhelming superiority of the enemy, which was considerably greater here than on the fronts of the two northern army groups. Our leadership distinguished itself by exceptional coolness and mastery, and the enemy gained ground but slowly.

The continual and violent assaults on the left wing of the 1st and on the 3rd Army caused the army group of the German Crown Prince to decide in the early days of October to break off the battle and to withdraw all the troops to the Hunding–Brunhild position, i.e., a line half-way to Laon–Marle–Sissone-the Aisne from Rethel upstream to Grand Pré. G.H.Q. was unable to give this group, which husbanded its men carefully, any reinforcements. The two northern groups needed too much. We approved of the movement, which was carried out as arranged in the days ending with the 13th October.

The Army Group of the German Crown Prince began in the early days of October to withdraw the troops before Reims behind the Suippes. In the night of the 10th–11th the whole front from the Chemin des Dames to the Argonne was abandoned after violent attacks had been beaten off by the 3rd Army. By the morning of the 13th October, the 7th, 3rd and 1st Armies stood ready to defend themselves in their new and well-constructed line, and the evacuation of the ground in front had been almost completed. The engagements of the two last-mentioned armies at the end of September and beginning of October present a fine example of completely successful defensive fighting, of which the leaders and the men may well be proud. The Army commanders, von Einem and von Mudra, and their Chiefs of Staff, von Klewitz and Hasse, once more rendered their country exemplary service.

The enemy followed up the retirement of the German Crown Prince's Army Group energetically between the Oise and the Aisne, and heavy fighting soon developed round our new positions. In the bend of the Aisne towards Rethel, the enemy advanced more cautiously. On the other hand, he soon attempted, at first without success, to capture the Vouziers–Grandpré bend of the Aisne. In the Aire valley, west of the Meuse, the American pressure against our 5th Army was unusually severe. The battle extended to the east bank of the Meuse also. In spite of their enormous numerical superiority, the attacks of the young American troops broke down with the heaviest losses. Their success on the 26th September was merely due to the failure of a German Reserve division, and to the fact that at another point their attack was met only by a division, which, though a brave one, was very battle-worn and had an extended front to hold.

For the present, an attack on the Michael line and the Army Group of Duke Albrecht seemed unlikely.

On the 17th the position was, that on the whole of the front west of the Meuse we had taken up a rear line. On the right wing the retrograde movement was still in progress. It was serious that, in falling back to the Hermann–Hunding–Brunhild position, we had to sacrifice a number of establishments that served the convenience of the troops. For example, we lost a number of delousing stations, which was extremely inconvenient. G.H.Q. anticipated a continuation of the attacks in the direction of Ghent and Maubeuge, between the Oise and the Aisne, and between the upper Aisne and the Meuse, the latter extending to the right bank of the Meuse. I also expected a serious drain on our strength and nerves. At many points we had fought victoriously, and at others the enormous superiority of the enemy had brought him only small gains. The result of the further fighting depended mainly on the maintenance of the men's *moral*. Every man had to hold firm at the front, and to be inspired with the utmost determination. The armistice offer had had an unfavourable effect on the men's spirits, and war weariness had increased. No stirring call from home came as a counterblast, and the work of explaining the situation seemed to have been abandoned there. On this point there were many complaints from the Army. In the end the nation and the Government would have to show their colours, and let it be seen whether they were really determined to fight, for only thus could we hope to improve the *moral* of the Army. The commands and explanations issued to the troops from Spa were not in themselves sufficient. The intimate connection between the Army and the home country could never be more clearly perceived than it was in these critical days. The Army wanted to know definitely what it could expect from the people at home.

The clearing of the country behind the new positions was carried on with all speed. The railways were continually worked to the utmost limit of their capacity. Enormous masses of war material had to be dealt with, involving weeks and months of work. I laid great stress on the importance of thorough preparation for the destruction of lines and bridges which could influence the course of operations, and upon the removal to Germany of our own material. I continually discussed with the Chiefs of Staffs the problems of evacuation and destruction. We dealt with the inhabitants with the greatest leniency, as we always had done. We have statements to this effect from the inhabitants themselves. It is true that they begged not to be forced to give evidence publicly for us, as they feared opinion in Paris. A neutral commission also came from Brussels to the front, and reported on the care we took of the inhabitants as well as of the devastation caused by the enemy artillery and airmen. What the population had to suffer were the results of the state of war, and not of the manner in which we carried on the war. This is quite plainly established. The Entente, however, needed accusations against us in order to influence Wilson further in their direction.

Further in the rear we were working hard on the Antwerp-Meuse line, and I had a new line surveyed along the German frontier.

The Italian front was quiet, but there was talk of an imminent Entente attack. This could only be looked forward to with increasing anxiety, in view of the poor fight the Austro-Hungarian troops had put up in Serbia.

In the Balkan peninsula the situation had developed still further to our disadvantage, Bulgaria having surrendered to the Entente.

The submarine station at Cattaro was abandoned and moved to Pola.

In Serbia, General von Kövess had taken over the command, with a view to the defence of Hungary. Under his command were the troops that had retired under General von Pflanzer-Baltin from Albania to Montenegro, and the allied troops on the Morava under the 11th German Army Head Quarters—General von Steuben. General von Kövess had a difficult task. The Austro-Hungarian troops were of little value, the Germans were only the old classes and their strengths were low. The Alpine corps was worn out.

Austro-Hungarian troops were supposed to cover the deployment of the German and Austro-Hungarian divisions in the Morava valley south of Nish. They did not fight well. On October 12th the concentration which was to have been on the heights north of the town had to be fixed further back. We had to anticipate a further retreat. On the 16th we were already on the heights north of Alexinatz on both sides of the Morava. The German troops which had retired through Mitrovitza had got into touch north of the western Morava.

The formations which retired by way of Sofia had gone further back to Lom-Palanka, to be transported across the Danube. French divisions were in pursuit. They reached the Danube on the 17th. Unrest was increasing in Rumania.

Scholtz's Headquarters Staff had been removed to Rumania. Here, under instructions from Field-Marshal von Mackensen, it undertook the defence of the Danube. The reinforcements from the Caucasus and the Ukraine were arriving.

The line in Serbia and on the Danube was thus not secure, but it had not yet collapsed.

At Adrianople and from the Maritza downstream there were already English troops. The Turkish frontier guard was unusually weak there. The German troops and officials in Constantinople were preparing, in the event of an Entente attack on the town, to leave by sea and proceed to Odessa.

This was the military situation that I had to consider in deciding my attitude to the second Wilson Note.

X

In his answer to our second Note Wilson gave us nothing ; he did not even tell us whether the Entente took its stand on the fourteen points. He demanded, however, the suspension of the submarine war campaign, stigmatized our conduct of the war in the West as a violation of international law, and once again sought in obscure phrases to meddle with intimate questions of our domestic politics. No doubt was any longer possible as to the intentions of our enemies, or as to the predominating influence of Clemenceau and Lloyd George. Wilson was not prepared to stand against the comprehensive claims of France and England. We had heavy decisions to take. We now stood clearly before the question, were we to surrender unconditionally to the Entente, or was the Government to call on the people to fight a last desperate battle ? We had to return a firm and dignified reply to the Note, to emphasize once more our honourable anxiety for an armistice, but at the same time to warmly uphold the honour of our brave Army. We could not allow ourselves to be deprived of our submarine weapon, for this would amount to capitulation.

The Note was discussed on the 17th October at a meeting of the War Cabinet in Berlin. Colonel Heye and I were present. I had also requested General Hoffmann to attend. On this very day the 18th Army was fighting a desperate battle at the front.

The Chancellor again asked a number of questions and, turning to me, made a statement to the following effect : that a new Note had arrived from Wilson, containing new and larger demands ; that Wilson had plainly been placed in a difficult position through pressure from outside ; that he apparently hoped that we would give him the opportunity to continue negotiating with us and to overcome the opposition of the " Never-endians." In order to reply to the Note, it was necessary to understand quite clearly what Germany's military position required.

I had a different view as to the sentiments of the enemy, and could now see nothing but their intention to destroy us.

To the many questions that were put to me, I took up in general the following attitude :

" On a previous occasion I have been asked a number of questions to which it is impossible to give precise answers. War is not a sum in arithmetic. There are in war many probabilities and improbabilities. What will actually happen no man knows. When we went to East Prussia in August, 1914, and the orders were given for the Battle of Tannenberg, even then none knew how things would go, or whether Rennenkampf would or would not move. He did not move, and we won the battle. Part of war is luck, and luck may come Germany's way again.

" I can only tell you my convictions. For what I tell you the responsibility is mine, and has been mine for four long, weary years."

In particular the question was discussed whether by transferring all our divisions from East to West, or even a part of them, the front could be so strengthened that we could hold out for a long time. To deal with this, we had to know how much G.H.Q. could withdraw from the East. I had therefore to have an answer from the Government to my two earlier questions as to the danger of Bolshevism and the importance of the Ukraine to us. If the Government had changed its attitude of the previous February it must tell me so. At this time we had in the East, in Russia and Rumania, 26 divisions composed only of men over 35. Battalion strengths were low. In Lithuania there was one soldier to every 18 square kilometres. In the West there were 185 divisions; many had had to be broken up. Divisions recently removed from East to West had not done well under their new conditions and I had had very unfavourable reports of them. In spite of the shortage of men, drafts from the East were received with the greatest reluctance. They brought a bad *moral* and had an unfavourable effect on their fellows. According to the explanations of General Hoffmann, the temptations to which the men were exposed from the corruption of Jew traders in the East and from Bolshevik propaganda, as, indeed, from propaganda from home, had broken their fighting spirit. How far this had gone was not known until the beginning of November. The views of the General as to the possibility of employing these divisions in the West were quite in accord with my own experience. Nothing that they could do could produce any such alteration in the military situation as would bring the enemy to negotiate with us. They lacked the necessary vigour to fight in the West. For any work that might fall to them in the East, even for an attack on the Soviet troops, they seemed still fully capable.

Our blockade against the Bolsheviks was now everywhere very thin and only just effective. General Hoffmann and I explained that the danger from Bolshevism was very serious, and that the maintenance of this frontier *cordon* was essential.

The Government as such did not appear to take any definite stand on principle against Bolshevism. It did not speak clearly or decisively. In spite of the objections of General von Lynder, the president of the Imperial Military Court, it had released Liebknecht from prison, and it stood idly by while Herr Joffe distributed money and pamphlets, and prepared for the revolution. Our warnings, as well as those of the Headquarters Staff in the Marches, received no attention. It appears that about this time General Hoffmann, through his relations with Herr Solf, at last succeeded in opening the eyes of some members of the Government. As a party, the Majority Socialists recognized the great danger of Bolshevism. But while *Vorwärts* on the one hand issued warnings against this power, on the other it gave it the greatest help by its attacks on constituted authority and its advocacy of class hatred. At last, at the end of October, Joffe was sent away. We were thus once again at war with Russia, and the need to take precautions against Bolshevism became all the greater.

At this meeting I emphasized once more the infinite economic importance of the territory under the control of the C. in C. in the East.

No decision could be taken as to evacuating the Ukraine, the necessary preliminary discussions not having yet taken place, and the question being one quite impossible to settle out of hand. Count Roedern wanted to abandon the Ukraine, as the civil population got little benefit from it.

Secretary Solf insisted on the great value of the Ukraine, and desired that it should be retained on humanitarian grounds also. I could not look at the question from any other point of view than that of Germany's advantage.

Secretary von Waldow threw no further light on the matter, but enlightenment was essential, and I begged the Chancellor to have the question exhaustively examined. G.H.Q. had occupied the Ukraine in February in agreement with the Government, the latter being then fully convinced of the absolute necessity for the step, not merely to avert the danger of Bolshevism, but also to secure the food situation of the Quadruple Alliance. In the summer, Austria-Hungary had only been kept alive with the help of the Ukraine. We in Germany had obtained from the country cattle and horses and much raw material, even if we had not had the corn we expected. The war was not over. Rumania's harvest was a complete failure. By early threshing we had had to mortgage our future again. We and our Allies had to look somewhere for additional foodstuffs, and the Ukraine was the only possible source. Without this aid, there would be a severe crisis in the early summer of 1919. The Government never cleared up this question of the value of the Ukraine in the autumn of 1918. Had we evacuated at this stage, which would have taken us a considerable time, we should have gradually released ten divisions which were not really fit for the line. The advantages would not have been equal to the disadvantages that we should have brought upon ourselves by evacuation.

I am confident that not a man too many was kept in the East.

We now turned to discuss the vital question, how much could and would the people still give to the Army. Everything else depended on this. I had hoped that the Government would have been clear on this point. The new Minister of War gave me a more optimistic account of the prospects for reinforcements than I had hitherto received. He estimated a figure of 600,000 men. I could not check his figures. I was very greatly impressed by the statement that 60,000 to 70,000 men were immediately available from the Home Army. Why had they not been sent sooner? I said: " If I have these reinforcements now, I can face the future with confidence, but I must have them immediately." The Minister promised not to lose a day.

I now turned to the question of the *moral* and state of feeling prevailing at home and in the Army. I expressed myself as I have so often done in this book. I emphasized that the Army, especially at this moment, was in need of support.

The Chancellor requested the three Parliamentary Secretaries of State to give their views.

Secretary Gröber did not speak quite to the point on the matter.

Secretary Scheidemann spoke very seriously. He was glad to believe that we could still release hundreds of thousands of men for the Army, but it would be quite wrong to suppose that these men would improve the spirit in the Army. Everywhere working men were beginning to say : " Better a terrible end than terrors without end." Scheidemann stated that the cause of this regrettable attitude was the lack of food, which he attributed partly to the shortage of waggons. I instantly agreed to adopt, so far as lay in my power, every measure that could relieve the shortage. In general his statement constituted a serious indictment of our Government, which had allowed the splendid spirit of 1914 to be so terribly changed. Secretary Scheidemann's speech amounted to a declaration of bankruptcy of the domestic policy of the Chancellor and the Majority parties.

Secretary Haussmann thought that an appeal to the people would have considerable effect.

Secretary Erzberger was not present. He had recently lost his son in the service of his country.

Vice-Chancellor von Payer did not take so serious a view of the state of public feeling as Scheidemann. He shared my views and spoke more or less to the following effect :

" The arrival of the second Wilson Note strengthened public opinion, as people saw that it was a question of life and death, but the mood has changed again. Men realize that the nation is to be destroyed, especially economically. If we say to the nation : ' There is just a chance, if you hold out. But if you cannot hold out for a few weeks, then you must expect Germany to be more or less wiped out from among the nations. You must expect an absolutely crushing burden of indemnities '—you may rouse them once more.

" If you succeed in dealing with the note in such a way that the nation feels : ' We are, true, in an anxious situation, but we are not throwing up the sponge '—all is not lost."

Secretary Friedberg spoke to the same effect, adding that in any case we must act quickly.

In addition to the question of reinforcements, there was always the question of nerve strain, on which everything depended. Why had not these gentlemen, who knew of these available men, called them up sooner ? This is to me an insoluble and disastrous riddle.

The Last Phase. Summer and Autumn, 1918.

Of the general military situation I had nothing new to say. Of the West front I repeated what I had said on the 10th October : " I regard a break-through as possible, but not probable. If you ask me on my conscience, I can only answer that I do not expect it."

I stated, however, that the position might grow worse at any moment. The recent fighting had brought no surprises. The front had held neither better nor worse than before. Our troops had done what we expected of them. The vigour of the enemy's attacks seemed to be waning.

The negotiations with Wilson had so far led to no result. We were in every respect masters of our own actions and could break off or continue the negotiations. We had a free hand to do either. Is it a crime to fight on when one honestly wants peace and cannot get it ? Is it a crime to abandon the hope of a compromise for which one has honestly striven, when the opponent demands more than one can give ? Did anyone accuse Trotsky of dishonesty when at the beginning of February he did not sign the peace treaty? None could doubt that we honestly desired peace. On the other hand, we had every right to protect our life and our honour to the last. The Government owed a duty to the people to use every possible means in any case not to break off too abruptly the negotiations for the compromise that they had so honestly sought. It was a principle of elementary common sense : the stronger we were in the field, the better we could negotiate.

It came to this, that it was our duty to continue the fight, unless we were prepared to surrender unconditionally to an enemy from whom we had nothing to hope. Negotiations might improve our position, but, in any case, could not make it worse. The best elements of the Army, and a large part of the people, expected us to negotiate.

The majority of the German people were ready and willing to sacrifice the last ounce of their strength to the Army, and it was the duty of the Government to translate that willingness into action. I spoke to that effect. Like the Chancellor in his speech of the 5th October, I also suggested that Ebert, as leader of the Social Democrats, should be given some leading position, so that he could strengthen the resistance of the people and reinforce the prosecution of the war. I agreed with Admiral Scheer in holding it impossible to abandon submarine warfare, which was continually reducing England's resources. To throw down a weapon at the enemy's bidding would be the grossest confession of weakness imaginable, and would immeasurably increase the enemy's demands.

Secretary Solf accused me of a change of front. I replied in astonishment that the Government had also been willing to continue the fight if the worst came to the worst. Even if I had now spoken with more confidence than before, the Secretary could and should be glad to hear a more favourable opinion of the situation, since the negotiations must thereby be rendered more easy for him. Besides, I was not thinking of breaking off negotiations at the moment, but was only pressing for clearness in our thought and final aims. I summed up my views once again in the following phrases :

" Now, as before, I hold that if it be in any way possible, we must initiate armistice negotiations. We cannot, however, accept any conditions that do not provide for an orderly evacuation of the territory. This involves a time limit of not less than two or three months. Nor must we accept anything that makes it impossible for us to renew hostilities. The note forces one to assume that this is the object of the enemy. The conditions are designed to put us out of the field. Before we go further, the enemy must tell us clearly what his terms are. We do not wish to break off with Wilson out of hand. On the contrary, we must say : ' Tell us clearly what we are to do ! But, if you ask anything inconsistent with our national honour, or desire to render us incapable of fighting further, our answer must be " No ! " ' "

" In saying this, I am not departing from my previous position in the least."

I then dealt with the destruction which the Entente alleged we had indulged in during our retreat.

" We have, in accordance with our duty, done everything to

limit the destruction as far as is consistent with military needs It would be absolutely inexcusable to leave houses undestroyed, for billets are of great help to the enemy. The enemy themselves destroyed the houses afterwards. In Lille we left untouched the electric light installation, the water supply and the tramway line, but destroyed the telegraphs, telephones and railways. The worst damage was done by the English guns and airmen.

" The Army is not responsible for isolated cases of brutality I have done my best to stop any such abuses. I request that this be emphasized in the note to Wilson, for the Army has a right to that."

The meeting then closed. Secretaries Gröber and Haussmann, by whom I was sitting, told me how glad they were that I had so raised their spirits. I travelled back to Spa in confident mood.

There was some discussion at this meeting about a catastrophe which G.H.Q. was said to have reported at the end of September or the beginning of October. This, and Secretary Solf's idea that I had changed my views, led me to discuss once again with Major Freiherr von dem Busche his speech of the beginning of October. He could again only refer to his notes. Colonel von Haeften, too, had never spoken of any such catastrophe.

This improved state of mind in Berlin lasted until noon on the 19th October, when optimism vanished. I have no further knowledge of events there. Why did not the Secretaries of State, who had expressed themselves so confidently on the 17th, press for action ? They knew well what was at stake. It is wholly incomprehensible to me that, on the 12th May 1919, Secretary Konrad Haussmann should say, amid great applause : " If our Army, if our workers, had known on the 5th and the 9th November that the peace would take this terrible form, the Army would not have laid down its arms, but would have fought on." What has actually happened was plainly to be expected on the 17th October. That is an historical fact that cannot be denied. We warned them against capitulation. All that was required was to look the facts in the face, to cease deceiving themselves and the people, and translate resolve into action just as G.H.Q. did.

On the 20th we received the new draft answer at Spa. The submarine campaign was abandoned, and the way to capitulation, with all its disastrous consequences, was taken. The Field-Marshal and I drew attention to this point of view once again, and again warned them of the consequences. We proposed issuing a call to arms to the people. We refused to take any part in drafting such an answer. The War Cabinet became very excited at this ; why, I do not know. We were men with views of our own and we followed the course which we regarded as the right one, a course we had always pursued.

The answer to Wilson was dispatched on the 20th. The submarine campaign was abandoned. This concession to Wilson was the heaviest blow to the Army and especially to the Navy. The injury to the *moral* of the fleet must have been immeasurable. The Cabinet had thrown up the sponge.

The Chancellor did not alter the situation by his speech on the 22nd October : " The man who takes his stand honourably on the peace of justice also takes upon himself the duty not to accept without resistance a peace of violence. A Government which did not realize this would deserve and earn the contempt of the fighters and workers." Even this speech was not followed by action. Nothing was done to raise *moral* at home or in the field. Prince Max has pronounced judgment on himself and his colleagues.

The Minister for War alone did something towards providing the reinforcements. But this again came to nothing, for many of the men refused to go to the front, and the Government yielded !

XI

On the 23rd or 24th October Wilson's answer arrived. It was a strong answer to our cowardly note. This time he made it quite clear that the armistice conditions must be such as to make it impossible for Germany to resume hostilities, and to give the nations allied against her unlimited power to settle themselves the details of the peace to be accepted by Germany. In my view there could no longer be doubt anywhere that we must continue the fight. From the impressions I gained at the meeting of the 17th October, I felt quite confident that the people, even after the loss of all these valuable days, were still to be won over to that course.

In the West events hereafter took the following course : the 4th Army completed its rearward movement into the Hermann line, in the closest contact and in constant fighting with the pursuing enemy. Bruges, Thielt and Courtrai were evacuated on the 19th. On the 20th there was fighting on the Lys, the enemy securing the eastern bank at Deinze. He attempted to force us back from the Lys by strong pressure between the Lys and the Scheldt. On the 25th the fighting again took the form of a battle in which the enemy, pressing forward towards the Scheldt, slowly gained ground towards Ghent–Oudenarde. Between the Lys and the Scheldt he also attacked the 6th Army.

The 6th and 7th Armies had abandoned Lille and Douai on the 17th, and had fallen back, in touch with the 4th, behind the Deule canal, in the direction of Avelghem, Tournai and Valenciennes. On the 20th the enemy was approaching these towns. The civil population again took part in the fighting.

The southern wing of the 17th Army and the 2nd and 18th were involved in heavy fighting, the enemy attacking heavily on the 17th and 18th between Le Cateau and the Oise. We were forced to withdraw the front behind the Sambre-Oise canal, from the south-west of Landrecies as far as the Oise. After a pause on the 19th, the enemy attacks extended from the 20th onwards towards the north. The enemy pressed on past Solesmes and Le Cateau, in the direction of Landrecies. Our losses were heavy, and the troops did not fight well at all points. Other troops, however, behaved magnificently. We witnessed the same phenomenon as before.

At first the Army Group of the German Crown Prince had left the left wing of the 18th Army in its position on the Oise downstream from La Fère. The enemy's efforts to cross the Oise were defeated. On the 20th the Hermann line, between the Oise and the Serre, was occupied. The enemy attacked this line in force, and violent battles developed.

The 7th and 1st Armies were attacked between the Serre and the Aisne. In the main, they maintained their positions, and on the 25th they threw back a powerful enemy attack with heavy losses.

The enemy was also applying strong pressure on the Aisne, as far as Vouziers and Grand Pré, in the Aire valley, and towards the heights on the left bank of the Meuse. The fighting was heavy and costly, but did not lead to any important changes in our line. As before, the battle extended to the eastern bank, without producing any essential change here either. Further south, as far as the Swiss frontier, the line was quiet.

On the evening of the 25th the Western Front was enduring the greatest strain. There was fighting from the Dutch frontier to Verdun. No more help was coming from home. Not a word of encouragement was given. It was miraculous that the troops fought so heroically.

The work of evacuation went on, in spite of the terrible condition of the railways.

The construction of the Antwerp–Meuse line progressed slowly. The work of fortification was beginning. G.H.Q. had to reckon with the possibility of withdrawing the front back to that line at the beginning of November, to shorten it still further. Of course, this would be of advantage to the enemy also. Owing to the destruction of the railways, the enemy attacks in the north would be bound to lose impetus. It was to be expected that they would now attack in Lorraine.

In Italy, the Italian attack began on the 24th. At first it was directed to the mountain front, but from the 26th onwards it was raging with full force on the Piave. By the evening of the 25th there had been no important developments. The Austro-Hungarian front was still holding. Nevertheless I expected that Austria-Hungary would soon make peace. In co-operation with the Bavarian Ministry of War, the first pro tective measures on the Tirolese frontier were arranged.

In Serbia, General von Kövess found it necessary to order the retirement behind the Danube. There was no change on the Danube frontier of Rumania, and on the line of the Rumanian Army beyond the Sereth. Matters there still hung in the balance.

A rallying of the German people would in any case have improved matters. It is impossible to say for how long we might have continued the struggle. The enemy *moral* was not too clearly known to us. If only it had a firm will, a great people was not to be easily destroyed. France in 1870–71 had proved that, as had the Boers in their war with England. Winston Churchill's estimate of the military position is given in the *Sunday Pictorial* of the 12th January, 1919, in the following words :

"A very little more, and the submarine warfare, instead of bringing America to our aid, might have starved us all into absolute surrender. . . .

"It was neck and neck to the very end. But because the whole nation worked without flinching . . . we have at last come safely through.

"The more one knows about the struggle, the more one realizes on what small, narrow, perilous margins our success turned."

On the 25th October the Field-Marshal and I placed our views before His Majesty in Berlin, whither we had again travelled. We expressed the view that we must fight on. The new Chief of the Civil Cabinet, His Excellency von Delbrück, was present. While keeping his own opinions in the background, he adopted the same standpoint as Prince Max. We were surprised to learn that he was ignorant of the fact that we had discussed the question of peace with the Chancellor as early as the middle of August. His Majesty came to no decision, but he showed full confidence in me. He referred us to the Chancellor. The latter was ill and von Payer received us and Admiral Scheer at nine o'clock in the evening. He seemed personally ill-disposed towards us, in contrast to his previous attitude. He knew well that the

Cabinet wanted me to go, as I was for fighting on ! The Minister for War was also called in. He had not stood up for the Emperor and the Army in the Reichstag and within the Government for had he done so he would have had to resign. It was a very sad hour, as it was clear that the Government did not intend to fight any more. They thought it was necessary to sacrifice everything. Could they already hear the murmurs of the revolution of the 9th November ? Did they hope to save the country from the revolution by capitulating to foreign enemies ? I spoke seriously and was deeply moved. I uttered a warning against the enemy's desire to destroy us, and against any hope being placed in Wilson.

I also spoke warningly of the spread of Bolshevism in Germany, and of the agitation against the officers, which was then assuming large proportions. That had been the decisive turning-point in Russia too.

I warned them not to do anything to shake the position of the Emperor. I reminded them that His Majesty was our Highest War Lord and that the whole army looked up to him as its head. We had sworn loyalty to him. These imponderabilia were not to be underestimated, for they were part of our flesh and blood and united us to the Emperor. Whatever affected the Emperor affected the cohesion of the army.

The weakening of the position of the Corps of Officers and of the Supreme War Lord at a moment when the army was being put to the severest test was the most short-sighted act imaginable. It constituted the heaviest blow against order in the army and the State, at a time when the army was called on to be the guardian of civil order. At a later stage, it did more to undermine the discipline of the army than the hasty evacuation of the whole left bank of the Rhine, to which we allowed ourselves to consent.

At the beginning of November I spoke in the same sense to certain of the Social Democratic leaders. They, too, could not grasp what the Emperor meant to the army, not merely to us regular officers, but also to the rank and file. My view has been confirmed by many incidents happening since the 9th of November.

I did not discuss with von Payer the incidents in the Reichstag in the morning, which were aimed at G.H.Q. I had received but one report, and that an incomprehensible one, on the matter. On the evening of the 24th, shortly before leaving Spa, there was brought to me the following proclamation, already signed by the Field-Marshal, which expressed the views prevailing at G.H.Q. about the third Wilson note. It appeared essential that G.H.Q., in its dealings with Berlin, should take up a definite standpoint with regard to the note, in order to lessen its evil effects on the army. The telegram to the army ran thus :

" FOR THE INFORMATION OF ALL TROOPS :

" Wilson says in his answer that he is ready to propose to his allies that they should enter into armistice negotiations, but that the armistice must render Germany so defenceless that she cannot take up arms again. He will only negotiate with Germany for peace if she concedes all the demands of the allies as to the internal constitutional arrangements of Germany ; otherwise, there is no choice but unconditional surrender.

" Wilson's answer is a demand for unconditional surrender. It is thus unacceptable to us soldiers. It proves that our enemy's desire for our destruction, which let loose the war in 1914, still exists undiminished. It proves, further, that our enemies use the phrase ' Peace of Justice ' merely to deceive us and break our resistance. Wilson's answer can thus be nothing for us soldiers but a challenge to continue our resistance with all our strength. When our enemies know that no sacrifices will achieve the rupture of the German front, they will be ready for a peace which will make the future of our country safe for the great masses of our people.

" In the Field, 24th October, 10 p.m.

(Signed) " VON HINDENBURG."

I had been so busy that the Major who had to draft the telegram had taken it first to the Field-Marshal and then to me. Usually all documents for signature by the Field-Marshal were submitted to me first to be countersigned. This Army Order was not consistent with the answer sent to Wilson on the 20th. I was surprised, and asked the Major whether the tone of the Order was really in harmony with the views of the Government. He said that it was, and that the Order was wholly consistent with the explanations given to the representatives of the Press in the Foreign Office by Colonel von Haeften and Privy Councillor von Stumm. I became hopeful again, and added my signature. It appeared later that the opinion that the wording of the telegram corresponded with the views of the Government was incorrect, and Colonel Heye stopped the publication of the Order. From Kovno, where revolutionary organizations already controlled the telephones, it came to the knowledge of the Independent Socialists, and thus to that of the Reichstag. It was also given out confidentially in the Press discussion in the usual way. At the Reichstag meeting on the 25th at noon a storm of indignation burst over G.H.Q. The Government did not move a finger to protect us, although we were still the head of a mighty army. It was not until late in the evening of the 25th that I heard of this incident, or I would have discussed it with von Payer. Subsequently the history of the genesis of this Order was explained in all its context to the Government. Meanwhile, however, the distortion of the facts had achieved its end, and I was dismissed.

The discussion on the 25th in the Ministry of the Interior lasted about one and a half or two hours. General von Winterfeldt and Colonel von Haeften waited for me below. In deep inward anguish I could only say : " There is no hope. Germany is lost." These two were greatly moved.

In the German note of the 27th October we capitulated.

At 8 o'clock on the morning of the 26th, still in the mood of the previous evening, I wrote tendering my resignation. In this I adopted the point of view that, in the discussion of the previous day with Vice-Chancellor von Payer, I had gained the impression that the Government would not act in the crisis, that His Majesty, the country and the army were thus placed in an untenable position, that I was considered anxious to prolong the war, and that, in view of the attitude taken by the Government to Wilson, my departure might ease their position. I therefore begged His Majesty graciously to accept my resignation.

In accordance with his usual practice, the Field-Marshal came to see me at 9 o'clock on the morning of the 26th. I had placed my letter on one side, as I had made up my mind not to speak to him of it until the letter was before His Majesty. The Field-Marshal was master of his own destiny, and I did not want to influence him. He saw the writing, however. The form of the letter attracted his attention, and he begged me not to dispatch it, but to retain office. I ought not to desert the Emperor and the army at this time. After an inward struggle I consented. I became convinced that I ought to retain my post, and proposed to the Field-Marshal that we should make another effort to see Prince Max. He did not receive us, being still ill. While I was waiting for news on this point, Colonel von Haeften reported to me that the Government had succeeded in persuading His Majesty to dismiss me, the ostensible reason put forward being the Order above-mentioned. His Majesty would shortly send for me to the Bellevue Castle. I was no longer capable of astonishment, and had no anxiety about myself personally. Before this conversation ended, we were suddenly called, at this unusual hour, to attend His Majesty.

On the way from the General Staff Office to the Bellevue Castle I told the Field-Marshal what I had just heard. Later I heard it stated that Prince Max had put the question of my dismissal forward to His Majesty as a cabinet question.

The Emperor seemed wholly changed in comparison with the previous day. Speaking to me alone, he expressed himself particularly against the army order of the evening of the 24th. There followed some of the bitterest moments of my life. I said respectfully to His Majesty that I had gained the painful impression that I no longer enjoyed his confidence, and that I accordingly begged most humbly to be relieved of my office. His Majesty accepted my resignation.

I went back alone. I did not see His Majesty again. After my return to the General Staff Office, I said with the deepest anxiety to my officers there, among them Colonel von Haeften, that in a fortnight there would no longer be an Emperor in Germany. They clearly held the same view. On the 9th November Germany and Prussia were republics.

A moment later the Field-Marshal came to me in my room. I could only show him my letter of resignation which three hours before he had prevented me from dispatching. We then separated.

I gave up my post at once. I sent off the letter which I had written in the morning ; I should have now worded it differently.

On the evening of the 26th I went back to Spa, to say farewell to my officers with whom I had shared joys and sorrows through so many years, and to put my personal affairs in order.

On the morning of the 27th I was at G.H.Q. In the afternoon I said good-bye. I was much moved. It was very hard for me to leave my officers and the army at this anxious time. But, however hard it was, I could do nothing else, in consideration of my view of an officer's duty towards his All-Highest War Lord.

In my life as a soldier I have trodden but one path, the straight path of duty. One, and only one, great thought has moved me, the love of my country, of the army, and of the hereditary Ruling House. For them had I lived, even in these last four years. My one aim was to break the enemy's desire for our destruction, and to secure Germany's future against new hostile attacks.

On the 27th October I stood in Spa, in full possession of my powers, at the end of a military career which had brought me an enormous field of labour, and with it responsibility such as falls to the lot of few men.

In the evening I left Spa. In Aix-la-Chapelle I sought out my first war quarters. I thought of Liége. There I had staked my manhood, and had not changed since. My muscles braced themselves. I went back home.

ICELAND

NORWAY

SWEDEN

ATLANTIC OCEAN

Shetland Iⁿ

Orkney Iⁿ

SCOTLAND

Cristiania

Stockholm

IRELAND

NORTH

SEA

BALTIC

DEN-MARK

Copenhagen

ENGLAND

London

The Hague

HOLLAND

Berlin

The Channel

Brussels
BELGIUM

Luxemburg

Paris

Reims
Verdun

Vienna

Bordeaux

Rhône

Berne
SWITZ^D

Venice

Trieste

Adriatic Sea

PORTUGAL

Madrid

Andorra

Cette

Marseille

Corsica

Rome

Lisbon

Gibraltar

Sardinia

Sicily

MEDITERRANEAN

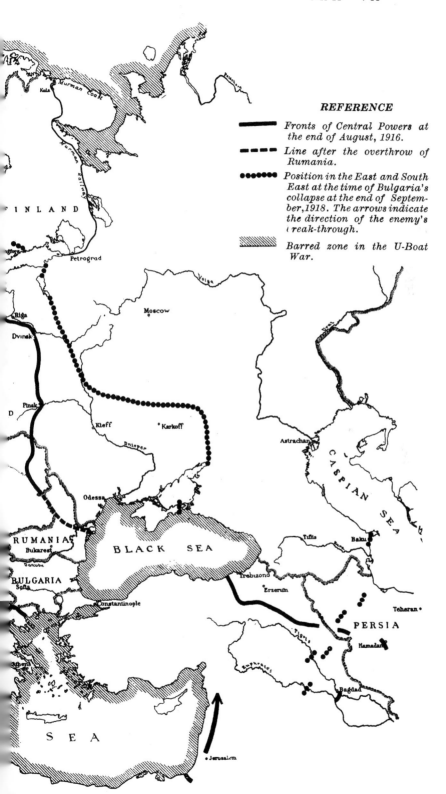

REFERENCE

——— Fronts of Central Powers at the end of August, 1916.

- - - Line after the overthrow of Rumania.

•••••• Position in the East and South East at the time of Bulgaria's collapse at the end of September, 1918. The arrows indicate the direction of the enemy's break-through.

▨▨▨ Barred zone in the U-Boat War.

FINLAND

Kola Murman Coast

Petrograd

Volga

Moscow

Riga

Dvinsk

Pinsk

Kleff   Karkoff

Dnieper

Astrachan

CASPIAN SEA

Odessa

RUMANIA   Tiflis   Baku

Bukarest

Danube

BLACK SEA   Trebizond

BULGARIA   Erzerum   Teheran

Sofia

Constantinople   PERSIA

Tigris   Hamadan

Athens   Euphrates

SEA   Bagdad

Jerusalem

EPILOGUE

FROM the end of October events followed one another at an increasing pace. In the West, on the 4th November, the German Army was withdrawn in good order to the Antwerp–Meuse line under the pressure of the enemy from Verdun upwards. The Alsace-Lorraine front, well-organized, awaited an enemy attack.

The Austro-Hungarian Army had completely dissolved as a result of the fighting in Upper Italy between the 24th October and the 4th November.

Hostile forces were moving on Innsbruck. G.H.Q. took comprehensive measures for the protection of the southern frontier of Bavaria. In the Balkan theatre we held the Danube.

We stood alone in the world.

At the beginning of November the Revolution, the work of the Independent Socialists, broke out, starting in the navy. The Government of Prince Max had not the strength to nip the outbreaks in the bud, although they were only local at first, on the Russian model. It was incapable of leadership, and let things run their course.

At noon on the 9th November Prince Max, on his own initiative, announced the abdication of the Emperor. The old Government issued orders to the troops which amounted to a prohibition to use their arms, and immediately afterwards it disappeared.

The Emperor was confronted with a *fait accompli*. On the advice of G.H.Q. at Spa, he went to Holland. The Crown

Prince followed him, after Berlin had refused his unconditional offer of further service. The princes of the States abdicated.

On the 9th November Germany, lacking any firm guidance, bereft of all will, robbed of her princes, collapsed like a house of cards. All that we had lived for, all that we had bled four long years to maintain, was gone. We no longer had a native land of which we might be proud. Order in state and society vanished. All authority disappeared. Chaos, Bolshevism, terror, un-German in name and nature, made their entry into the German fatherland. Soldiers' and Workmen's Councils, an institution prepared in long, systematic underground work, were now established. Men had worked at this who might by service at the front have secured a successful issue of the war, but who had been dubbed " indispensable," or had deserted.

The bulk of the troops in depots, among whom the idea of revolt had long been gaining ground, went over to the side of the revolutionaries.

The L. of C. troops, including those stationed in the occupied territories, both in East and West, who had no doubt also been prepared for the Revolution, lost all discipline and order, and streamed home in wild confusion, plundering as they went. The troops in Rumania and on the Danube front marched off into Hungary, there to be interned.

On the fighting front in the West, Soldiers' Councils, with approval from high quarters, could not be formed fast enough.

The new rulers and their *bourgeois* camp followers abandoned all resistance, and without a shred of authority signed our unconditional capitulation to a merciless enemy.

In the West the army crossed the frontier in an orderly manner and passed beyond the Rhine, there to dissolve in turn through too hurried demobilization and contact with the revolutionary hordes at home.

Men who had fought magnificently against the enemy lost their nerve and abandoned the army and the country, thinking of nothing but themselves. Even officers were among them, forgetting the duties of their class and their historical mission. We lived through scenes that no Prussian had thought possible since 1806. All the more highly must we value the loyalty of the officers, N.C.O.'s and men who, even in the new circumstances, held themselves at the service of their country in accordance with their old sentiments.

Army property was wasted in all directions, and the defensive power of the country completely undermined. Material of incalculable value was lost.

The proud German Army, after victoriously resisting an enemy superior in numbers for four years, performing feats unprecedented in history, and keeping our foes from our frontiers, disappeared in a moment. Our victorious fleet was handed over to the enemy. The authorities at home, who had not fought against the enemy, could not hurry fast enough to pardon deserters and other military criminals, including among these many of their own number, themselves and their nearest friends.

They and the Soldiers' Councils worked with zeal, determination and purpose to destroy the whole military structure. Such was the gratitude of the new homeland to the German soldiers who had bled and died for it in millions. The destruction of Germany's power to defend herself—the work of Germans— was the most tragic crime the world has witnessed. A tidal wave had broken over Germany, not by the force of nature, but through the weakness of the Government, represented by the Chancellor, and the paralysis of a leaderless people.

Those who for decades had confused the people and made them false promises, who have always agitated against authority in State and army and have now destroyed it, soon found themselves forced to abandon the principles they had hitherto propagated. A new authority had now to be created, a new army formed, in order to oppose force with force at home, in a way that had never been necessary before. It is not the troops formed by the Revolution, but the voluntary formations with the spirit and discipline of the army of 1914, that are rescuing Germany, an illuminating sidelight on this fateful time. Mankind was, after all, not ready for the alleged blessings of the Revolution. What the Revolution thinks that it has achieved might have been won on constitutional lines without suicide. It was a terribly criminal game that was played with Germany in her hardest hour, and Germany is paying for it with her life and her ideals.

Before all these events the world has stood astonished ; it could not believe its eyes when it saw the collapse of this proud and mighty Germany, the terror of her foes. The Entente feared us even in our destruction, and could not take enough advantage of the opportunity to weaken us still further internally by propaganda and by imposing a helots' peace upon us.

Germany, by her own fault, has been brought low. She is no longer a great power ; she is not even an independent State. Her present and future existence are in danger.

Out of this world struggle she comes weakened and diminished in every respect, and robbed of districts and peoples which have been hers for generations.

She loses her colonies.

Her right to defend herself is taken away. The German has lost the right to serve his country in the army.

Germany's merchant fleet disappears from the high seas. Her industrial strength is broken, and the fragments that remain are placed under enemy supervision. The livelihood of 70,000,000 Germans is insecure.

The indemnities we have to pay are beyond our power.

The guilt which lies at the door of the Revolution does not end merely with this Peace. It makes the heavy yoke, with which it has sent the German people into bondage, into an absolutely crushing one.

It places a premium on idleness, and destroys the feeling that work is greater than money reward. It hinders the employment of creative energy, and obliterates personality, replacing it by mob rule and mediocrity. The impulse towards reconstruction inherent in all political and economic life is jeopardized, if not dead for years to come. The homeland, weakened by the Peace, cannot support its population.

In Germany there is civil war. German property is being destroyed. The public moneys are wasted and put to selfish

Epilogue

uses ; the finances of the Empire, the States and the towns become rottener day by day. The people, sunk to the lowest depths, wallow unrestrained in the " freedom " of the Revolution ; the lowest instincts of mankind have free rein. We are witnessing the reign of disorder, shirking, deceit and over-reaching, accompanied often by the most disgusting frenzies of luxury—and this at the graveside of the millions who have died for the country, and in the sight of the many cripples on whom our eyes rest. Germany offers a hideous and contemptible spectacle, filling every true German heart with indescribable grief, but arousing among our enemies and neutrals nothing but contempt.

German men come forward and accuse their country of crimes to the enemy, to please the foe and secure lenient treatment for themselves. Germans who fought loyally for their country are delivered up by their Government to the enemy, to figure in his triumph. That is the depth of our humiliation, which fills one with shame and disgust at the German people.

By the Revolution the Germans have made themselves pariahs among the nations, incapable of winning allies, helots in the service of foreigners and foreign capital, and deprived of all self-respect.

" In twenty years' time the German people will curse the parties who now boast of having made the Revolution." A true word, a terrible word, uttered at the second Congress of Councils in Berlin, in April, 1919, by a Social Democrat to his fellows.

The history of the German people is concluded for the moment by the Peace. The future lies dark before us, the only bright spot being the acts of the men of Scapa Flow.

All delusions have vanished, mass suggestion begins to fail. We look into nothingness. Self-deception, empty words, the practice of trusting to others or to phantoms, lip courage, meaning vain promises for the future and weakness in the present ; all these will never help us, as they have never helped us in the past.

Something else is needed.

Fearless thinking, manly action from each one of us, the subordination of self and the submission of the individual to national discipline—these are what we require. They alone can restore our national self-respect, the recovery of which is a condition precedent to the renaissance of Germany. That is the first commandment !

Love of country, love of the daily task, devotion to work and tireless creative energy, ruthless industry, unfettered activity in our economic life, with due consideration for one's neighbour, the co-operation in full confidence of rich and poor, of hand and head, in the same dutiful tasks, freedom for honourable work— these are the basis of German wealth and the condition of our revival. That is our second commandment !

Loyal, honest, truthful and brave must the German be once more. Moral seriousness must govern his thoughts and actions. That is the third commandment ! The saying of Fichte, that to be a German and to have character are unquestionably the same thing, must again become the truth. Only so can we recover our self-respect, which alone can win us that of others.

In national self-restraint and education, in German achievement, in untiring work, and human dignity, looking clearly into the hard reality of our bare and cheerless future, thus and thus alone will the Germans find themselves again. Such action will help us once again to win ourselves a country, and to recover the old selfless patriotism which gives us strength to live (and, if fate demands, to die, as the heroes of this great struggle have died) for our ideals, for all that is Germany, for the prosperity and security of our German homeland, and for her restoration to her old greatness.

In the four years of war our people did mighty deeds, which bore eloquent testimony to that inherent strength which to-day is being wasted by the Revolution. A people of such achievements has the right to live. May it now have the strength to throw off the fetters it has laid upon itself ; may it now find men to lead it who are as ready to accept responsibility as the commanders in the field, men of strong purpose and firm will, capable of breathing fresh vigour into our feeble national life—

Epilogue

men who, followed by all that is best in the nation, will unite all our creative forces in great constructive work.

After our great downfall, let us, in memory of the heroes who have fallen believing in Germany's greatness, the heroes whom the country now so badly needs, learn once again to be Germans, and to be proud that we are Germans.

God grant it !

INDEX

Index

Caucasus, 175, 256, 347, 620, 621, 656.
Censorship, 7, 373, 377.
Central Purchasing Co., 359.
  ,,   Supply Office, 355.
Cerna, 293, 412.
Cernavoda, 295, 356, 568.
Chalons-sur-Mer, 663.
Champagne, 140, 172, 410, 425, 426, 668, 718.
Channel Tunnel, 519.
Charles, Emperor, 437, 440, 441, 443, 487, 564, 662, 685 et seq., 703.
Charles, Archduke, 229, 232, 235, 247, 259, 279, 280, 295.
Charleville, 265, 324, 325, 739.
Château Thierry, 630, 663, 670.
Chauny, 604.
Chavignon, 492.
Chemin des Dames, 424, 430, 479, 493, 663, 744.
Chentziny, 81.
Cherson, 622.
Chile, 415.
Choat, American Ambassador, 416.
Cholm, 153, 165, 555.
Chorshele, 132, 152.
Churchill, Winston, 759.
Ciechanov, 108, 132, 155.
Cividale, 485, 497, 500.
Clemenceau, 5, 371, 372, 513, 530, 554, 592, 632, 641, 652, 702 et seq.
Close Arrest, 611, 612.
Coal and Coalfields, 10, 257, 345, 346, 469, 482, 517, 518, 519, 525, 622, 657, 698.
Coast Defence Force, 59.
Cobadinu, 286, 288.
Coblenz, 41, 44, 46.
Codroipo, 500.
Colonial Secretary, 262.
Colonies (German), 521, 522.
  ,,   (French), 60, 263, 305.
Combles, 278, 599.
Commissariat Department, 353.
Communications, 68, 83, 152, 153, 164, 174, 177, 186, 190, 237, 568.
Compiègne, 616, 674.
Conrad, General von, 60, 67, 75 et seq., 85 et seq., 95, 100, 102, 108, 109, 113, 114, 138, 139, 247, 250,

258, 265, 279, 282, 301, 322, 326, 398, 501.
Conscription in England, 177.
Constantine, King, 502.
Constanza, 295, 356, 357.
Constitution of Germany, 264.
Constantinople, 214, 235, 354, 355, 503, 715, 747.
Conta, General von, 236.
Coronel, 214.
Corfu, 174.
Corps of Officers, 362, 392, 646 et seq.
Cossacks, 68, 82, 625, 655 et seq., 699
Coupette, General, 341.
Courcy-la-Ville, 604.
Courland, 142, 149, 155, 159, 192, 206, 443, 467, 471, 520, 531, 552, 561, 661.
Cracow, 74, 77, 79, 80, 93, 101, 105, 108, 109.
Craiova, 297.
Cramon, General von, 257, 610, 685, 703.
Crantz, Major von, 17, 626.
Craonne, 140.
Crimea, 623.
Croiselles, 598, 599, 695.
Crown Council, 516.
  ,,   Prince, 20, 29, 244, 265, 266, 275, 388, 411, 419, 476, 481, 650.
Crozat Canal, 408, 696.
Curtea de Arges, 298, 299.
Cuts, 690, 694.
Cyclist Brigade, 31, 488, 506.
Czecho-Slovaks, 566, 654, 655.
Czechs, 116, 325, 326, 354, 367.
Czernin, Count, 11, 322, 325, 326, 349 et seq., 439, 455, 531, 545, 546, 550, 554, 555, 568, 569, 662.
Czernowitz, 222, 436, 437, 484.
Czestochova, 93 et seq., 99, 100 et seq.

Dagö, 487, 507.
Daily Mail, 684.
Damaschke, 466.
Damascus, 619, 715.
Dankl, General von, 80.
Danube, 172, 174, 249, 287 et seq., 360, 571.
  ,,   Flotilla, 287.

Index

Index

Libau, 144, 164, 165, 181, 182, 187, 198, 215, 488, 506.
Lichnowsky, Prince, 641, 686.
Lida, 158, 167, 169, 180, 183.
Liége, 1, 24, 32 *et seq.*, 41, 342, 353, 519.
Lignite, 518.
Lille, 590, 596, 755, 757.
Liman Pasha, Marshal, 254, 256, 395.
Liman, General von, 619.
Limanova, 109, 111.
Limburg-Stirum, Count, 263, 702, 718.
Lisingen, General von, 103, 114, 115, 138, 139, 180, 221, 228, 230, 231, 247.
Lipsk, 126.
Lithuania, 142, 146, 149, 155, 159, 187, 192, 442, 446 *et seq.*, 520, 531 *et seq.*, 561, 662, 704, 705.
Litovsk, 154, 155.
Litzmann, General von, 107, 122 *et seq.*, 159, 161, 233.
Livonia, 535, 552, 559, 560, 561.
Lloyd George, 5, 311, 323, 368, 371, 372, 450, 49e, 513, 515, 530, 554, 592, 603, 706, 707, 719.
Lobau, 51, 52, 53.
Lochow, General von, 140, 141.
Lodz, 81, 92, 94, 105 *et seq.*, 240.
Lomnitza, 435.
Lomza, 119, 120, 123, 125, 130, 133, 134, 147, 152, 157, 158.
Loncin, Fort, 37, 39.
London, 518, 594, 700, 701, 723.
Longwy, 69, 345.
Lorraine, 59, 69, 117, 404, 410, 517 *et seq.*
Loos, 172.
Lossow, General von, 258, 620, 622.
Loszberg, General von, 21, 266, 278, 422, 478, 489, 490, 674, 678, 689.
Lötzen, 45, 52, 61, 63, 64, 71, 135, 136, 146, 164, 179.
Louvisa, 627.
Lowicz, 90, 93, 105, 106, 109.
Luce, 680.
Ludendorff. Position on outbreak of war, 24. Transfer to Dusseldorf, 27. His family, 29, 30,
73. Parentage, 42. Director of Military Operations, 44. Receives Iron Cross, 58. Appointed Chief of Staff of the Southern Army, 69. Visit to Austrian H.Q., 74. Visit to Berlin, 1914, 95. Life in Posen, 97, 111. Lecturer at the Kriegsakadamie, 103. Negotiations with Austria-Hungary, 111. Visit to Munkacs, 115 *et seq.* Leaves Posen, 122. H.Q. at Lotzen, 135. Visit to Posen, 148. H.Q. at Kovno, 178. Visit to Berlin, 210. Visit to Mitau, 213, to Pless, 227, to Kowel, 230, to Wladimir-Wolynsk, 231, to Lemberg, 232, to Brest-Litovsk, 234. Appointed Q.M.G., 239 *et seq.* Visit to the Western Front, 265 *et seq.* Peace negotiations, 320. Speech at Kovno, 323. Enemy propaganda against, 362, 369. Birthday at Kreuznach, 421. Consultation on prospects of peace, 440. Resignation tendered, 454. Arrival in Berlin, 454, 455. The Ludendorff Fund, 465. Visit of Tsar of Bulgaria, 469. Railway accident, 483. Death of eldest son, 483. The Papal Peace Note, 514. Crown Council, 516. Views on peace, 521. As Chancellor, 530. Conference in Berlin, 532, 533. Conference at Kreuznach, 534. Relations with the Kaiser, 547 *et seq.*, 607. Conference at Homburg, 557 *et seq.*, 587, 588. Relations with F.O., 560. Views on Rumanian peace, 568, 569. G.H.Q. at Spa, 595. Death of youngest son, 602. Appreciation in Finland, 628. Resignation, 762 *et seq.* Views on peace, 706, 707 *et seq.*
Lukoff, General, 253, 712.
Lusitania, 216, 417.
Lutsk, 170, 219 *et seq.*, 281, 294.
Luttwitz, General von, 226.

Index

Index

Index

PRINTED AT
THE CHAPEL RIVER PRESS,
KINGSTON, SURREY.